Social
Theory
—and—
Modernity

Social
Theory
—and—
Modernity

Critique,
Dissent,
and
Revolution

Timothy W. Luke

SAGE PUBLICATIONS
The International Professional Publishers
Newbury Park   London   New Delhi

For information address:

SAGE Publications, Inc.
2455 Teller Road
Newbury Park, California 91320

SAGE Publications Ltd.
6 Bonhill Street
London EC2A 4PU
United Kingdom

SAGE Publications India Pvt. Ltd.
M-32 Market
Greater Kailash I
New Delhi 110 048 India

Printed in the United States of America

Library of Congress Cataloging-in-Publication Data

Luke, Timothy W.
    Social theory and modernity : critique, dissent, and revolution /
by Timothy W. Luke
        p.   cm.
    Includes bibliographical references.
    ISBN 0-8039-3860-8. — ISBN 0-8039-3861-6 (pbk.)
    1. Social history—20th century.   2. Marxian school of sociology.
I. Title.
HN18.L78   1989
301'.01—dc20   90-8234
                                                                CIP

FIRST PRINTING, 1990

Sage Production Editor: Kimberley A. Clark

Contents

Acknowledgments   5

Part I. Marxologies: Critical Social Theory and Modernity

Introduction and Overview   9

Part II. Technology, Technique, and Social Transformation

1. On Techno-Power:
    Technics and Marx's Materialist Conception of History   21

2. Technique in Marx's Method of Political Economy   51

3. Gramsci and Revolution: On the Theory
    of Workers' Councils and the Working-Class Party   69

Part III. Instrumental Reason and Popular Revolution

4. The Dialectics of Social Critique
    in Rousseau: On Nature and Society   93

5. A Phenomenological/Freudian Marxism?
    Marcuse's Critique of Advanced Industrial Society   128

6. After One-Dimensionality:
    Culture and Politics in the Age of Artificial Negativity   159

Part IV. Power, Discourse, and Culture in the Developing World

7. Cabral's Marxism:
   An African Strategy for Socialist Development   185

8. Discourses of Modernization and
   Development: Theory and Doctrine After 1945   211

9. Foucault and the Discourses of Power:
   Developing a Genealogy of the Political Culture Concept   241

   Index   269

   About the Author   274

Acknowledgments

In the process of writing these studies and working on this book, several people have given a great deal of their time and energies to improve this project. In particular, I would like to thank Ben Agger, Carl Boggs, Janet Coleman, Lawrence Joseph, John H. Kautsky, Victor T. LeVine, Paul Piccone, Edward B. Portis, Herbert Reid, Barbara Salert, Lawrence Scaff, and Florindo Volpacchio. I also would like to give special thanks to my colleague Stephen K. White, who took time to provide invaluable advice and criticism at every stage of this book's development.

I also would like to express my thanks to the journals through which most of these studies initially found an audience. Chapter 1 originally was published in a different version in the *Indian Journal of Political Science* (Vol. 41, December 1980, pp. 695-728), and Chapter 2 appeared in *Social Science Journal* (Vol. 18, April 1981, pp. 118-150). Parts of Chapter 3 were published in *Telos* (Vol. 31, Spring 1977, 237-242; and Vol. 32, Summer 1977, pp. 241-246). Chapter 4 was expanded and revised from *History of Political Thought* (Vol. 5, Summer 1984, pp. 211-243). Chapter 5 initially appeared in *Political Science Review* (Vol. 20, April-June 1981, pp. 118-150), and Chapter 6 is a revision of a paper from *Telos* (Vol. 35, Spring 1978, pp. 55-72). Chapter 7 is reprinted from *Studies in Comparative Communism* (Vol. 14, 1981, pp. 307-330). Chapter 8 is an expanded version of a paper originally published in *Journal of Political Studies* (Vol. 24, September 1981, pp. 1-26), and Chapter 9 first appeared in *History of Political Thought* (Vol. 10, 1989, pp. 125-149).

The real work of producing the text was done by Kathy Akers, Kim Hedge, Terry Kingrea, and Maxine Riley, in the Department of Political Science at Virginia Polytechnic Institute and State University. I am very grateful for their dedication and patience in dealing with my writing and revisions. And, finally, my thanks go to my wife, Kay Heidbreder, who once again was an ideal reader and editor for this entire manuscript.

PART I

Marxologies:
Critical Social Theory
and Modernity

Introduction and Overview

Marxologies? What exactly does this expression suggest? Working analytically with the word itself, this neologism fuses *Marx* with the suffix
ologies, which ordinarily means a subject of study, discourse, a character
of language, theory, a branch of knowledge, or science. My point in using
a curious term like *Marxologies* is to jostle our thinking about *Marxism*,
displacing Marx from many of the conventional settings in which he and
his thought appear. Much of what is today called "orthodox Marxism"
now stands almost totally discredited as both political theory and practice.
Yet there is still a vital core in Marx's project that frequently finds voice
in disparate contexts at different times. By rearticulating some of these
voices of critique, dissent, and revolution, this book reconsiders the merits
of displacing and recontextualizing Marxian/Marxist thinking as different
kinds of social, political, and cultural theorizing.[1] At the same time, my
reconsideration of these various idioms of critique, dissent, or revolution
works in another Marxological dialect rooted in critical theory.[2] All of
these dimensions in Marxology, therefore, can be interwoven into the
narratives of the following chapters as essays in critical theory written
about, from, around, beyond, or alongside Marx.

The motivation behind these studies is my desire to display the potential
of critical theory as a powerful combination of insightful social analysis
and useful social guidance in several different political contexts. As
critical theories tied to Marx, such studies blend notions from cultural
critique, sociology, history, anthropology, and political economy in an
empirically informed analysis of present-day political problems, which
are intent upon winning emancipation from oppression, drawing rationality out of irrationality, and resisting domination to realize greater

autonomy.[3] These intentions are addressed more immediately in the book's three major thematic sections.

What role, for example, does technology or technique play in advancing or retarding social transformation? The chapters in Part I, on technology, technique, and social transformation, directly raise this concern as they reconsider the significance of the means of production in the structuration of society. Chapter 1 looks into how the power of technology is appraised by Marx and Engels in the constructs of historical materialism as a driving force behind major changes within and between different historical modes of production. Marx's historical materialism frequently is cast by many political analysts as a purely nineteenth-century project that did not anticipate the transformations in industrial capitalism over the last century. In Chapter 1, I argue that this stance is not entirely correct. I make this point by comparing and contrasting Marx's vision of technological change with Lewis Mumford's interpretation of technical development, revealing how Mumford's model amplifies and extends many of Marx's insights.

Chapter 2 also suggests that this limited historical interpretation of Marx is somewhat flawed. Marx's method of political economy does account partially for some of the obvious class contradictions raised by the First Industrial Revolution of the 1780s-1850s era. What is more, his discussion of modern techniques also anticipated and can explain effectively many of the complex class contradictions, cleavages, and conflicts provoked by the organizational intensification of production in the Second Industrial Revolution during the 1880s-1950s period. Likewise, his critical framework of analysis might be kept in mind today in our efforts to understand what many see as a Third Industrial Revolution, marked by intensive computerization, extensive telecommunications, and transnational forces of production, unfolding across the world-system in the 1980s and 1990s.[4]

In Chapter 3, on the other hand, I look at how Gramsci dealt with technological and institutional dynamics in modern industrial capitalism, particularly in Italy, in his own vision of workers' councils and a workers' party to stage a socialist revolution. The difficult challenge of organizing an effective revolutionary strategy in relatively advanced industrial societies, then, is the focus of Chapter 3. Gramsci's theoretical understanding of workers' councils and the party, as they evolved in the context of Italy in the 1920s, is carefully reevaluated as an evolving discourse of revolutionary critique. By reexamining his early newspaper writings as well as the *Prison Notebooks*, I compare and contrast Gramsci's contributions to revolutionary discourse with other competing strategic discourses of revolutionary action, which reveal the originality and significance of this project.[5] In each of these three essays, the importance of technology as a mediation of the owning classes' agendas of control and domination is closely reconsidered to reveal different facets of Marx's and Gramsci's critical analysis of instrumental reason.

The power of instrumental reason and its significance as the mediation of domination in modern modes of advanced industrial capitalism are continued as themes from Part I in the studies presented in Part II, on instrumental reason and popular revolution. Chapter 4 engages in a distinctive rereading of Rousseau as a critical thinker who anticipates and prefigures much of the Marxian project—the critique of instrumental reason, social inequality, alienation, and domination—in his confrontation with the Enlightenment project. As an outspoken exponent of radical political critique, Rousseau is often dismissed as time bound in approach and his work as historically obsolete for present-day practice.

Given the discursive focus on Nature and participatory democracy in contemporary ecological politics, I argue that many of Rousseau's insights are as suggestive today as they were two centuries ago. Rousseau is one of the first systematic critics of the instrumental rationality, commodity fetishism, and depoliticized passivity that now is endemic to advanced industrial society. Similarly, his moral agenda for repoliticizing public life by recapturing and revitalizing civic virtue remains an important starting point for understanding the potential impact of political ideas on social institutions.

Continuing many of the sophisticated philosophical insights of Marx in the radical spirit of Rousseau, Marcuse directly confronts the problematic of instrumental reason, as the contradictory mediation of human domination and liberation, in his attempts to revitalize Marxist critique for the contemporary era. Chapter 5 investigates the strengths and weaknesses of his phenomenological/Freudian Marxist critique of advanced industrial capitalist and communist societies. By teasing out the nature of domination under advanced industrial society, Marcuse reveals the important role played by instrumental rationality in modern economy, politics, and society.

Marcuse's analysis of technological reason as the source of both domination and emancipation remains a starting point for contemporary critiques of the present social-political system. His discussion of postproletarian strategies for political emancipation continues to be important despite his largely misguided faith in preconceptual, libidinal forces as revolutionary means of liberation. Even so, his fundamental belief in the redemptive potential of "Outsiders"—such as racial minorities, student groups, or modernizing peripheral societies in the Third World—as potential revolutionary agents echoes the call for radical participatory transformations advanced by Rousseau (as discussed in Chapter 4) or Cabral (see Chapter 7).

Some of the critical flaws in Marcuse's analysis of the present historical situation are identified in Paul Piccone's interpretation of "the crisis of one-dimensionality." To overcome these shortcomings, he has advanced the thesis of "artificial negativity" as a means of more effectively appraising the political conflicts and cultural contradictions of advanced capitalism in the 1980s and 1990s. In Chapter 6, I expand upon this thesis, exploring how culture and politics change during the crisis of one-dimensionality. After identifying and articulating some of the strategies of artificial negativity in post-1945 American society, this chapter closes with some thoughts about developing and nurturing an organic negativity in the present-day political situation. While this discussion does not solve all of the shortcomings of Marcuse's analysis, it does set the stage for a continuing debate over how to organize and act politically in contemporary advanced capitalist societies.

The focus of Parts I and II falls mainly upon the developed societies of Europe and North America. The chapters in Part III, on power, domination, and culture in the developing world, however, concentrate upon a different set of Marxological concerns. Although I continue the political theme of the previous chapters, Chapter 7 breaks new ground as I explore the reasoning of one of Black Africa's most inventive and insightful Marxist thinkers—Amilcar Cabral. Most important, this chapter reconsiders the origins and grounding of Amilcar Cabral's vision of an "African" and "socialist" model of development. Reflecting his doubts about imported European socialist strategies, Cabral's theories of colonial exploitation and popular revolution echo Gramsci's sensitive analyses of class, cultural hegemony, and state power, which were discussed in Chapter 3, in a particular national context. By situating his theoretical critique within the specific contradictions and crises of Portuguese colonialism and West Africa, Cabral advances a visionary program of revolutionary transformation that essentially is unparalleled anywhere else in sub-Saharan Africa.

The essential validity of culture as a mediation of both domination and liberation, which is at the core of Cabral's critical project, continues as a central theme in Chapters 8 and 9. The Marxological thrust of Chapter 8 delivers an ideology critique of modernization and development thinking in the developed countries, especially in the United States, about the nature and situation of the developing countries of Africa, Asia, and Latin America. The peculiar qualities of this "American ideology" of modernization and development perpetuate an imperialist order in postimperialist theoretical trappings, spinning around discourses of metrocentric political analysis. The impulses of domination are deeply embedded in a broad spectrum of modernizationist ideologies disguised as empirical social scientific research. I see them suffusing even the most basic language and concepts of the discourses of development with inescapable nuances of arbitrary control, cultural manipulation, and forced enlightenment.

Discourses, and their instrumental uses in reconstituting individual and collective subjectivity, also are investigated closely in Chapter 9. By reevaluating the origins and operations of the political culture concept in the post-1945 world-system, this discussion continues the ideology critique of Chapter 8 into the spheres of mass politics, individual political participation, and collective action in the developing countries, as they have been understood and discussed in the United States since World War II. Here, I also carefully reconsider the entire thrust and larger scope of Foucault's system of social and political analysis to illustrate why his image of disciplinary strategies can be used to understand how power might work today. To make his point, I employ Foucault's notion of genealogy to outline how the political culture concept has been used in professional explanations of Third World political stability and instability by social scientists and government officials. In particular, this chapter argues from a Marxological standpoint that an entire discourse of normalizing naturalistic analysis is embedded within this genre of political culture studies, which legitimates the cultivation of depoliticized passivity in the current world-system and mediates a new mode of transnational domination through the policing of individual and collective subjectivity.

Each of these studies, then, is not done from within the boundaries of yesterday's now withering orthodox Marxist approaches. Instead, I see them as expressions of a new critical theory written alongside, beyond, or around Marx, continuing what is alive today in Marxian/Marxist project by displacing it from its outmoded usages and reapplying it to new theoretical puzzles. As these chapters attempt to demonstrate critical theory's possibilities for disclosing essential cultural conflicts and vital political contradictions, in turn, a number of recurrent motifs mark most of these Marxologies.

First, almost all of them deal with the limits of instrumental reason in theory and practice, stressing the need to remain vigilant against the instrumentalist agendas of technocratic power. While this theme surfaces in Part I, it is very strong in all of the chapters in Parts II and III. To find some means of resisting these forces, several of the chapters stress the need for new strategies of revolutionary pedagogy grounded in the specific context of resistance, the challenge of creating alternative forms of party organization or social movements tied to real democratic values, and the necessity of developing authentic expressions of autonomous individual subjectivity free from the disciplinary deformations of mass culture and bureaucratic dependence. Here, the contradictory potential of instrumental rationality both to advance liberation and to retard emancipation is a central theme of this Marxological discourse.

Second, as discourses of critique, dissent, and revolution, several of these chapters also are serious efforts to revise and particularize the project of historical materialism in different political circumstances. Like Marx's own often inadequate outings for this purpose, these narratives are by no means always accurate or effective. Chapters 1 and 2, of course, are explicit attempts to redirect thinking about the function of technology and technique in the materialist conception of history from the perspective of today's "neotechnical" or "informational" capitalist society. Chapters 3, 5, and 7, on the other hand, are studies in how Gramsci, Marcuse, and Cabral all sought to reengage historical materialism in their own Marxian analyses of the "unorthodox" conditions of Italy after World War I, the United States in the 1960s, and decolonizing Black Africa following World War II, respectively. Similarly, Chapter 6 in its own way strives to respecify some of the dynamics of critical political economy in its critique of the United States during the 1980s and 1990s. These attempts usually fail to be completely satisfying. Nonetheless, they still are necessary exercises in order to refit and revise continually the surviving insights of historical materialism to the ever-changing conditions of contemporary capitalism.

Third, many of these essays reexamine the sublimation of politics in modernity. The displacement of political decisions and options by basic technological choices in the reproduction of the relations of production strongly anchors the critical narrative in Chapters 1, 2, and 3. As Chapter 4 indicates, Rousseau's dissatisfaction with humanity's increasing imperfection as a moral and political subject, growing with its perfection as a technological subject beholden to progress in the Enlightenment's arts and sciences, guides him to call for a revitalization of politics in civic virtue. On the other hand, Marcuse's critique of technological rationality and individual subjectivity in one-dimensional advanced capitalism leaves him embracing the aesthetic dimension and the politics of militant Outsiders as antidotes to counteract modernity's depoliticization and depersonalization. In turn, Chapters 7, 8, and 9 investigate how the processes of cultural modernization and economic development undercut political autonomy in the developing world through outright imperial coercion or discourses of disciplinary normalization.

Finally, virtually every one of these essays asks serious questions about the origins and outcomes of modernity. The understanding of modernization as technological progress, bringing greater rationalization, secularization, or technification into the enactment of everyday life simply in order to accumulate capital and power, is disputed in Chapters 1, 2, and 3. The technification of freedom, power, and community addressed in Part I also is a central concern in Part II's discussion of instrumental reason. Rousseau's rejection of the Enlightenment project as well as his vision of Nature and the General Will are pointed critiques of modernity, even though Rousseau himself made them, in part, from within a philosophy of rational consciousness tied to individual and collective subjectivity. At the same time, Marcuse's massive attacks on the "one-dimensionality" of modernity and the thesis of "artificial negativity," which are presented in Chapters 5 and 6, stand out as alternative approaches for reconstructing modern life along more emancipatory lines. Part III looks into the destructive impact of modernization, with its disciplinary practices of normalization and rationalization, in the once less affected regions of the Third and Fourth Worlds. Cabral's African Marxist project is a comprehensive critique of modernity as colonization as well as one design for reconstituting a society in this semitraditional/semimodern condition through revolutionary wars of national liberation. Chapters 8 and 9, at the same time, reread the discourses of modernization and development thinking and empirical social science in the United States to uncover clues about the destructive nature of modernity as it has been imposed upon the developing countries from within and without since 1945.

To summarize, by exploring several different but important discourses of critique, dissent, and revolt, these essays in critical social theory illustrate the need to blend the analytical insights of political theory, history, comparative politics, sociology, cultural studies, anthropology, and social philosophy together as a method of critical analysis. Actually, as the chapters of this book illustrate, these zones of discourse or areas of research complement each other very well. On the one hand, the concerns of critical theory present new issues for comparative political analysis to deal with historically and cross-culturally in relation to questions of instrumental reason, social change, and individual resistance. On the other hand, the methods and practices of comparative analysis provide fresh perspectives for political theory in setting out the possible effects of ideological critique and political opposition on the functioning of oppressive social institutions. Continuing to respect the current niches of sociology, political theory, history, cultural studies, anthropology, or comparative politics as discrete enterprises in the contemporary intellectual division of labor leads almost everyone concerned down too many endless conceptual trails and into fruitless analytical dead ends. Yet, combining elements from many areas of research in the critical study of dominant ideas and powerful institutions might promote the discovery of new puzzles, fresh approaches, and unanswered questions that must be confronted to win greater human emancipation on the rough, shifting terrain of advanced capitalist economies and societies.

Notes

1. For a survey of the idiomatic and doctrinal variations in Marxian/Marxist thinking, see Stanley Aronowitz, *The Crisis in Historical Materialism: Class, Politics and Culture in Marxist Theory* (New York: Praeger, 1981); Alex Callinicos, ed., *Marxist Theory* (Oxford: Oxford University Press, 1989); Alvin W. Gouldner, *The Two Marxisms: Contradictions and Anomalies in the Development of a Theory* (New York: Seabury, 1980); Dick Howard and Karl E. Klare, eds., *The Unknown Dimension: European Marxism Since Lenin* (New York: Basic Books, 1972); Russell Jacoby, *Dialectic of Defeat: Contours of Western Marxism* (Cambridge: Cambridge University Press, 1981); Martin Jay, *Marxism and Totality: The Adventures of Concept from Lukács to Habermas* (Berkeley: University of California Press, 1984); Leszek Kolakowski, *Main Currents of Marxism*, vols. 1-3 (Oxford: Oxford University Press, 1978); George Lichtheim, *Marxism: An Historical and Critical Study* (New York: Praeger, 1961); and C. Wright Mills, *The Marxists* (New York: Dell, 1962).

2. To get some sense of the critical theory perspective, see Andrew Arato and Eike Gebhardt, eds., *The Essential Frankfurt School Reader* (New York: Urizen, 1978); John Forester, ed., *Critical Theory and Public Life* (Cambridge: MIT Press, 1985); and Stephen Eric Bronner and Douglas MacKay Kellner, *Critical Theory and Society: A Reader* (New York: Routledge, 1989).

3. For additional discussion of critical theory as an intellectual project, see Seyla Benhabib, *Critique, Norm, and Utopia* (New York: Columbia University Press, 1986); Richard J. Bernstein, *The Restructuring of Social and Political Theory* (Philadelphia: University of Pennsylvania Press, 1978); Brian Fay, *Social Theory and Political Practice* (London: George Allen & Unwin, 1975); Brian Fay, *Critical Social Science* (Ithaca, NY: Cornell University Press, 1987); David Held, *Introduction to Critical Theory* (Berkeley: University of California Press, 1980); Martin Jay, *The Dialectical Imagination* (Boston: Little, Brown, 1973); Douglas Kellner, *Critical Theory, Marxism and Modernity* (Cambridge: Polity, 1989); John O'Neill, ed., *On Critical Theory* (New York: Seabury, 1976); Scott Warren, *The Emergence of Dialectical Theory: Philosophy and Political Inquiry* (Chicago: University of Chicago

Press, 1984); Albrecht Wellmer, *The Critical Theory of Society* (New York: Seabury, 1974); and Stephen K. White, *The Recent Work of Jürgen Habermas: Reason, Justice and Modernity* (Cambridge: Cambridge University Press, 1988).

4. For additional discussion of this question, see Alvin W. Gouldner, *The Dialectic of Ideology and Technology* (Oxford: Oxford University Press, 1976); and Timothy W. Luke, *Screens of Power: Ideology, Domination and Resistance in Informational Society* (Urbana: University of Illinois Press, 1989).

5. See Paul Piccone, *Italian Marxism* (Berkeley: University of California Press, 1983), for an excellent discussion of Gramsci's Marxism versus Leninism.

PART II

Technology, Technique, and Social Transformation

1

On Techno-Power:
Technics and Marx's
Materialist Conception of History

This chapter explores the analytical foundations of a much used, much abused, and usually misunderstood conceptual system, the Marxian materialist conception of history. Unlike many critics, however, I will not pretend to reveal "what Marx really meant" or "what Marx really said" in the various statements of his principles of historical materialism. Nor do I intend, like the analytical Marxists or rational choice Marxists, to provide a "definitive" proof or disproof of the logic expressed in this widely employed analytical framework.[1] Such exercises are almost always limited by the narrow constraints and assumptions needed to give such formalizations any sort of closure. Instead, my study simply illuminates a critical factor in Marx's system, namely, the ambiguous role played by technology in change. More important, I will examine how changes in the material structures of instrumental rationality contribute to the transformation of larger social formations in the historical process of economic, political, and social change.

A considerable amount of existing scholarship on Marx already addresses itself to the technological question. However, beyond Cohen's functional analysis of historical materialism, these accounts largely do not systematically or critically reexamine the meaning of technological forces for the Marxian project.[2] This investigation will carefully compare and contrast Marx's historical periodization with the development of European technics described by Lewis Mumford, whose analyses of technological development have not been given the critical attention that they merit. And, by systematically refining Marx's definition of technology, this analysis illustrates how *technical* change—or changes in the forms of energy utilization, raw materials consumption, labor and skills, and the technical organization of production—can effectuate important changes in economic and social relations. Plainly, changes in the economic and social relations of production also cause important changes in the technical forces of production or even become, as Chapter 2 will suggest, a productive force by themselves. But these are separate questions to be treated elsewhere. Undoubtedly, then, this critical approach also might create more puzzles than it solves. However, such an outcome is both desirable and unavoidable, given the intricacy of these problems in Marxological discourses.

The Argument: Approach and Method

With regard to my approach to the materialist conception of history, three assumptions must be immediately spelled out. First, like Georg Lukács, I wish to apply Marxism as a *method* that "must be constantly applied to itself" so that it can be "developed, expanded, and deepened only along the lines laid down by its founders." [3] Also, like Marx, I will confine my discussion mainly to the European historical context to maintain the internal integrity of the developmental scheme. Of course, this precedent should not necessarily prevent anyone from deploying the same method, should they choose to do so, when and where it is applicable, to non-Western systems, especially to those participating in Western technological forms.

Second, I also assume, strictly for the purposes of this discussion, that Marx intended to contribute in some fashion to what we recognize today as a positive, or empirically oriented predictive, social science as he propounded the materialistic conception of history. Of course, other studies persuasively argue that Marx's theoretical project is not the work of a "blinkered empiricist." [4] This school contends that Marx adhered to a "negative dialectic" or a "philosophy of praxis" predicated upon materialist premises, but not rooted in an identitarian logic of argument. While this position carries a great deal of weight, it does not preclude the fact that Marx's political economy, as Engels observes, "requires historical illustration and continuous contact with reality. A great deal of such evidence is therefore inserted, comprising references both to different stages in the actual social development and to economic works, in which the working out of lucid definitions of economic relations is traced from the outset." [5] Therefore, I will assume that Marx's historical materialism follows the spirit of those methodological procedures set down in *The German Ideology*, namely, that "empirical observation must in each separate instance bring out empirically, and without any mystification and speculation, the connection of the social and political structures with production." [6]

Third, I am assuming, again only for this analysis, that Marx and Engels, as social theorists, were working on a common project even though Engels remained, by his own admission, the junior partner of the two. Again, Avineri, Lukács, and Marcuse convincingly argue that Marx and Engels must be separated as social theorists if we are truly to understand Marx and to realize how Engels revised the critical spirit of "Marxism" after Marx's death. [7] Yet, given the 40-year partnership of Marx and Engels, I will treat Engels as an integral force in Marxian scholarship. For better or worse, as Robert Tucker notes, "classical Marxism is an amalgam in which Engels's work constitutes an essential and inalienable part." [8]

Given these provisional assumptions, what are the conceptual principles of historical materialism? Succinctly summarized:

> The materialist conception of history starts from the proposition that the production of the means to support human life and, next to production, the exchange of things produced, is the basis of all social structure; that in every society that has appeared in history, the manner in which wealth is distributed and society divided into classes or orders is dependent upon what is produced, how it is produced, and how the products are exchanged. [9]

In other words, the ultimate cause of social change as well as the final basis of all social change and structures arises in the means of production and the system of distributive exchange. Marx and Engels loosely outline a five-stage schema of historical development—primitive society, ancient society, Asiatic society, feudalism, and capitalism—as well as a threefold subdivision of capitalism: simple cooperation, manufacture, and industrial capitalism. A sixth and yet-to-be-realized historical stage of communism, lying beyond the transitional state of socialism, is seen as awaiting human development in the future that lies within capitalism. For the most part, however, *property* and *property divisions*, seen as the *legal* elaboration of the productive relations required by the technical productive forces, serve as their basic indicator for organizing this succession of historical ideal types.

The origins of class cleavages, property distributions, and social changes are located in controlling and owning the modes of producing wealth. However, certain questions are unanswered. What exact changes in the modes of production or exchange are the most crucial? Are the social divisions of classes, wealth, and labor more dependent upon *what* is produced or upon *how* it is produced or upon *how* the products are exchanged? Marx and Engels do not consistently refer to technological change in their historical analysis. The technical means of production, or the instruments of labor, repeatedly are included in their account as important factors, but never are referred to with univocal certainty. The autocratic state, or the *superstructure*, often plays as crucial a role as the technical *base* because change frequently employs "the power of the State, the concentrated and organized force of society, to hasten, hothouse fashion, the process of transformation of the feudal mode of production into the capitalist mode, and to shorten the transition. Force is the midwife of every old society pregnant with the new one. *It is itself an economic power.*" [10] In fact, as the next chapter suggests, fragments of the superstructure often can act forcefully in the *base* to guarantee the germination of new technological changes within the existing modes of production.

Thorstein Veblen has suggested that, "while the materialist conception of history points out how social development goes on—by a class struggle that proceeds from maladjustment between economic structure and economic function—it is nowhere pointed out what is the operative force at work in the process."[11] Obviously, Marx and Engels posit that the "operative force" at work in the historical process can be found in the mode of production. Still, their position remains indeterminate in that the mode of production combines within itself both the *productive forces*, or technical and economic factors, and the *productive relations*, or legal and political institutions.

The productive forces can be divided further into the actual labor force of human workers, the means or instruments of production, and the means of labor or raw materials.[12] On the other hand, the relations of production have been broken down into the even more ambiguous "(a) *formal-legal relations of production* and (b) *work relations*." [13] The formal-legal relations are tied to property ownership, or access rights to the productive means of society, while the work relations are social relationships, created in the cooperative process of labor, that actually become a productive force. Yet, from this array of factors, neither Marx nor Engels pinpoints unequivocally which element ultimately is the operative force at work in their explanation of social change,[14] which leads to Veblen's line of criticism by many other critics.

Indeed, if anything at all emerges from Marx's schema, it is an affirmation of suspicions about the inconsistencies of the conceptual model. The transition from primitive society to ancient and Asiatic society is linked to, respectively, the founding of communal associations out of tribes and the establishment of a despotic political state, which maintains the ruling classes' hegemony by means of a powerful communal or bureaucratic state. Feudalism develops because of the decay of ancient society's economy and the peculiarities of the Germanic tribes' family-military organization. Early capitalism forms from the practices of the urban middle classes' coordinating feudal craft production more rationally, while industrial capitalism comes on the scene to supply the quantitatively expanded needs of world trade. If the productive forces change at all, the alteration does not apparently come from the means of production or the instruments of labor. On the contrary, shifts in the labor force or the objects of labor are seen as being caused by conquest, trade, invasion, migration, or new social associations; as a result, these nontechnical factors are cited as causes for historical advancement through the stages of the materialist conception of history. Technology is used by Marx and Engels as an *indicator* of these changes, but it is not actually cited as their *cause*. Only with the rise of industrial capitalism and its intrinsic promise for the communist society does technology become salient for Marx and Engels.

Admittedly, one can reconcile these ambiguities in the Marxist account by noting that complete certitude clashes with Marx's essentially dialectical method. However, I would like to assume that a stricter analytical approach is possible for the materialist view of history. Thus I want to discover what might be "the ultimate cause and great moving power of all important historic events in the economic development of society"[15] as explained by historical materialism. What element in the modes of production is most important for a materialist conception of historical evolution? At this juncture, H. B. Acton proposes two possible answers:

Did Marx intend to assert the ultimate source of social and historical change is to be found in the forces of production alone? Did he hold, that is, that no important social or historical change takes place except as a consequence of changes in the forces of production? If he did hold this, then he was really putting forward a technological theory of history. If he held, on the other hand, that it is changes in the basis as a whole, in the productive relations as well as productive forces, that bring about all other important social and historical changes, then his theory would be better described as an economic-technological theory of history.[16]

Marx, in many respects, was advancing "a technological theory of history." Hence the "operative force" at work in this process of historical development largely flows from elements within the technical forces and instruments of production. And changes in the technical component of the productive forces, or the means of production, and not changes in the basis as a whole, are the most basic factors in this process.[17]

Marx and the Meaning of Technology

Clearly, many critics of Marx argue that technology is of only secondary importance to social relations in historical materialism.[18] To forestall these counterarguments, this discussion requires a more exacting definition of *technology*. The major flaw of most treatments of the Marxian "technological theory of history" has been their use of *technology* as a concept. Is it part of the base or the superstructure? Is it an idea, an object, a process, a thought, or a thing? Evasive definitions of the term result in its incorrect use as a conceptual sponge full of value connotations and fuzzy definitions.

Marx associates technology with the instruments of labor, its tools, or, in other words, with "things." He contends that "relics of by-gone instruments of labor possess the same importance for the investigation of extinct economic forms of society, as fossil bones for the determination of extinct species of animals. It is not the articles made, but how they are made, and by what instruments that enables us to distinguish different economic epochs." [19] In this sense, technological change, as he states in *The Poverty of Philosophy,* from the hand mill to the steam mill is "thing-change" and can be documented through examining transformations in the instruments of labor, as material "things," with the passing of time. Engels adheres to this notion of technological evolution in *Anti-Dühring* as he explains the shift from simple cooperation to industrialization as the progression from the spinning wheel, the hand loom, and the blacksmith's hammer to the spinning machine, the power loom, and the steam hammer.[20]

This inference from material relics to the conditions of production provides a valid insight into the workings of technology upon the division of labor. Yet, while tools are admittedly an aspect of the concept of technology, the term implies more than "tools" as "things." In common usage, *technology* is a generic concept that variously specifies such particulars as tools, apparatus, technical languages, applied science, ensembles of techniques, technical methods, or most generally the totality of means employed in society to provide the objects necessary for human subsistence and comfort. Most criticism of Marx utilizes the last and most indefinite sense of the term—the totality of means employed by society to provide material objects. By doing so, Marx's schema is attacked for lacking conceptual specification of the causal relations within the technical totality that might actually change and thereby cause economic or social change. I want to specify the concept of technology more precisely by understanding it to have three distinct but interrelated dimensions: as *tools,* as *technics,* and as *techniques.*

Tools are relatively simple, mainly passive implements that must be used with a definite craft or skill as well as the application of human energy to be effective. That is, tools do not function independent of the skills and energy of the human tool users. As Marx notes, a tool "is itself passive in relation to the labourer, and active in relation to the object of the labor." [21] A tool can become "active" in relation to the laboring subject, as is the case, for example, with primitive agricultural implements like the hoe, the shovel, or the scythe. Here, the tool, in a sense, is active inasmuch as it directly limits the scope and productivity of the laboring subject's agricultural activity. Still, as tools, such implements are passive entities that require both human energy and skill in direct application to function as tools. Consequently, "the essential distinction between a tool and a machine lies in the degree of independence in operation from the skill and motive power of the operator: the tool lends itself to manipulation, the machine to automatic action." [22]

Basically, Marx's insight into the workings of technology as tools is accurate, but his own account of this problem is incomplete and confusing. Following Benjamin Franklin, Marx defines man "as a toolmaking animal." As was noted above, he also maintains that the technical relics of all societies are impregnated with social meanings that enable the social theorist to infer judgments about the economic productivity and productive relationships of these societies. By documenting how wealth is produced and by what kind of instruments, technical relics "not only supply a standard of the degree to which human labor has attained, but they are also indicators of the social conditions under which that labor is carried on." [23]

Although this method proved rather effective in documenting the changes that resulted in the transition from feudalism to capitalism, tool change *alone* seems an inadequate measure for scrutinizing the changes *between* other historical stages or the variation of tools across cultures *within* historical periods. Tools changed quite radically in the transition from feudalism to capitalism, but changed hardly at all during the transformation of ancient society into medieval feudalism.

Technics, as another aspect of technology, denotes the use of machines and the applied techniques of mechanical organization that integrates and monitors the operation of automatically acting machines. Machines are, in a simple mode, basically tools; yet, as they become complex through the addition of nonhuman energy sources and vastly more complicated mechanisms, the increasing automatism of machines objectifies the skill or craft of the laboring subject as part of the machine in addition to displacing human energy with nonhuman motive force. Hence the power loom, in a real sense, does away with the human weaver by weaving cloth automatically, without the weaver's guidance or energy. Of course, this development implies a tremendous specialization of function within the machine; whereas the human weaver could weave many varieties of cloth from many different materials, the power loom often can weave only one kind of cloth from one kind of material. A simple tool is usually capable of being put to several diverse uses by the laboring subject, while the machine is more often designed to serve only a single special function. Therefore, a specific complex of technics, or machine concentrations, demands a particular type of labor, a unique range of skills, a peculiar set of raw materials, and a definite kind of energy in order to maintain its necessary operations. [24]

Moving from this perspective, it might be feasible to reconstruct a historical picture of human technology evolving in social change that would be comparable in scope and impact to Darwin's theory of evolution. As Marx claims in *Capital*, "Technology reveals man's dealing with nature, discloses the direct productive activities of his life, thus throwing light upon social relations and the resultant mental conceptions," [25] but never fully illustrates how technology "discloses" the productive relations or how it "throws light" on social relations.

Technology has this power, in Marx's mind, because it ultimately determines the division of labor: "Labor is organized, is divided differently according to the instruments it disposes over. The hand-mill presupposes a different division of labor from the steam-mill." [26] This technically determined division of labor, in turn, leads to or defines both social relations and ideational superstructure. Once this linkage is uncovered, however, serious conceptual problems arise, because Marx never systematically substantiates his theory by matching his periods of historical evolution—primitive society, Asiatic society, ancient society, feudalism, capitalism, and communism—to historical stages of technics defined by terms of changes in labor forms, kinds of technical skills, sources of energy, or types of basic raw materials.[27]

Finally, technology can be defined as *technique*, or the purposeful organization and combination of systematic procedures that usually does not assume a material embodiment of tangible form. Rather, technique implies an ensemble of methods organized for attaining certain practical purposes that usually becomes an "objectified" process. As Ellul notes, "Technique refers to any complex of standardized means for attaining a predetermined result. Thus, it converts spontaneous and unreflective behavior into behavior that is deliberate and rationalized." [28] The use of tools and the operation of technics can take place with spontaneous, unreflective craft skills, but it also may require the implementation of techniques.[29] At the same time, however, techniques are commonly created without being related to the operation of tools or technics, as, for example, in management or military techniques, which will be examined in greater depth in Chapters 2 and 3.

By taking these three interrelated aspects of technology's meaning—as tools, as technics, and as techniques—I hope to develop the technological logic of historical materialism more fully by examining how technics—or changes in technics, as Mumford's analyses of these shifts suggest—are one of the key operative forces at work behind social change in the materialist conception of history.

Mumford and the Development of Technics

At this juncture, Lewis Mumford's discourse of technics becomes quite informative. Indeed, this historical schema of technological civilization's emergence in Europe and Asia might further concretize the Marxian perspective by comparing and contrasting its narratives with the technical stages defined by Mumford. Marx claimed that "machinery, properly so-called, dates from the end of the eighteenth century." [30] Many subsequent historians of industrialization usually honor this date as the beginning of the Industrial Revolution.[31] Speaking in relation to Europe, however, Mumford follows another school of the historical reconstruction of technical evolution, pushing the advent of machine civilization, or modern technics, back to the tenth century, and then periodizes the subsequent evolution of technics with three developmental phases. These overlapping stages—eotechnics (beginning around 1000 A.D. and running up to 1750), paleotechnics (1750 to 1910), and neotechnics (1910 to the present)—can be supplemented by a fourth stage, "prototechnics," which he sees as emerging intermittently in various areas of the world since antiquity.

More important, however, Mumford's system of historical development rests upon careful criteria for analyzing social transformations:

> While each of these phases roughly represents a period of human history, it is characterized even more significantly by the fact that it forms a technological complex. Each phase, that is, has its origin in certain definite regions and tends to employ certain special resources and raw materials. Each phase has its specific means of utilizing and generating energy, and its special forms of production. Finally, each phase brings into existence particular types of workers, trains them in particular ways, develops certain attitudes and discourages others, and draws upon and further develops certain aspects of the social heritage.[32]

Technics, and technics change, then, enables one to divide history explicitly into stages by explaining changes from stage to stage in terms of how shifts in these technical factors entail larger social and economic changes. By critically juxtaposing Mumford with Marx, I wish to suggest that shifts in these technological complexes, or technical changes in the use of energy, the productive consumption of raw materials, the training or skills of workers, and the technical organization of production cause change in society's productive relations and superstructure.

Prototechnics

Though Mumford does not precisely describe the state of technics prior to eotechnics, it is possible to construct an image of premodern technics from Mumford's writings. For the most part, the centuries prior to the tenth century A.D. were characterized by the use of tools rather than technics, or organized complex machines; still, in certain areas of the Eurasian region[33] at definite historical junctures, one can document the formation of civilizations rooted in technics that might be called "prototechnics," or the use of human and animal energy, supplemented by water and wood energy, and the utilization of stone and wood as basic raw materials. Essentially, prototechnics is a slave labor, stone, and animal and water energy complex. Although the prototechnical civilization clearly antedates, both historically and structurally, modern technics, the profound changes worked by this technical complex should not be ignored. Indeed, cultural anthropologists and archaeologists frequently refer to prototechnical structures and their historical diffusion as the "first industrial revolution." [34]

According to Mumford, these technics emerged with the ancient union of Throne and Altar, in which the monarchs presume to possess godlike powers on earth under the cloaking myths of divine royal descent and right to rule. In order to act like gods—that is, as omnipotent and omniscient agents—these kings construct "collective human machines" to undertake engineering, agricultural, and administrative tasks. In terms of the primitive neolithic villages that had predominated up to the rise of the prototechnical kingdom, these prototechnical "mechanisms" produced power, products, and services unsurpassed by any neolithic culture. In fact, the prototechnical society's productive forces could even be compared with the processes and products of late feudalism and early eotechnics.

These "collective human machines" contained three components: the standing professional army, the slave labor gang, and the state bureaucracy. For Mumford, however, the slave labor gang was the greatest mechanical innovation of the prototechnical king as "royal engineer." The organized standing army, which he had created for large-scale destruction, provided a model for large-scale production, with its hierarchical organization, rigorous discipline, and permanent mobilization. Instead of relying upon irregularly organized and intermittently mobilized labor levies, these ancient states or city-states formed "standing armies" of laborers, basically slaves, who were commanded by cadres of builders, engineers, and bureaucrats.

Once formed, these standing labor armies were put to extensive use in royal "civil action projects," that is, the building and operation of public works such as temples, pyramids, urban ziggurats, highways, canals, harbors, dams, aqueducts, and cities of incredible scale and durability given the sophistication of prototechnical implements. The king and his royal bureaucracy gave the commands, determined the designs, wielded the administrative power, and assembled the massive slave gangs under the regimen of mechanical organization.[35] Likewise, Mumford argues that the king's standing army maintained social order and popular compliance, while at the same time serving as the means of procuring more slaves and raw materials for royal production through continual foreign conquests.

> From the beginning, this human machine presented two aspects: one negative and coercive, the other positive and constructive. In fact, the second factors could not function unless the first were present. Though the military machine probably came before the labor machine, it was the latter that first achieved an incomparable perfection of performance, not alone in quantity of work done, but in quality.[36]

Still, much of the "quality" of the labor machine derived from the third component of prototechnical society: the state bureaucracy.

As what Wittfogel called "agro-managerial regimes," [37] prototechnical societies featured a bureaucratic ruling class, which also was often a bureaucratic clergy or gentry, that loosely managed the state's agricultural productivity, engineering activity, and public administration. As Mumford records, these bureaucracies became and remained potent organizational forces because of their mastery of: (a) a practical body of quasi-scientific knowledge, partly grounded in religion and partly based upon mathematics, astronomy, and engineering principles; and (b) rationalized hierarchical organizations—an "army of scribes, messengers, stewards, superintendents, gang bosses, and major and minor executives" [38] that formed a crude but literate bureaucratic command-and-monitoring system for the king's and clerical bureaucracy's operations. As the prototechnical society's tax collector, energy regulator, manpower organization, production foreman, applied scientist, distributive commissariat, and engineering contractor, "the bureaucracy was, in fact, the third type of 'invisible machine,' co-existing with the military and labor machines, and an integral part of the total structure." [39] The specialization of function and standardizing operating procedures within the prototechnical bureaucracy, Mumford suggests, made possible its large-scale coordination of both smallholding village agriculture and primitive household crafts that composed the productive forces of the society.

Using these technical advancements, it became possible for proto-technical societies to irrigate, cultivate, and administrate large tracts of territory in the river systems of Meso-America, Mesopotamia, the Mediterranean basin, and Asia. The resulting increase in wealth, in turn, created a permanent economic surplus for consumption by the ruling class and administrative intelligentsia of these theocratic-bureaucratic empires. Hence it was a *technical revolution* that lifted Eurasian cultures, as well as other non-European groups, out of their primitive society and into the urban civilization of ancient and Asiatic formations. "By royal command," according to Mumford, "the necessary machine was created: a machine that concentrated energy in great assemblages of men, each unit shaped, graded, trained, regimented, articulated to perform its particular function in a unified working whole." [40]

Mumford notes that an autocratic monarchy usually underwrote the efficient performance of the prototechnical society; however, an urban commune did emerge as a functional equivalent of a royal court in many ancient Western societies. Often preceded by some sort of kingship, the city-states of ancient society organized a prototechnical society based on the authority of a commune of property holders who also staffed the city's army and provided much of its administrative personnel. Consequently, it would appear that *technical change* can best be seen as providing the key causal forces in the development of ancient and Asiatic society as they have been described by Marx and Engels. In Mumford's analysis, the prototechnical revolution lifted certain Eurasian cultures out of the neolithic society's—or the "primitive society" of historical materialism—simple reliance upon tools.

Eotechnics

Eotechnics is the next unique technological complex described by Mumford. Organized in the river valleys and coastal regions of western and central Europe, its major energy came from the mechanical exploitation of wind, water, and wood energy. Wood also served as the main raw material in the eotechnical phase. By rebuilding and rediscovering technical apparatus known to ancient society—such as windmills and water mills—and by reclaiming certain prototechnical devices—such as Roman roads, highways, and aqueducts—medieval Europeans launched a new technical revolution. Lifting themselves out of a "tool"-based pretechnical mode, which had characterized the modes of social production since the collapse of the Western Roman Empire and the neglect of its technical achievements by the Merovingians, post-Carolingian Europe discovered new mechanical bases for a "technical" society.

In doing so, the Europeans first greatly deemphasized animate—human and animal—energy in favor of wind and water energy. As Robert Latouche notes, "The watermill took the place of the stone roller and the grindstone which needed men to work them. Its use became general in Carolingian times." [41] Second, with the systematic application of inanimate energy to productive tasks, it became possible to fabricate instruments that incorporated automatic mechanisms in their design, such as power looms, power saws, power grinders, power planers, automatic pumps, water clocks, and ore crushers. And, third, these new technical mechanisms did away with the need for slavery and forced labor. Eotechnics gradually led to increasingly skilled and free laborers.

This technical complex eventually spread across the Atlantic and into Asia; however, its major area of development was along the coastlines of the North and Baltic Seas as well as the river valleys of Western Europe, as wind and water power opened up new land for cultivation in coastal estuaries and riverine basins. Wood also reigned supreme as a structural material and a supplemental energy source. Strong, durable, easily worked, it performed as iron and steel do in modern times. "As a raw material, as tool, as machine-tool, as utensil and utility, as fuel, and as final product wood was the dominant resource of the eotechnic phase." [42]

Eotechnics, at the same time, demanded relatively simple skills and minimal labor time to function effectively. Most mechanical parts were of wood or stone, the cost of building such technical emplacements was low, wear and tear on this simple capital was minor in comparison to later mechanical systems, and energy in the form of wind and water power was relatively cheap. Consequently, a major increase in energy utilization and production was achieved without recourse to slavery and in spite of scarce capital resources. Eotechnical production, moreover, had to occur where the greatest amount of wind and water power were found; hence a diffuse deconcentration of capital installations became possible. Labor, capital, and population were not drawn exclusively toward the cities; rather, eotechnical mills frequently were built in the countryside to take advantage of good wind currents and river sites. And, as Mumford records, "the diffusion of power was an aid to the diffusion of population: as long as industrial power was represented directly by the utilization of energy, rather than by financial investment, the balance between the various regions of Europe and between town and country was pretty evenly maintained." [43]

As Engels observes, every man could produce his own satisfactions with his own tools, his own raw materials, and his own labor during the medieval period. Wood, water, and wind technics encouraged a spontaneous division of labor, individual craftsmanship, household production, rural cottage industry, and the relative unity of the city and the countryside in the division of labor. Almost anyone could learn to manipulate the various skills of woodworking or the skills required for operating wood utensils. Local mills provided power for diverse needs without concentrating huge populations in teeming cities. The eotechnical productive forces were simple, decentralized, and humane in the sense of being closely adjusted to immediate human needs and a spontaneous division of labor.

Still, the eotechnical evolution took on a self-augmenting character. Having surpassed the feudal tool-based economy, eotechnical productive forces, given their greater capital intensiveness, eventually came under the control of those with some capital, the bourgeoisie, which, in turn, began to rationalize and reorganize these plants' limited productive capabilities for greater productivity. Following Marx, eotechnics made possible primitive accumulation. And primitive accumulation with eotechnics led to simple cooperation and, in the last analysis, to manufacturing.

Though eotechnic productive forces grew from within feudal society, and in their early stages adapted to the technical relations of feudal production, eotechnics transcended feudal restrictions. Often wind and water mills had to be placed in the country, making it difficult for the urban guilds to control their laborers. By the same token, many rural lords had difficulty cashing in on this industrial revolution because their holdings did not contain feasible mill sites. Hence eotechnics encouraged individual and local initiatives among the urban middle classes, the other town dwellers, and the better-off peasantry to serve as millers, factors, craftsmen, and mill builders. As a result, new social forces came to master eotechnical expertise and to accumulate some considerable wealth from their productive abilities.

Once eotechnical industry became the hegemonic technical form, its productive mechanisms were extensively concentrated and intensely organized to increase their output. In fact, Mumford maintains that many of the salient innovations of eotechnical society were devices for increasing regularity and standardization. "The primary mechanical inventions of the clock and the printing press were accompanied by social inventions that were equally important." [44] To be sure, these mechanical inventions partly caused and partly followed the new "social inventions" of the university, the scientific academy, the laboratory, and the factory. These social inventions both created and indicated the eotechnician's concern for greater rationality and efficiency in social production. Wind energy's unreliability and the limited numbers of exploitable water mill sites made necessary the utmost efficiency and rationality in the use of such energy.

In the eotechnical factory, however, this concern became most manifest. Though eotechnics permitted the general diffusion of productive forces, the use of wind and water power for industrial purposes required a particular concentration of capital, labor, and raw materials within any given individual installation. As long as many individual craftsmen were concentrated in one place to improve the logistics of production, little alteration occurred within the work process. Yet, to improve productivity beyond extensive concentration, the individual entrepreneur had to decompose an organic production process into its constituent operations and "reassemble" it into simpler and more mechanical tasks. Just as the printer breaks down a written passage into its component words and letters for reassembly into print, the eotechnical manufacturer began to dissect craft skills into mechanical tasks ultimately to be reassembled by less skilled laborers under his management. [45] With the new regulative instruments of the clock and printed records, eotechnical energy made possible factory organization, greater productive output, and ever-increasing rates of capital accumulation.

Eotechnics also facilitated the rebirth of maritime commerce and modern military organization in Europe. The eotechnician's sophistication in woodworking soon led to the reinvention, and invention, of naval and navigational technology that allowed Europeans of the eotechnical period to build ships capable of global trade. [46] The mechanistic rationality fostered by the clock and the printing press resulted, in part, in the reintroduction of standardized drill and battle tactics in European military procedures. Armed with firearms and standardized military organization, the armies and navies of European eotechnical states soon were the primary consumers of their economies' surplus as well as the major instrument for winning those economies new markets and commercial outlets. Eventually, however, the fragility of the eotechnical era prompted its supersession. The undependable and basically nonexpansive energy of wind and water, the exhaustion of wood supplies, and the new technical rationality that had sprouted from within eotechnical culture soon led to the discovery of new technical forms.

Paleotechnics

In an important way, technical causes pushed European society into the paleotechnical stage as the general deforestation of Europe precipitated both a raw materials shortage and an energy crisis. Eotechnical society persisted in areas with extensive timber reserves—Scandinavia, New England, and Russia—up until the middle of the nineteenth century, but it faltered up to a century earlier in England and France, which turned to coal for energy and to iron for structural materials.

Coal had to be mined, but mines could go down only so far before their primitive pumping systems were overwhelmed. When wood failed as a fuel, however, the demand for coal increased. New, deeper mines became necessary, which led to the gradual perfection and expanded application of the atmospheric steam engine to run more efficient pumps. At the same time, such engines and pumps required metals in their structural makeup, so metals mining also gained new importance, especially iron mining. Additionally, iron refining and ironworking were the first industries to feel the bite of the late medieval "wood crisis." Cheap new sources of coal and iron extended their productive capacity and launched their technical improvement.

The ultimate outcome of the eotechnical energy and materials shortage, then, was the inception of a wholly different technical complex: the paleotechnic stage of coal, steam, and iron civilization. Just as eotechnics reveals itself to be an important cause of primitive accumulation, which leads to the capitalist phases of simple cooperation and manufacturing, paleotechnics—from the standpoint of historical materialism—assists the advent of industrial capitalism. Although the emergence of the bourgeoisie, the spread of wage labor, the rise of commodity production, and the anarchy of social production come first in eotechnics, paleotechnics universalizes them in industrial capitalism.

Paleotechnics overlaps eotechnics as it surfaces as Europe's increasingly dominant form of social production by 1750. Mumford contends:

The great shift in population and industry that took place in the eighteenth century was due to the introduction of coal as a source of mechanical power, to the use of new means of making that power effective—the steam engine—

and to new methods of smelting and working up iron. Out of this coal and iron complex, a new civilization developed.[47]

Werner Sombart marked the turning point to modern capitalism with Europe's, especially England's, change from the organic textile industry to the inorganic mining industry. This shift also captures the development from eotechnics to paleotechnics in that, "more closely than any other industry, mining was bound with the first development of modern capitalism." [48]

Mining was the first industry that required massive capital infusions to begin operations. The need for extra capital led to miners' turning to the urban middle classes as partners for loans and seed money, which in turn encouraged the rise of absentee ownership, capitalist speculation, and wage labor. Miners were also among the first workers to become pure wage laborers working for entrepreneurs under wage contracts. Mining supplied, in the last analysis, the basic model for paleotechnical living—coal, iron ore, various metals for the machine industries, and the initial testing of steam power. Moreover, mines, with their gangs of wage laborers working in a totally artificial environment (regulated by the needs of technical planning and the capitalists' time regimentation) also set the norm for the paleotechnical factory.

The transportation and refining of the mine's bulky outpourings both demanded the construction of a whole new industrial infrastructure—ore ships, canals, docks, cranes, railroads, smelters, and mills. Paleotechnics's greatest invention, the railroad, was entirely fabricated out of components taken from mining technology. Iron rails, connecting cars, the steam engine, coal fuel, and iron construction all were first used in mining. As Mumford discerns, "In all its broader aspects, paleotechnic industry rested on the mine: the products of the mine dominated its life and determined its characteristic inventions and improvements." [49]

The paleotechnical mode of generating energy and of using materials divorced human skills and individual energy almost completely from the productive forces. Instead of the instrument serving the human being, the human being became the servant of the instrument, which vastly differentiated the human division of labor and created whole new kinds of workers. "Operated by steam, lighted by gas, the new mills could work for twenty-four hours. Why not the worker? The steam engine was the pacemaker." [50] The paleotechnical production of goods demanded new types of mechanics, machine tenders, and industrial repair workers. The distribution of new mass-produced goods—although rarely enjoyed by the rank-and-file worker—prompted the development of new tasks in transportation, communication, and administration that still other workers needed to perform. Finally, the more general consumption of mass-produced goods led to new mercantile jobs and to the germination of service industries.

Yet the production of basic products and the utilization of energy under paleotechnics presumed a massive capital base and a pool of knowledge that no one worker or any one small locality could ever hope to master. The worker, then, had to sell his labor power as a commodity to those owning the energy, the tools, and the raw materials that his labor could combine into new commodities. Likewise, the paleotechnics of production was complex, highly centralized, and totally "inhumane" inasmuch as the individual worker and the social division of labor were wholly extensions of inanimate machines. The artificial energy of coal-generated steam worked best when concentrated in huge shops. Hence drab new mill towns grew up in the coal and iron fields, while whole sections of port cities, crossroad towns, and railroad terminal cities were occupied by paleotechnical factories.

The effects of paleotechnics have already been well described by historical materialism. In fact, Marxism is a "paleotechnic" theory of society. And, as it is outlined by Mumford, paleotechnics directly indicates how it led to the productive relations and social formations of industrial capitalism. Whereas eotechnics, except in its later stages, nurtured a relatively settled life characterized by the growth of personal skills, individual ownership, personal appropriation of one's own products, decentralized production, and a social balance of town and country, paleotechnics fostered an endless battle of wages, the loss of personal skills to machinery, the loss of personal productive property for most working people, personal alienation from an increasingly depersonalized individual product, centralized production, and the total domination of the countryside by the city.[51]

Neotechnics

Writing in 1934, Mumford saw the paleotechnical stage ending in Europe, though it was only just beginning in Russia, China, and Japan. Like Marx, with his concern over the "anarchy of production," Mumford saw paleotechnics as the "planless" use of power: "During the paleotechnic period the changes that were manifested in every department of technics rested for the most part on one central fact: the increase of energy." [52] Yet this exponential increase in energy usage accompanied a total lack of rational planning outside of the workplace. The labor market, the levels of production, and the location of the industrial complexes were left almost exclusively to chance. Hence contradictions arose between rational and industrial design in individual plants and the global "anarchy of production" that framed the recurrent economic crises of paleotechnical capitalism.

Mumford detected, at the same time, a new technical complex gradually forming within the interstices of paleotechnics and slowly transforming its capitalist practices. "From around 1870 onwards the typical interests and preoccupations of the paleotechnical phase had been challenged by later developments in technics itself, and modified by various counterpoises in society itself." [53] With these challenges, the paleotechnical mode gave way to neotechnics, as the underlying instruments of labor once again were revolutionized. Neotechnics is marked by the conscious application of science to everyday life, the use of electricity and petrochemicals for energy, and the creation of new metallic alloys, plastics, and rare earth metals for use as structural materials.

Neotechnics, as the technical complex of electricity, artificial alloys, and petrochemicals, "brings the direct application of scientific knowledge to technics and the conduct of life." [54] Its development loosely parallels the emergence of Mandel's "late capitalism," Galbraith's "new industrial state," Baran and Sweezy's "monopoly capitalism," or even Hilferding's "finance capitalism." [55] Ultimately, it is the basis of the transnationalized, high-technology regime of the global economy after the 1960s. Fortuitous human invention is replaced by purposeful, systematic innovation accomplished by engineers and scientists and funded by large financial concerns. "Science, by joining on to technics, raised so to say the ceiling of technical achievement and widened its potential cruising area. In the interpretation and application of science a new group of men appeared, or rather an old profession took on new importance." [56] Engineers and engineering provided the manpower and designs for this qualitative transformation in technical evolution.

As the productive processes became more of a "social" activity, these specialists emerged to coordinate and advance the productive routine by systematically applying their scientific knowledge. "As the methods of exact analysis and controlled observation began to penetrate every department of activity, the concept of engineer broadened to the more general notion of technician." [57] Consequently, under neotechnics, the particular skills that are desired and the highly differentiated division of labor ultimately requires that the worker become some kind of technician, or at least procure a minimum of technical training. For only a trained technician can understand and use the new energy forms and materials necessary for the neotechnical mode of production.

"In the application of power," Mumford foresaw that "electricity effected revolutionary changes: these touched the location and the concentration of industries and the detailed organization of the factory—as well as a multitude of inter-related services and institutions." [58] Generated from any one of several sources of power, electricity is more readily transformed—into light, heat, mechanical energy, or circuitry—for mechanical applications than any other form of energy. Electricity with petrochemical backup power can be adapted to extensive decentralization, smaller productive units, and widely scattered plants, all kept under efficient administrative control by electronic communications and record keeping. Paleotechnical gigantism is no longer an economic virtue—a lesson that American industry has been struggling to learn and adapt to since the 1960s. The small workshop and the skilled worker might return with the realization of neotechnical production because of cheap versatile energy, instantaneous communications, and widespread access to technical education. As the productive forces of contemporary Japan reveal, "bigger no longer automatically means better: flexibility of the power unit, closer adaptation of means to ends, nicer timing of operation, are the new marks of efficient industry." [59]

Automation tends to phase out human labor as "power production and automatic machines have steadily been diminishing the worker's importance in factory production." [60] Moreover, the robotlike labor of paleotechnic machine-tending workers can be superseded by the new mechanical automata; likewise, those workers who do remain in the installation need improved skills. The worker becomes a supervisory force over the machine rather than an active but subservient component of the machine. The worker's actions still are fully attuned to the machine, but "the qualities the new worker needs are alertness, responsiveness, and an intelligent grasp of the operation parts: in short, he must be an all-around mechanic rather than a specialized hand." [61] The division of labor, all the same, becomes even more complex and the ownership of the workplace even more remote from individual workers as its capital-intensiveness leads to more and more corporate joint-stock undertakings.

With neotechnics, the more challenging nature of work, the higher levels of skill, the ultraproductivity of the machines, and the vastly improved system of benefits mitigate for the workers the problems posed by the paleotechnic factory. In fact, electrical power, new materials, and more widespread technical education, to a certain degree, allow one worker or small groups of workers to build their own workplaces to do subcontracting or high-value precision work unsuitable to large-scale operations.

The neotechnic productive formations, then, shifted away from paleotechnic technical patterns and tended back toward eotechnical structures. The division of labor became more complex; yet, it was feasible to decentralize the labor process to approximate a more "humane" mode of living. City and country, Mumford maintains, tended to reintegrate and become more contemporary through the industrial organization and application of science to agriculture. Ultimately, the neotechnical society drew itself toward a new social formation: the planned society managed by technicians. The versatility of electrical power, the rapidity of petroleum-driven transport, the speed of electronic communications, the worldwide distribution of neotechnics' raw materials, and the increasingly "social" nature of scientific knowledge dictated increasing social coordination and uniformity on a global scale. Mumford describes the necessary "socialization" of neotechnical production that attends the globalization of capitalism:

> Note the importance of these facts in the scheme of world commodity flow. Both the eotechnic and paleotechnic industry could be carried on within the framework of European society; England, Germany, France, the leading countries, had a sufficient supply of wind, wood, water, limestone, coal, iron ore; so did the United States. Under the neotechnic regime their independence and self sufficiency are gone. They must either organize and safeguard and conserve a worldwide basis of supply, or run the risk of going destitute and relapse into a lower and cruder technology. The basis of the material elements in the new industry is neither national nor continental but planetary: this is equally true, of course, of this technological and scientific heritage. A laboratory in Tokyo or Calcutta may produce a theory or an invention which will entirely alter the possibilities of life for a fishing community in Norway. Under these conditions, no country and no continent can surround itself with a wall without wreaking the essential international basis of its technology: so if the neotechnic economy is to survive, it has no other alternative than to organize industry and its polity on a worldwide scale.[62]

In other words, as Marx and Engels assert, the "socialized production" of neotechnics ultimately must create the outlines of the "socialized society" as well—even if it initially takes the forms of contemporary global Fordism. That is, neotechnic productive forces seem to have laid many of the essential foundations of a socialist, if not the communist, society that Marx and Engels foresaw succeeding industrial capitalism. In terms of the conditions of labor and social productivity, neotechnic instruments of labor portend fully socialized production.

Still, in the mid-1950s, Mumford believed that neotechnical society mainly provided some future promise, instead of actually changing present reality, because it retained the "obsolete capitalist and militarist institutions of the older period." [63] In that decade as well as in the 1970s and 1980s these institutions clung to their need for control, or to "paleotechnic purposes with neotechnic means: that is the obvious characteristic of the present order." [64] Such trends notwithstanding, Mumford remains convinced that the neotechnical regime works, at least in part, in several areas of the contemporary world, especially in Scandinavia.

Interpretations and Implications

Mumford's historical reconstruction of technical evolution in Western Europe throws new light on many of the conceptual nuances hidden only *in nuce* within historical materialism, including a preliminary understanding of today's global Fordism or transnational modes of production. Most important, however, Mumford's model greatly clarifies the intuitive appeal of historical materialism taken as a *technological* theory of history. It complements Cohen's functionalist defense of the materialist conception of history, because it concretely elaborates how technical change sparks the substantive economic and social transformations in Marx's schematic system. Or, as Marx would have it, Mumford's concepts more exactingly reveal how man's dealings with nature disclose the direct productive activities of his life, while throwing much more light upon the nature of social relations and their associated cultural conceptions.

If one understands "technology" in the Marxian formula to mean *technics,* then the "operative force at work in the process" of historical materialism can be seen as technical change. Whereas Marx and Engels simply look at various changes in property relations and in tool usage to infer how changes in the mode of production entailed changes for the entire society, Mumford's schema more strictly stipulates what to look at and why to look at it when sizing up social changes as technical change. It is plausible to maintain that definite shifts in the technical means of production, or the actual instruments of labor, cause the larger mode of production to conform to its technical demands for energy, raw materials, working skills, and structure of production. And, in turn, these structural tendencies toward conformity with the technical instruments of labor transform the larger sociocultural superstructure. Each historical stage of technics presupposes a distinct form of energy utilization, a peculiar variety of raw materials, a definite kind of skilled laborer, and a unique technical organization of production. These productive forces prefigure and, then, precipitate a social division of labor that settles into a class system, with its particular ideological veils.

By juxtaposing Mumford with Marx, one can explain primitive society and feudal society as nontechnical *tool-based* periods of history, while ancient society, Asiatic society, capitalism, and communism are essentially *technics-based* stages of history. In primitive society, men deal with their environment through simple tools that involve only human energy and rudimentary manipulative skills. The primitive household remains the primary productive force, which rarely develops complex relations of production. Yet, from within this social setting, and by using available energy supplies and materials, ancient and Asiatic societies emerged through the invention of prototechnical mechanisms. This technical base, created by either an urban commune or a theocratic despotism, likewise underwrites ancient or Asiatic societies. The collapse of such systems, however, in ancient Europe resulted in a relapse to the crude productive base of nontechnic feudalism. Though feudalism was not a return to primitive society, its closest analogue, the feudal mode of production, also was trapped within the fairly primitive household economies of the manorial demesne and the peasant village. Here, the hand mill did give society the feudal lord because the instruments of labor could be employed effectively by a few individuals working with simple tools on many scattered petty manors.

But, with the eotechnical revolution, European economies surpassed feudalism with a radical new technical revolution, which made possible "primitive accumulation" and the advance to simple manufacturing. The inherent limitations of eotechnical materials and energy, however, inexorably led to its supersession by the more reliable paleotechnic complex of coal, steam, and iron mechanisms. At this juncture, industrial capitalism emerges with the exploitation of fossil fuels and mass production. And, finally, the internal logic of the neotechnic base develops from within the womb of paleotechnics and makes historically possible the establishment of "socialized societies" promising the fully "socialized production" of human necessities.

Marx and Engels do not declare explicitly that technological change is the "operative force at work in the process" of historical development. Nevertheless, through the clarification of Mumford's technical narrative, I have tried to demonstrate in this chapter, at least experimentally, that it is quite desirable and actually possible to *see* socially constituted technics *as* a crucial motive force, and not merely the indicator, of historical changes in European modes of social production. By exploring how variations in the use of energy, materials, and skills can alter the social division of labor, my experiment sought to deepen this aspect of historical materialism by exactly demonstrating how technics might change the structures of production and, in turn, the rest of society.[65]

Still, one can ask quite rightly if such a comparison, even as an experiment, is completely fair. In keeping the unidirectional causation of the technical base on the social superstructure, Mumford's system, like Marx's, has gaps. It clarifies, in part, how technics might initiate the shift *between* stages in the evolution of modes of production from primitive societies through feudalism and capitalism and into the historical stage of communist society. Nevertheless, as I argue in Chapter 2, other nontechnical factors appear to be more important *within* stages, for example, in explaining why prototechnics leads to an urban republic in ancient Athens and to a royal despotism in Asiatic societies despite their common slave-labor technics. By the same token, as "convergence" theories have suggested, certain structural factors allow both the Soviet Union and the United States from the 1940s through the 1990s to use neotechnic mechanisms for mainly paleotechnic ends.[66]

Only with the advent of *perestroika*, the end of the Cold War, and the contemporary successes of high-technology Japanese industries have the elites in both societies begun to consider how they might adapt more completely to the forces of modern neotechnical production. The essentially "socialized qualities" of neotechnics—neither "capitalist" nor "communist" in character—have not resulted in an essentially socialized or fully transnationalized economy in either nation. In other words, certain conceptual problems arise when one attempts to explain *intraperiod* tendencies in terms of technics. Technics mainly assist one in examining *interperiod changes*, but cause confusion when one strives to account for *intraperiod variations* in social development by using technics. Hence Mumford's system, while clarifying certain points of the

Marxian system, confronts historical materialism with yet another set of puzzles. The influence of *technique*, as opposed to technics, might account for these inconsistencies, which will be discussed in Chapters 2 and 3.

Notes

1. See, for example, Jon Elster, *Making Sense of Marx* (Cambridge: Cambridge University Press, 1985); or John Roemer, *Analytical Marxism* (Cambridge: Cambridge University Press, 1986). Similar discussions also can be found in Marshall Cohen, Thomas Nagel, and Thomas Scanlon, eds., *Marx, Justice and History* (Princeton, NJ: Princeton University Press, 1980); and Alex Callinicos, *Marxist Theory* (Oxford: Oxford University Press, 1989).

2. G. A. Cohen, *Karl Marx's Theory of History: A Defence* (Princeton, NJ: Princeton University Press, 1978). Cohen's presentation is essentially a functionalist defense of historical materialism inasmuch as he argues that the nature of productive forces explains the emergence of definite relations of production. In turn, particular relations of production stimulate the continuing development of the forces of production. For more conventional treatments of technology and historical materialism, see Kostas Axelos, *Alienation, Praxis, and Techne in the Thought of Karl Marx* (Austin: University of Texas Press, 1976); H. B. Acton, *What Marx Really Said* (New York: Schocken, 1971); Mandell Morton Bober, *Karl Marx's Interpretation of History* (New York: Norton, 1965); Anthony Giddens, *Capitalism and Modern Social Theory: An Analysis of the Writings of Marx, Durkheim, and Max Weber* (Cambridge: Cambridge University Press, 1971); Sidney Hook, *Marx and the Marxists* (New York: Van Nostrand, 1955); Henri Lefebvre, *The Sociology of Marx* (New York: Vintage, 1969); David McLellan, *Karl Marx: His Life and Thought* (New York: Harper & Row, 1973); C. Wright Mills, *The Marxists* (New York: Dell, 1962); Joseph A. Schumpeter, *Capitalism, Socialism, and Democracy* (New York: Harper & Row, 1962); and William H. Shaw, *Marx's Theory of History* (Stanford, CA: Stanford University Press, 1978).

3. Georg Lukács, *History and Class Consciousness: Studies in Marxist Dialectics* (Cambridge: MIT Press, 1968), xiv, 1.

4. Shlomo Avineri, *The Social and Political Thought of Karl Marx* (Cambridge: Cambridge University Press, 1970), 5-40. For additional support of Avineri's thesis, namely, that Marx merely bent the dialectic of Hegel to fit his own materialist needs, see Karl Marx, "Afterword to the Second German Edition," *Capital* (vol. 1), ed. by Frederick Engels (New York: International, 1967), 17-20; Antonio Gramsci, "Problems of Marxism," *Prison Notebooks,* ed. by Quintin Hoare (New York: International, 1971), 381-419; Max Horkheimer, "Traditional Theory and Critical Theory," *Critical Theory: Selected Essays* (New York: Seabury, 1972), 230-243; Lukács, *History and Class Consciousness,* 38-39, 42-43; and Herbert Marcuse, *Studies in Critical Philosophy* (Boston: Beacon, 1972), 4, 47-48. Also see Marcuse's *Reason and Revolution: Hegel and the Rise of Social Theory* (Boston: Beacon, 1960), 273-322; and "On the Problem of the Dialectic," *Telos* 27 (Spring 1976), 35-40.

5. Frederick Engels, "Karl Marx, 'A Contribution to the Critique of Political Economy' " (review), *A Contribution to the Critique of Political Economy* (Moscow: Progress, 1970), 227.

6. Karl Marx and Frederick Engels, *The German Ideology* (New York: International, 1947), 13.

7. Avineri, *Social and Political Thought of Karl Marx,* 66, 69; Lukács, *History and Class Consciousness,* xiv; Marcuse, *Studies in Critical Philosophy,* 48.

8. Robert C. Tucker, ed., *The Marx-Engels Reader* (New York: Norton, 1972), xxxiv.

9. Frederick Engels, *Socialism: Utopian and Scientific* (New York: International, 1935), 54.

10. Marx, *Capital* (vol. 1), 751.

11. Quoted in Murray Wolfson, *A Reappraisal of Marxian Economics* (Baltimore: Penguin, 1966), 10.

12. Ibid. Also see Marx, *Capital* (vol. 1), in which Marx asserts, "The elementary factors to the labour-process are 1, the personal activity of man, i.e., work itself, 2, the subject of work, and 3, its instruments" (p. 178).

13. Irving M. Zeitlin, *Marxism: A Re-examination* (New York: Van Nostrand, 1967), 64-65.

14. Such analytical ambiguity is not necessarily a flaw in historical materialism. In fact, it allows for a certain open-endedness and pragmatic approach to the perplexities of historical inquiry. As Engels suggests, "According to the materialist conception of history, the *ultimately* determining element in history is the production and reproduction of real life. More than this neither Marx nor I have ever asserted. Hence, if somebody twists this into saying the economic element is the only determining one, he transforms that proposition into a meaningless, abstract senseless phrase. The economic situation is the basis, but various elements of the superstructure . . . can also exercise their influence upon the course of historical struggle and in many cases preponderate in determining their *form*." Frederick Engels, "Letters on Historical Materialism," *The Marx-Engels Reader,* ed. by Robert C. Tucker, 540.

15. Engels, *Socialism,* 16.

16. Acton, *What Marx Really Said,* 53-54.

17. In fact, I disagree with Acton that it is necessary to discriminate between changes in the productive forces taken by themselves and changes in the "basis as a whole." As both Marx and Engels claim, the productive forces ultimately are more basic than the relations of production. Hence shifts in the forces of production entail necessarily concomitant alterations in the productive relations. And, as a result, Acton's first formula—the purely technological one—almost by definition entails the second notion—the economic-technological—within its own implications.

18. Robert C. Tucker, *The Marxian Revolutionary Idea* (New York: Norton, 1969), 14.

19. Marx, *Capital* (vol. 1), 179-180.

20. Frederick Engels, *Anti-Dühring: Herr Eugen Dühring's Revolution in Science* (Moscow: Progress, 1969), 319.

21. Alfred Schmidt, *The Concept of Nature in Marx* (London: New Left, 1971), 102.

22. Lewis Mumford, *Technics and Civilization* (New York: Harcourt, Brace, 1934), 10.

23. Marx, *Capital* (vol. 1), 180.

24. Mumford, *Technics and Civilization,* 169.

25. Quoted in V. I. Lenin, "Karl Marx," *Selected Works* (vol. 1) (Moscow: Progress, 1970), 37-38.

26. Karl Marx, *The Poverty of Philosophy* (Moscow: Progress, no date), 105.

27. In *The Origins of the Family, Private Property, and the State,* Engels reproduces this Marxian logic and attempts to consummate fully these insights on technology and "the execution of a bequest" made by Marx. Unfortunately, Engels ultimately pays more attention to changes in the social superstructure than he does to the means of production that are changing it from the technical base. Also, to a certain extent, Nikholai Bukharin, in his *Historical Materialism: A System of Sociology,* struggles to confirm Marx's insights on technology; yet, his arguments are confined mainly to the change from feudalism to capitalism. See Frederick Engels, *The Origins of the Family, Private Property, and the State* (New York: International, 1970); and Nikholai Bukharin, *Historical Materialism: A System of Sociology* (Ann Arbor: University of Michigan Press, 1969).

This problem provides a basis for Cohen's functionalist account of historical materialism. That is, "*the production relations are of kind R at time t because relations of kind R are suitable to the use and development of the productive forces at t, given the development of the latter at t. . . .* When relations endure stably, they do so because they promote the development of the forces. When relations are revolutionized, the old relations cease to exist because they no longer favour the forces, and the new relations come into being because they are apt to do so. Dysfunctional relations persist for a time before being replaced. During that time the character of the relations is explained by their suitability to a *past* stage in the development of the forces." Cohen, *Karl Marx's Theory of History,* 160-161.

28. Jacques Ellul, *The Technological Society* (New York: Vintage, 1964), vi.

29. Still, the use of tools may develop without "techniques" per se. *Technique* implies a complex set of standardized predetermined means for attaining deliberate ends, and the use of many tools requires actually this kind of influence. Yet, at the same time, tools may be used by virtue of the "craft," or "art," which implies seeking deliberate ends, but through unrationalized, nonstandardized, and spontaneously determined means.

30. Marx, *Poverty of Philosophy,* 132.

31. See Phyllis Dean, *The First Industrial Revolution* (Cambridge: Cambridge University Press, 1967); Clark Kerr et al., *Industrialism and Industrial Man: The Problems of Labor and Management in Economic Growth* (Cambridge, MA: Harvard University Press, 1980); David S. Landes, *The Unbound Prometheus: Technological Change and Industrial Development in Western Europe from 1750 to the Present* (Cambridge: Cambridge University Press, 1969); John U. Nef, *Industry and Government in France and England: 1540-1640* (Ithaca, NY: Cornell University Press, 1969); and Thorstein Veblen, *Absentee Ownership and Business Enterprise in Recent Times: The Case of America* (Boston: A. M. Kelley, 1967).

32. Mumford, *Technics and Civilization,* 109-110.

33. Clearly, "prototechnical" civilizations have arisen and flourished in non-European areas: Meso-America, the Indian subcontinent, Indochina, and the river valleys of China. The civilizations and their particular "prototechnical" structures, however, do not concern us here simply because the materialist conception of history speaks most directly to European experience in historical development.

34. For further discussion of this sort of argument, see V. G. Childe, *Man Makes Himself* (New York: New American Library, 1952); Peter Drucker, "The First Technological Revolution and Its Lessons," *Technology, Management and Society* (New York: Harper & Row, 1970); M. Sahlins and E. Service, *Evolution and Culture* (Ann Arbor: University of Michigan Press, 1960); Julian Steward, *Theory of Culture Change* (Urbana: University of Illinois Press, 1955); and Leslie A. White, *The Science of Culture: A Study of Man and Civilization* (New York: Farrar Straus, 1971). Also see Lewis Mumford, "The First Megamachine," *Interpretation and Forecasts* (New York: Harcourt Brace Jovanovich, 1973), 260.

35. Mumford contends that "to call these collective entities machines is no idle play on words. If a machine be defined more or less in accord with the classic definition of Releux, as a combination of resistant parts, each specialized in function, operating under human control, to transmit motion and to perform work, then the labor machine was a real machine: All the more because its component parts, though composed of human bone, nerve and muscle, were reduced to their bare mechanical elements and rigidly restricted to the performance of their mechanical tasks." Mumford, "The First Megamachine," 239.

36. Ibid.

37. Karl Wittfogel, *Oriental Despotism: A Comparative Study of Total Power* (New Haven, CT: Yale University Press, 1959), 3, 8.

38. Mumford, "The First Megamachine," 264.

39. Ibid., 260.

40. Lewis Mumford, "Utopia, the City, and the Machine," *Interpretation and Forecasts* (New York: Harcourt Brace Jovanovich, 1973), 252.

41. Robert Latouche, *The Birth of Western Economy: Economic Aspects of the Dark Ages* (New York: Barnes & Noble, 1961), 271. Latouche continues his observations, recording that "thus a new driving power, that of water, replaced what man could no longer provide, which

explains why this particular invention, already known in the first century B.C., only came into general use at a comparatively late date. Its widespread adoption was delayed as long as slaves were available to work the grindstones." Ibid.

42. Mumford, *Technics and Civilization,* 109-112, 120.

43. Ibid., 115.

44. Ibid., 137-138. Surely it would not be outlandish to argue that the common use of clocks and of timekeeping in productive activity greatly assisted the rising bourgeoisie in outpacing their class rivals. The clock enabled the eotechnical entrepreneur to regulate his work by the hour and to regiment his employees by artificial universe of productive motion in which "time" became money as the clock produced seconds, minutes, and hours for the workman to match his money-wage-producing labor against. Clocks, then, became a primary force in urban life, which advanced toward increasing rationalization and organization by clock time. Likewise, the printing press brought into being the first industry for the mass production of standardized quantities of products for urban consumption. Here, printing fed into timekeeping in the development of mass communications, informed publics, record keeping, and literate rationality in early European society as it adapted to eotechnical production.

45. Ibid., 146. Mumford notes, "Here was both the process and result which came about through the increased use of power and machinery in the eotechnical period. It marked the end of the guild system and the beginning of the wage worker. It marked the end of internal workshop discipline, administered by masters and journeymen through a system of apprenticeship, traditional teaching, and the corporate inspection of the product; while it indicated the beginning of an external discipline imposed by the worker and the manufacturer in the interest of private profit—a system which lent itself to adulteration and to deteriorated standards of production almost as much as it lent itself to technical improvements." Ibid.

46. Ibid., 120. Of course, this observation is not to say that other cultures, undoubtedly based on "tool" usage alone, could not or did not build ships capable of global navigation and trade. The early medieval Norsemen, the Arab dhow trade, and the oceangoing Chinese junks clearly suggest that "nontechnical" cultures were quite capable of such attainments. Yet none of these cultures integrated its tool-use technologies into a comprehensive technical whole that might have turned seagoing ships into a qualitatively new means of production; hence eotechnical Europe mainly outpaced and, eventually, conquered the more "prototechnical" Arab, Indian, and Chinese societies.

47. Ibid., 156.

48. Ibid., 74.

49. Ibid., 158.

50. Ibid., 163. Or, as Marx foresees, "in agriculture as in manufacture, the transformation of production under the sway of capital, means, at the same time, the martyrdom of the producer; the instrument of labour becomes the means of enslaving, exploiting, and impoverishing the labourer; the social combination and organization of labour-processes is turned into an organized mode of crushing out the workman's individual vitality, freedom, and independence." Marx, *Capital* (vol. 1), 506.

51. Mumford, *Technics and Civilization,* 186-196.

52. Ibid., 196.

53. Ibid., 155.

54. Ibid., 217.

55. See Ernest Mandel, *Late Capitalism* (London: Verso, 1978); John Kenneth Galbraith *The New Industrial State* (3rd rev. ed.) (Boston: Houghton Mifflin, 1978); Paul Baran and Paul Sweezy, *Monopoly Capital* (New York: Monthly Review Press, 1966); and Rudolf Hilferding, *Finance Capital* (London: Routledge & Kegan Paul, 1981).

56. Mumford, *Technics and Civilization,* 219.

57. Ibid., 220.

58. Ibid.

59. Ibid., 226

60. Ibid., 228.

61. Ibid., 227.

62. Ibid., 233.

63. Ibid., 267.

64. Ibid. See also Lewis Mumford, *The Myth of the Machine* (New York: Harcourt Brace Jovanovich, 1970).

65. For the purposes of this conceptual experiment, however, I provisionally accept, by and large, the remainder of Marx's system, including how and why the mode of production transforms the ideological superstructure and why a rigorous historically grounded understanding of technology might further affirm a technological interpretation of historical materialism.

66. See Zbigniew Brzezinski and Samuel P. Huntington, *Political Power: USA/USSR* (New York: Viking, 1963), 9-14; and W. W. Rostow, *The Stages of Economic Growth* (Cambridge: Cambridge University Press, 1960), 129-136, 162-167.

2

Technique in Marx's Method
of Political Economy

This chapter continues the analysis begun in Chapter 1, illustrating further
the role played by technology in Marxian historical materialism. George
Lichtheim asserts that Marx rejected the traditional models of genetic
explanation fairly early in his career. That is, for Marx, simple descriptions of temporally connected events were insufficient explanations of
historical change. Instead, Marx held that "it was essential that the
patterns of events should display the kind of internal logic where each
successive stage is seen to arise as a matter of necessity, and not just
fact." [1] In keeping with Lichtheim's insight, this chapter will consider
how another "internal logic" in technology, understood in terms of "technique," might make certain massive social changes a "matter of necessity." Most important, it moves beyond Marx's tool-based and Mumford's
technics-based schemas of explanation to account for the new role played
by formal techniques of command and control, or instrumental reason as
such, in advanced industrial society.[2]

The Problem

Thorstein Veblen maintains that historical materialism tags the class
struggle as the central principle of social development, yet, "it is nowhere
pointed out what is the operative force at work in the process." [3] Marx
and Engels, of course, posit that the "operative force" at work in the
historical process can be found in contradictions within the mode of
production. Still, as I argued in Chapter 1, important questions are

unanswered. What concrete changes in the *mode* of production are the most crucial? Is the social division of classes, wealth, and labor more dependent upon *what* is produced and by what means or on *how* it is produced with what kind of instruments or on *how* the products are exchanged?[4] Actually, the "operative force" at work in the process of historical development, as Chapter 1 indicated, flows from changes in technology and not in the base structure as a whole.[5]

Many critics of Marx, however, have argued that technology is of only secondary importance in historical materialism. Robert Tucker claims that, "on the contrary to what one might suppose, this key concept of Marx's (the mode of production) is primarily social rather than technological in content, although it has a technological element."[6] Nevertheless, Tucker and others following this logic usually fail to define explicitly what they mean by *technology*, how the "social" differs from the "technological," and why there is only a negligible impact in the technological element of Marx's theory.

As outlined in Chapter 1, Marx associates technology with the instruments of labor, the means of production, tools, or, in other words, with "things." He contends that "relics of by-gone instruments of labor possess the same importance for the investigation of extinct economic forms of society, as fossil bones for the determination of extinct species of animals. It is not the articles made, but how they are made, and by what instruments that enables us to distinguish different economic epochs."[7] In this sense, technological change, as he claims in *The Poverty of Philosophy,* from the hand mill to the steam mill is "thing-change," and it is ascertained by documenting transformations in the instruments of labor as "things" with the passing of time.[8] Yet, while tools are admittedly *an* aspect of the concept of technology, the term implies more than "tools" and "things."

In common usage, *technology* is a generic concept that variously specifies such particulars as tools, technological apparatus, technical languages, applied science, ensembles of techniques, technical methods, or, most generally, the totality of means employed in society to provide the objects necessary for human sustenance and comfort.[9] Most criticism of Marx utilizes the last and most indefinite sense of the term—the totality of means employed by society to create material products. However, I already have specified more precisely the concept of technology by revealing its three distinct but interrelated modes: as tools, as technics, and as techniques.[10]

Although Marx's method proves somewhat convincing in documenting the changes that resulted in the transition from feudalism to capitalism, tool change alone seems an inadequate measure for scrutinizing the changes *between* other historical shifts or the variation of tools across cultures *within* historical periods.[11] As proposed in Chapter 1, one might contrast Marx's historical periodization with the evolution of European *technics* presented by Mumford. This effort might improve the Marxian scheme by highlighting the importance of technics in historical development.[12] My concern in this chapter, however, is to move past Marx's and Mumford's models to interpret technology not as tools or technics, but as *techniques*.[13] The work relations implied by the productive relations of society can be cast as *a productive force* or as *an instrument of labor in themselves*.[14] That is, formalized work relations often function as ensembles of deliberate, methodical, and rationalized procedure for producing wealth.[15] Even though this moment of production does not attain full development until the current stage of capitalism, every period in the historical evolution of society has its own "mode of cooperation," or techniques for the "intensive" increase of production, the "more rational" organization of resources, and the conscious "management" of distribution.[16] Therefore, instead of examining technological *hardware,* as tools or technics, as most previous analysts have done, I want to focus on technological *software* as techniques to discuss how organization affects production.

Technique and History:
Marx's Method of Political Economy

Basically, Marx's insight into the workings of technology on history is accurate, but his own historical account of this problem is incomplete and confusing. Following Benjamin Franklin, Marx defines man "as a tool-making animal." [17] He claims that the technological relics of all societies are impregnated with social meanings, enabling social theorists to make inferences about the economic productivity and productive relations of those societies. By revealing how wealth is produced and by what kind of instruments, technical relics "not only supply a standard of the degree to which human labor has attained, but they are also indicators of the social conditions under which the labor is carried on." [18]

From this premise, Marx believes that it is possible to reconstruct a historical picture of human technology evolving with society that would be comparable in scope and impact to Darwin's theory of evolution. In *Capital,* he claims that "technology reveals man's dealings with nature, discloses the direct productive activities of his life, thus throwing light upon social relations and the resultant mental conceptions." [19] Yet he never fully illustrates how technology "discloses" the productive relations or how it "throws light" on social relations. In Marx's thinking, technology has this power because it ultimately determines the division of labor: "Labor is organized, is divided differently according to the instruments it disposes over. The hand-mill presupposes a different division of labor from the steam-mill." [20] Once this linkage is uncovered, however, Marx never systematically substantiates it by matching his periods of historical evolution—primitive society, Asiatic society, ancient society, feudalism, capitalism, and communism—to stages of technical sophistication. [21]

Still, in addition to reviewing the case for seeing tools or technics as inducing social evolution, it is equally important to address Marx's political economy to encompass important changes that have emerged since his death. As Mumford discerns, "It was Marx's contribution as a sociological economist to see and partly to demonstrate that each period of invention and production had its own specific value for civilization, or, as he would have put it, its own historical mission." [22] In organizing his model of history, Marx correctly perceived the "historical mission" of capitalism and of the Industrial Revolution, namely, the transformation of animate productive forces into inanimate machinery and the global universalization of this mode of production.

Basically, Marx took the driving force of change in the nineteenth century, machine technology, and read its effects, in part, on the mode of production back into history as a key element in the evolution of society through the preceding centuries. In this vein, Marx observes:

> Bourgeois society is the most highly developed and most highly differentiated historical organization of production. The categories which serve as the expression of its conditions and the comprehension of its own organization enable it at the same time to gain insight into the organization and the relationships of production which have prevailed under all the past forms of society, on the ruins and constituent elements of which it has arisen, and of which it still drags along some unsurmounted remains, while what had formerly been mere intimation has now developed to complete significance. [23]

Moreover, he elaborates this largely technological theory of history quite consciously. As he states in the *Grundrisse*:

> The anatomy of the human being is the key to the anatomy of the ape. But the intimations of a higher animal in lower ones can be understood only if the animal of the higher order is already known. The bourgeois economy furnishes the key to ancient economy, etc.[24]

Thus, as a political economist thinking and working in a "bourgeois" age, he sensed that *all* of his categories, *"even from the scientific standpoint,"* [25] had a *bourgeois* tinge that distorted the previous stages of history to fit *bourgeois* thought.

In modern bourgeois society, Marx maintains that the categories of economic analysis are merely given, confining "forms of being, manifestations of existence, and frequently only one-sided aspects of this subject, this definite society." [26] Indeed, because of this temporally caused conceptual distortion, "it would be impractical and wrong to arrange the economic categories in the order in which they were determining factors in the course of history." [27] He argues in this manner because the categories of the modern political economist's analysis are "the exact opposite of what seems to be their natural order or the order of their historical development." [28] In fact, almost denying the project of the materialist conception of history, Marx notes, "What we are interested in is *not* the place which economic relations occupy in the *historical succession* of different forms of society." [29] Actually, at this juncture, Marx is not interested in reconstructing genetically the apparent historical evolution of economic relations because any such reconstruction is merely "apparent" and not truly accurate.

To escape these methodological problems in a genetic history, Marx turns instead to the phenomenological foundations of bourgeois society. In doing so, he suggests that bourgeois society contains, in all of its concrete particulars presently unified in the bourgeois mode of production, the abstract summation of all previous historical moments that led to its present structures. With this recognition, Marx does not mechanically reconstruct a specious historical chronicle of the evolution of historical modes of production. On the contrary, he phenomenologically reviews the "unassimilated remains" of past practices in bourgeois economic activity through the conceptual categories of bourgeois production, namely, the commodity form. Through this phenomenological reduction, Marx gains "an insight into the structure and the relations of production of all formerly existing social formations the ruins and component elements of which were used in the creation of bourgeois society." [30] Although these categories come into their "full validity" only with the attainment of bourgeois modes of production, they are nonetheless quite helpful for exploring the social relations "existing in all social formations." [31]

Bourgeois society and modern modes of production in Marx's explanation subsume the "relations of earlier societies often merely in very stunted form or even in the form of travesties," which may be "in an advanced, stunted, caricatured, etc., form, always with substantial differences." [32] The task of critical historical analysis, given these concrete survivals of historical practices, is to draw an understanding of the present and the past from these garbled forms of historical relations, while fixed within bourgeois categories of thinking. The more rudimentary forms of historical development are known only by and through a critical understanding of the present's more advanced forms of social activity; only knowledge of the "higher" animal—"bourgeois" modes of production— can lead one to sure knowledge of the "lower" animals—the historical antecedents of bourgeois society.

One need not be deterred by Marx's method of political economy.[33] To employ its logic one can validate real empirical relations, as Marx and Engels themselves suggest in *The German Ideology,* "in their actual empirically perceptible process of development under definite conditions." [34] Moreover, this method is far from outmoded. Contemporary empirical analysis can proceed under the same logic if one realizes that new social forms have developed beyond Marxian "bourgeois society." The present social forms are an equally "contradictory form of development"—the technological society—whose abstract categories, while partially valid in all previous historical epochs, have come to their "full validity" only "for and within the framework of these conditions," [35] namely, those of advanced technological society.

Granted the emergence of this still "higher" form of animal, it becomes necessary to *review* "the structure and relations of production of all formerly existing social formations," *now* including nineteenth-century "bourgeois society." On this basis, moreover, it must be conceded that "political economy, therefore, cannot be the same for all countries and for all historical epochs." [36] Each historical period can be comprehended *on its* own *terms*, but only *in terms of* its abstract summation with all other historical precursors as revealed in the concrete particulars of "the most advanced and complex historical organization of production," [37] which is now the advanced technological society.

By interpreting Marx's work in this fashion, it is possible to draw a new "technological" interpretation from the materialist conception of history.

As many social theorists, ranging from Max Weber to Ernest Mandel, have asserted, capitalist society has been transformed profoundly during the twentieth century.[38] What was an "intimation" of a "higher animal" of the twentieth century—the managerial society of Fordist monopoly capitalism based on advanced technological modes of cooperation—in the "lower animal" of nineteenth-century entrepreneurial capitalism, now has become "generally apparent" and requires the reinterpretation of the "lower" stages of society in order to understand the workings of the "mode of cooperation" in those earlier periods of social evolution.

Essentially, these new factors are the legacy of the "second industrial revolution," which, in a certain sense, reverses the dynamics of the "first industrial revolution."[39] As Marx discerned with regard to the "first" revolution, changes in *means of production,* or in material technics, are seen as the prime causal force in social change. In the "second" revolution, however, changes in the *mode of cooperation*, or the techniques for organizing work serving as a productive force, increasingly must be seen as an essential agent of historical development.[40] As Dahrendorf records:

> When, towards the end of the nineteenth century, many countries experienced what has sometimes been called a "second industrial revolution," the value of rationality stood behind it: at about this time, the "extensive" increase of industrial production was replaced by an "intensive" increase, i.e., by a "more rational" organization of existing resources. "Scientific management" and even "social engineering" were part of this trend.[41]

With this structural evolution in industrial capitalism, it seems plausible to assume that the new techniques of social planning, scientific management, or industrial organization embodied within these contemporary modes of cooperation have been or, at least, have had analogues that are a crucial *productive force* in all historical periods.

The Organization of Production as Technique

Rather than *seeing* the relations of production *as* a wholly negative factor expressing class conflict and property inequities, it is experimentally desirable to *see* the modes of cooperation, in part, *as* a positive force that directs and manages the productive capacity of society. By no means do I wish to maintain through this analytical distinction that these two views of the relations of production are mutually exclusive. In fact, when taken together, the formal property relations and work relations of production more fully exhaust the concept of the "relations of production" as Marx used it. Surely, the concept of property conventionally suggests two meanings: ownership and control. Marx accents ownership in regard to the productive process, because most nineteenth-century capitalists were both owner and controller combined, much like the entrepreneurial manufacturer of the late medieval period. Moreover, the owner of capital in Marx's time was the *controller* because he was also the *owner*. Control did not, as of that time, need to garner additional legitimation and rationalization through specialized administrative knowledge and/or scientific training. Instead this control justified itself by adding decisively to the cooperative processes of labor. The capitalist's invention and implementation of new techniques added an essential element to the productive process. That is, the managerial techniques deployed under the authority of the capitalist took the *less productive,* natural (*naturwüchsig*) division of labor and methodically reconstructed it as a *more productive, instrumentally rational* (*zweckrational*) division of labor, thereby reconstituting the modes of cooperation. Entering into these new productive structures, workers and machinery were immediately absorbed into its cooperative design. As Marx contends:

> Being independent of each other, the labourers are isolated persons, who enter into relations with the capitalist, but not with one another. This co-operation begins only with the labour-process, but they have then ceased to belong to themselves. On entering that process, they become incorporated with capital. As co-operators, as members of a working organism, they are but special modes of existence of capital. Hence, the productive power developed by the labourer when working in co-operation, is the productive power of capital. This power is developed gratuitously, whenever the workmen are placed under given conditions, and it is capital that places them under such conditions. Because this power costs nothing, and because, on the other hand, the labourer himself does not develop it before his labour belongs to capital, it appears as a power with which capital is endowed by Nature—a productive power that is imminent in capital.[42]

Marx, to be sure, foresaw intimations of the coming bifurcation of control and ownership. He discussed the organization of factory labor, the rise of joint-stock companies, and the nature of "the capitalist as commander." Undoubtedly, then, the two roles were as fused in Marx's mind as they were in actual activity. At the same time, this division between ownership and control also indicated to Marx that socialist forms of production, or the management of production by the producers, were developing within capitalism.

Nevertheless, such institutions notwithstanding, Marx could not *see* them *as* revolutionary because, to paraphrase Engels, managerial production "was as yet so little developed" in his time. This emergence of managerial authority becomes "generally apparent" only in the twentieth century, with what Dahrendorf calls the "decomposition of capital" into the distinct functions of ownership and management. Instead of reviewing the evolution of societies in terms of changes in "hardware" or the *technics* of labor, one might review these historical shifts in light of changes occurring in "software" or the *techniques* constituting the mode of cooperation. Even though this aspect of production does not attain full development until the stage of capitalism, every period in the historical evolution of society undoubtedly has its own "mode of cooperation," or techniques for the "intensive" increase of production, the more "rational" organization of resources, and the conscious "management" of distribution.[43]

The state, for example, in addition to being a coercive apparatus, in large part is an administrative mechanism with routinized productive techniques for supervising its economic forces.[44] Variations in the historical development of different states, at the same time, can result from variations in the invention and employment of techniques. The Asiatic agrobureaucrat, on the one hand, employed a certain kind of administrative technique in his religious-astronomical sciences, which legitimated and rationalized the despotic state's regulation of its hydraulic/agricultural production.[45] The feudal lord, on the other hand, with his manorial holdings, uses other distinct superintending techniques. Objectified in his juridical and military prerogatives, the feudal lord's rudimentary techniques often were the responsibility of "specialists"—such as the bailiffs, manciples, purveyors, reeves, stewards, summoners, and squires who mediated between the landed lords and the clerics, craftsmen, freemen, franklins, masters, serfs, and yeomen of the larger society. But, in both cases, the determinations and directions of administrative techniques brought these historical forms of cooperation into their peculiar productive patterns.

It seems that the historical development of European society can be linked directly to changes in techniques. In every historical period, the owning classes must develop certain managerial techniques for the intensive increase of production, the rational use of resources, and the conscious administration of distribution, even though these concerns do not become a hegemonic social influence until the capitalist phase. Plainly, the emergence of ancient and Asiatic society came about, in large part, with the perfection of military, bureaucratic, and administrative techniques for the management of their particular forms of production. Indeed, their creation of large, formal bureaucracy is of paramount importance in Marx's model of Asiatic society.

Likewise, feudal institutions of production may be viewed as the techniques used by landed property to direct serf production. With the collapse of the Western Roman Empire, "the German peoples, now masters of the Roman provinces, had to organize what they conquered." [46] Unable to adapt their clan-derived social constitution completely to their conquered subjects, and unable to sustain the slave-based productive forces of the moribund empire, the tribal military commanders and chieftains established small land grants as their economic and political dominions. The peasantry was bound to the land, but not enslaved, despite frequent mobilization for service in the lord's manor proper. A network of productive techniques, therefore, developed from the mutual obligations and estate privileges intrinsic to the Germanic military and kinship systems. Ultimately, these webs of social cooperation encompassed serfs, freemen, the petty nobility, and the higher sovereign lords, or kings, and the Church hierarchies as well. Thus these petty lords, as Engels suggests, imposed "a distinct mode of distribution and form of landed property, thus determining production." [47]

The techniques of manorial administration reflected the agrarian character of the Germanic tribal cultures. Each noble managed his own holdings through the labors of his family, his armed retainers, and his household functionaries. In addition to the production of his own estate, most lords extracted payments in kind and in labor from peasant households within and adjoining their manors. The peasants, either free or enserfed, managed their own plots and domestic economies as well as their villages by mutual cooperation. Nonetheless, they remained subject to the control and taxation of both the nobility and the clergy when large-scale cooperation was required. Of course, feudalism remained one of the least administered forms of social production because of its inherently small-scale and domestic-household-centered economy.

The invention and application of new productive techniques by the early capitalist, who more effectively rationalized the cooperative division of labor, also led to new developments in the social modes of production. Given the relatively low productivity of hand-driven feudal instruments of labor during primitive accumulation, which literally were those of "manu-facture," production could be amplified only by more rational organization. Since the technical means of production did not differ radically from those employed by individual craftsmen in the feudal guilds, the capitalists' arrangement of the craftsmen became the determinant element. Hence "a great number of laborers working together, at the same time, in one place (or, if you will, in the same field of labor), in order to produce the same sort of commodity under the mastership of one capitalist, constitutes, both historically and logically, the starting-point of capitalist production." [48]

Employing new managerial techniques (based on literacy and mechanical timekeeping) as an instrument of labor made possible the productive stage of simple cooperation. With precise mechanical timekeeping, time became money and required closer management to better organize its use. Here, for the laborers "the connexion existing between their various labors appears to them, ideally, *in the shape of a preconceived plan of the capitalist*, and practically in the shape of the authority of the capitalist, in the shape of the powerful will of another, who subjects their activity to his aims." [49] And the productivity of the craftsmen increases only under the authority and by the plans of the capitalist.

The sophistication of technique also made possible the capitalist phase of manufacture. The individually unique skills of the "craftsman" systematically are reduced by organization to the mechanical functions of the "workhand." "Manufacture," as Marx contends, "produces the skill of the detail labourer, by reproducing, and systematically driving to an extreme within the workshop, the naturally developed differentiation of trades, which it found ready to hand in society at large." [50] And, in keeping with the logic of technique, the absolutist monarch and his state ministries reproduce this administrative pattern, in keeping with the capitalists' expertise, within the mercantilist-autocratic reconstitution of the feudal state.

Manufacture and mercantilism are, as techniques, two sides of the same procedural coin. To meet the demands for even greater productive output, the manufacturing capitalist analyzed the modes of cooperation, atomized the work process into many independent detail operations, and then reassembled these operations into his more efficient operational organization: "the collective labourer." [51] The specialized techniques of superintendence enabled the manufacturing capitalist, and the autocratic monarch, to atomize and then recombine these preexisting natural motions into one productive instrument, the rational manufactory and the mercantilist state. "But," as Marx recognizes, "whatever may have been the particular starting point, its final form is invariably the same—a productive mechanism whose parts are human beings." [52] Techniques of concentration and regimentation refocus specialized and differentiated tasks in new productive integrations. It is these "integrative" techniques that are actually productive, as they reorganize the work of laborers, which "develops in them new powers." [53]

Finally, with the advent of machinery as part of industrial capitalism, technique prefigured the mechanization of the instruments of labor, with its mechanization of the workers' motions and activities. Under manufacturing, Marx refers to Andrew Ure, and notes that a truly effective industrial order was lacking; hence "Arkwright created order." [54] Quasi-military drill techniques were introduced under Arkwright and his followers to induce a mechanical level of precision in the factory's human machine tenders. As a manager of techniques, Arkwright's task was "to devise and administer a successful code of factory discipline, suited to the necessities of factory diligence." [55] These principles of factory discipline attempted to regulate labor exactly because mechanistic human activity was seen as a requisite for the efficient employment of mechanical tools.

Factory legislation, as Marx suggests, also embodied the logic of all social legislation in general:

> The factory mode in which capital formulates, like a private legislator, and at his own good will, his autocracy over his workpeople, unaccompanied by that division of responsibility, in other matters so much approved of by the bourgeoisie, and unaccompanied by the still more approved representative system, this code is but the capitalistic caricature of that social regulation of the labour-process which becomes requisite in co-operation in a large scale, and in the employment in common, of the instruments of labour and especially of machinery.[56]

Here, once again, technique proves crucial in directing, superintending, and adjusting production as the capitalist's mechanical regulation of the labor process within the factory extends the state's rationalization of social production. In fact, when scrutinizing the industrial capitalist state's provision for social production, Marx contends, "factory legislation, that first conscious and methodical reaction of society against the spontaneously developed form of the process of production, is, as we have seen, just as much the necessary product of modern industry as cotton yarn, self-actors, and the electric telegraphs." [57]

In other words, through factory legislation, public works taxation, military appropriation, chartering public utilities, corporate and commercial taxation, and bureaucratic regulation, the modern state with its dominant managerial forces—the bourgeois classes—tends to apply techniques for the "intensive" increase of material production. Within both the modern industrial plant and the modern industrial society, mechanically precise administrative procedures based on industrial psychology and scientific management direct the course of the laborers' productivity.[58] And, under advanced capitalism, these Fordist techniques gain significant new autonomy from direct state stimulation as new administrative techniques are generated by corporate organizations and scientific institutions to manage not only production but consumption as well.[59] Still, one of the major mediations of modern technique remains the institution of state administration. In this phase of managing productive cooperation, it is the state that intervenes to regulate the money supply, credit availability, unemployment levels, labor training, industrial development, agricultural production, technological innovation, and the course of the business cycle.[60]

More Interpretations and Implications

Technique, as the autonomous science of modern technical and bureaucratic administration, does not attain its "full validity" until the twentieth century, with its formal rationalization of the management sciences. As Marx argues, "The most advanced and complex historical organization of production" is the only key to understanding all of its historical precursors. Modern administration could allow one to understand familial-tribal cooperation, urban communal organization, agromanagerialism, feudal manorialism, simple capitalist cooperation, manufacturing management, and industrial capitalist organization more completely; yet their historical differences must not be obliterated, nor should all of these cooperative forms be treated as identical. Historically, each form was mediated through different social formations; in so doing, each complex of techniques implied a special division of labor, a certain organization of work relations, and a definite mobilization of the "collective laborer," which can be comprehended *on its* own *terms*, but only *in terms of* its abstract summation in the *present* concrete forms of technique.

Veblen's suspicions about the consistency of historical materialism, in part, can be avoided by noting how technique advances historical development and diversity. The transition from primitive society, rooted in familial-tribal work relations, arises with the social techniques of the urban communal state, as in ancient society, or from the creation of an agromanagerial state, as in Asiatic society. Yet, the same *tool base* gives totally different relations of production *because,* at this juncture, urban communal and agromanagerial *techniques* presuppose a distinct division of labor, organization of work, and "collective laborer." Likewise, feudal institutions, and their concomitant manorial techniques, arose to organize production after the conquest, and partial decay, of ancient and Asiatic societies, whose techniques were no longer effective managerial aids.

Early capitalism, by the same token, emerges from the urban middle classes' reorganization of feudal modes of production. Industrial capitalism grows with the centralized mercantilist state, which built the market and the general conditions of social production needed for the mass manufacture of industrial goods.[61] The same technics base may give rise to wholly different modes of production, and essentially distinct technics may allow for the formation of the same kind of superstructure. From this perspective, techniques—especially as they are mediated through the state—often totally reconstitute the modes of cooperation in order to concentrate and administrate more rationally the "collective laborer" within diverse social situations. This dynamic was behind the Fordist organization of production that emerged during and after World War I, and it is this same recognition that underlies the current transnational competition to rationalize the neotechnical economy of advanced industrial societies along "Japanese" lines in order to emulate what is believed to be contemporary Japan's highly rational "post-Fordist" organization of production.[62]

Through the concept of technique, I have shown, at least tentatively, that it is quite useful to *see* techniques *as* an important technical cause of the unique capitalist and technological development of European society. Historically, government has been a critical source of these new techniques and of changes in them as the modes of governance seek improvements in the systematic ensembles of deliberate, methodical, and rationalized administrative procedure. This point will be raised again in Chapter 5 with regard to Marcuse's discussion of "one-dimensionality" and in Chapter 9 in relation to Foucault's notion of disciplinary normalization. And, by examining how variations in techniques might affect social production, this discussion has probed another crucial dimension in the *technological* logic of historical materialism. Chapter 3 continues these themes as it addresses Gramsci's stance on workers' councils and the party as revolutionary forms of resistance against as well as institutional adaptations to modern technologies of production. In turn, these theoretical concerns with instrumental reason and its social formations in Chapters 1, 2, and 3 will be addressed in greater detail in Chapters 4 and 5 with regard to Rousseau's critique of enlightenment and Marcuse's critical reappraisals of technology as domination.

Notes

1. George Lichtheim, *Marxism: An Historical and Critical Study* (New York: Praeger, 1964), 142.

2. For more conventional treatments of technology and historical materialism, see Kostas Axelos, *Alienation, Praxis, and Techne in the Thought of Karl Marx* (Austin: University of Texas Press, 1976); H. B. Acton, *What Marx Really Said* (New York: Schocken, 1967); Anthony Giddens, *Capitalism and Modern Social Theory: An Analysis of the Writings of Marx, Durkheim, and Max Weber* (Cambridge: Cambridge University Press, 1971); Sidney Hook, *Marx and the Marxists* (New York: Van Nostrand, 1955); Henri Lefebvre, *The Sociology of Marx* (New York: Vintage, 1969); David McLellan, *Karl Marx: His Life and Thought* (New York: Harper & Row, 1973); C. Wright Mills, *The Marxists* (New York: Dell, 1962); and Joseph A. Schumpeter, *Capitalism, Socialism, and Democracy* (New York: Harper & Row, 1962).

3. Quoted in Murray Wolfson, *A Reappraisal of Marxian Economics* (Baltimore: Penguin, 1966), 10.

4. See, for example, Acton, *What Marx Really Said,* 53-54.

5. Again, I disagree with Acton that it is necessary to discriminate between changes in the productive forces taken by themselves and changes in the "basis as a whole." As both Marx and Engels claim, the productive forces ultimately are more basic than the relations of production. Hence shifts in the forces of production entail necessarily concomitant alterations in the productive relations. And, as a result, Acton's first formula—the purely technological one—almost by definition entails the second notion—the economic-technological—within its own implications. For a complex analysis of this problem in functional terms, see G. A. Cohen, *Karl Marx's Theory of History: A Defence* (Princeton, NJ: Princeton University Press, 1978).

6. Robert C. Tucker, *The Marxian Revolutionary Idea* (New York: Norton, 1969), 14.

7. Karl Marx, *Capital* (vol. 1), ed. by Frederick Engels (New York: Modern Library, 1967), 179-180.

8. Engels adheres to this notion of technological evolution in *Anti-Dühring*, in which he explains the shift from simple cooperation to industrialization as the progression from the spinning wheel, the hand loom, and the blacksmith's hammer to the spinning machine, the power loom, and the steam hammer. This inference from material relics to the conditions of production plainly provides a valid insight into the workings of technology upon the division of labor. Frederick Engels, *Anti-Dühring: Herr Eugen Dühring's Revolution in Science* (Moscow: Progress, 1969), 319.

9. For examples of common usage, see, for instance, *Webster's Ninth New Collegiate Dictionary* (Springfield, MA: Merriam-Webster, 1988), 1211.

10. As Marx maintains, a tool "is itself passive in relation to the labourer, and active in relation to the object of labor." The tool can become "active" in relation to the laboring subject, as is the case, for example, with primitive agricultural implements like the hoe, the shovel, or the scythe. Here, the tool, in a sense, is active inasmuch as it directly limits the

scope and productivity of the laboring subject's agricultural activity. See Alfred Schmidt, *The Concept of Nature in Marx* (London: New Left, 1971), 102.

11. See Lewis Mumford, *Technics and Civilization* (New York: Harcourt, Brace, 1934), 10.

12. Ibid.

13. For a definition of technique, see Jacques Ellul, *The Technological Society* (New York: Vintage, 1964), vi.

14. For a sustained analysis of work relations as productive forces, see Harry Braverman, *Labor and Monopoly Capital* (New York: Monthly Review Press, 1974); and Michael Burawoy, *The Politics of Production* (London: Verso, 1985).

15. See Marx, *Capital* (vol. 1), 334.

16. This conception, unlike that of Marx and Engels, maintains that these management activities flow from the intentional application of technique as a means of production rather than from the unconscious ideologies of the superstructure. Marx and Engels undoubtedly would consign such techniques to the superstructure because they are systems of ideas, whereas this discussion asserts that such ideational systems play an undeniably important role in the technical base by their rationalization and organization of that base.

17. Marx, *Capital* (vol. 1), 179.

18. Ibid., 180.

19. Quoted in V. I. Lenin, "Karl Marx," *Selected Works* (vol. 1) (Moscow: Progress, 1970), 37-38.

20. Karl Marx, *The Poverty of Philosophy* (Moscow: Progress, no date), 105.

21. In *The Origins of the Family, Private Property, and the State*, Engels reproduces this Marxian logic and attempts to consummate these insights on technology fully as "the execution of a bequest" made by Marx. Unfortunately, Engels ultimately pays more attention to changes in the social superstructure than he does to the means of production that are changing it from the technical base. Also, to a certain extent, Nikholai Bukharin, in his *Historical Materialism: A System of Sociology*, struggles to confirm Marx's insights on technology; yet, his arguments are confined mainly to the change from feudalism to capitalism. See Frederick Engels, *The Origins of the Family, Private Property, and the State* (New York: International, 1970), and Nikholai Bukharin, *Historical Materialism: A System of Sociology* (Ann Arbor: University of Michigan Press, 1969).

22. Mumford, *Technics and Civilization*, 5.

23. Karl Marx, *The Grundrisse*, ed. by David McLellan (New York: Harper & Row, 1971), 134.

24. Ibid., 39.

25. Karl Marx, *A Contribution to the Critique of Political Economy* (Moscow: Progress, 1970), 212.

26. Marx, *The Grundrisse*, 40.

27. Ibid., 41-42.

28. Ibid.

29. Ibid.; emphasis added.

30. Marx, *Contribution to the Critique*, 211.

31. Ibid., 210.

32. Ibid., 211.

33. Here, in a sense, *The German Ideology* serves as the theoretical codebook to the entire materialist conception of history, and rightly so. Though Marx continued to develop his theoretical project further, especially in *The Grundrisse*, one can find *in nuce* all of historical materialism in *The German Ideology*. See Karl Marx and Frederick Engels, *The German Ideology* (New York: International, 1947). As Benedetto Croce discerns, it is "a youthful work in which Marx and Engels, as a matter of fact, fixed once and for all their historico-philosophical standpoint." See Benedetto Croce, "The Historical Materialism of Marx and His Alleged Promotion of Communism from Utopia to Science," *Philosophy, Poetry, History: An Anthology of Essays* (London: Oxford University Press, 1966), 622.

34. Marx and Engels, *The German Ideology,* 15.

35. Marx, *Contribution to the Critique,* 210.

36. Engels, *Anti-Dühring,* 178.

37. Marx, *Contribution to the Critique,* 210.

38. For an in-depth sample of this theoretical perspective, see Ralf Dahrendorf, *Class and Class Conflict in Industrial Society* (Stanford, CA: Stanford University Press, 1959); Lucien Goldmann, *Cultural Creation in Modern Society* (St. Louis: Telos, 1972); Jürgen Habermas, *Towards a Rational Society* (Boston: Beacon, 1970); Rudolf Hilferding, *Finance Capital* (London: Routledge & Kegan Paul, 1981); Max Horkheimer, *The Eclipse of Reason* (New York: Seabury, 1974); Otto Kirchheimer, *Politics, Law, and Social Change: Selected Essays of Otto Kirchheimer,* ed. by Frederic S. Burin and Kurt L. Shell (New York: Columbia University Press, 1969); Serge Mallet, *Essays on the New Working Class,* ed. by Dick Howard and Dean Savage (St. Louis: Telos, 1974); Ernest Mandel, *Late Capitalism* (London: Verso, 1975); Herbert Marcuse, *One-Dimensional Man* (Boston: Beacon, 1964); Franz Neumann, *Behemoth: The Structure and Practice of National Socialism, 1933-1944* (rev. ed.) (New York: Harper & Row, 1944); Franz Neumann, *The Democratic and Authoritarian State: Essays in Political and Legal Theory,* ed. by Herbert Marcuse (New York: Columbia University Press, 1957); Friedrich Pollock, *The Economic and Social Consequences of Automation* (Oxford: Oxford University Press, 1957); Friedrich Pollock, "State Capitalism: Its Possibilities and Limitations," *Studies in Philosophy and Social Sciences* 9, no. 2 (1941); Max Weber, *General Economic History* (New York: Collier, 1961); and Max Weber, *The Protestant Ethic and the Spirit of Capitalism* (New York: Scribner, 1958).

39. Dahrendorf, *Class and Class Conflict,* 68-69.

40. Ernest Mandel also locates the "second industrial revolution" in a "second technological revolution" based upon the adoption of electric power technology; "the emergence of the second technological revolution—above all in the technology of electric motors—was a compelling reason for the formulation of trusts and monopolies." Mandel, *Late Capitalism,* 188.

41. Dahrendorf, *Class and Class Conflict,* 68.

42. Marx, *Capital* (vol. 1), 333.

43. That is, every stage of historical development generates its own peculiar mode of cooperation, yet it can be spoken of only in relation to the model of capitalist cooperation, which represents its most organized moment. Or, as Marx suggests, "from the standpoint of these [precapitalist modes of cooperation], capitalistic co-operation itself appears to be a historical form peculiar to, and specifically distinguishing, the capitalist process of production." Marx, *Capital* (vol. 1), 334.

44. See, for example, Max Weber's definition of the modern state: "The primary formal characteristics of the modern state are as follows: it possesses an administrative and legal order subject to change by legislation, to which the organized corporate activity of the administrative staff, which is also regulated by legislation, is oriented." This understanding of the state clearly emphasizes the crucial managerial and administrative role played by political authority in organizing the economy and society. Max Weber, *The Theory of Social and Economic Organization,* ed. by Talcott Parsons (New York: Free Press, 1964), 156.

45. Karl Wittfogel, *Oriental Despotism: A Comparative Study of Total Power* (New Haven, CT: Yale University Press, 1959), 25-45.

46. Engels, *Origins of the Family,* 126.

47. Marx, *Contribution to the Critique,* 201.

48. Karl Marx, "Capital," *The Marx-Engels Reader,* ed. by Robert C. Tucker (New York: Norton, 1972), 272.

49. Ibid., 273; emphasis added.

50. Marx, *Capital* (vol. 1), 339.

51. More exactly, Marx elaborates on this concept in the following manner: "The collective labourer, formed by the combination of a number of detail labourers, is the machinery specially characteristic of the manufacturing period. The various operations that

are performed in turns by the producer of a commodity, and coalesce one with another during the process of production, lay claim to him in various ways. In one operation he must exert more strength, in another more skill, in another more attention; and the same individual does not possess all these qualities in an equal degree. After manufacture has once separated, made independent, and isolated the various operations, the labourers are divided, classified, and grouped according to their predominating qualities. If their natural endowments are, on the one hand, the foundation on which the division of labor is built up, on the other hand, manufacture, once introduced, develops in them new powers that are by nature fitted only for limited and special functions. The collective labourer now possesses, in an equal degree of excellence, all of the qualities requisite for production, and expends them in the most economical manner, by exclusively employing all his organs, consisting of particular labourers, or groups of labourers, in the performing of their special functions." See Marx, *Capital* (vol. 1), 348-349.

52. Ibid., 338.

53. Ibid., 349.

54. Ibid., 368.

55. Ibid., 424.

56. Ibid.

57. Ibid., 480.

58. See Braverman, *Labor and Monopoly Capital*; and Burawoy, *The Politics of Production*. For an early Marxist analysis of these tendencies, see Antonio Gramsci, "Americanism and Fordism," *Selections from the Prison Notebooks,* ed. by Quintin Hoare and Geoffrey Nowell Smith (New York: International, 1971), 277-318.

59. See Stuart Ewen, *Capital of Consciousness* (New York: McGraw-Hill, 1976); Christopher Lasch, *The Culture of Narcissism* (New York: Norton, 1979); Henri Lefebvre, *Everyday Life in the Modern World* (New York: Harper & Row, 1971); William Leiss, *The Limits to Satisfaction: An Essay on the Problem of Needs and Commodities* (Toronto: University of Toronto Press, 1976); and Alan Wolfe, *The Limits of Legitimacy: Political Contradiction of Contemporary Capitalism* (New York: Free Press, 1977).

60. See Timothy W. Luke, "The Modern Service State: Public Power in America from the New Deal to the New Beginning," *Race, Politics, and Culture: Critical Essays on the Radicalism of the 1960s,* ed. by Adolph Reed, Jr. (Westport, CT: Greenwood, 1986), 246-251.

61. In this regard, Marx argues that, "while in each individual workshop it enforces uniformity, regularity, order, and economy, it increases by the immense spur which the limitation and regulation of the working-day give to technical improvement, the anarchy and the catastrophes of capitalist production as a whole, the intensity of labour, and the competition of machinery with the labourer. By the destruction of petty and domestic industries it destroys the last resort of the 'redundant population' and with it the sole remaining safety-valve of the whole social mechanism." Marx, *Capital* (vol. 1), 503. Hence modern technique comes to reconstitute both the living place and the working place of modern society totally.

62. See, for example, Herman Kahn, *The Emerging Japanese Superstate: Challenge and Response* (Englewood Cliffs, NJ: Prentice-Hall, 1970); Zbigniew Brzezinski, *The Fragile Blossom: Crisis and Change in Japan* (New York: Harper & Row, 1972); Rodney Clark, *The Japanese Company* (New Haven, CT: Yale University Press, 1979); Ezra F. Vogel, *Japan as Number One: Lessons for America* (Cambridge, MA: Harvard University Press, 1979); William Ouchi, *Theory Z: How American Business Can Meet the Japanese Challenge* (Reading, MA: Addison-Wesley, 1981); Richard Bolling and John Bowles, *America's Competitive Edge: How to Get Our Country Moving Again* (New York: McGraw-Hill, 1982); William Ouchi, *The M-Form Society: How American Teamwork Can Recapture the Competitive Edge* (Reading, MA: Addison-Wesley, 1984); Chalmers Johnson, *MITI and the Japanese Miracle: The Growth of Industrial Policy* (Stanford, CA: Stanford University Press, 1982); and Kevin P. Phillips, *Staying on Top: The Business Case for a National Industrial Strategy* (New York: Random House, 1984).

3

Gramsci and Revolution:
On the Theory of Workers' Councils
and the Working-Class Party

What roles could technique and technology, as they have been treated in Chapters 1 and 2, play in organizing revolutionary resistance? How do existing means of production constrain revolutionary action? These and other questions are addressed effectively in Gramsci's political writings for the working-class press in Italy. During the decade preceding his arrest by Mussolini's police in November 1926, Antonio Gramsci, by his own accounting, "wrote enough words to fill up fifteen to twenty volumes of four hundred pages apiece." [1] Later, he modestly judged these writings as "stuff written for the day it appeared and I always thought it would be dead the day after." [2] Gramsci, however, was severely mistaken about the worth of the "stuff" he wrote for the days during World War I and the ensuing "Biennio Rosso." [3] It clearly is instead a "profoundly original body of thought," [4] as one can discover by reading Gramsci's daily and weekly contributions to the journals *Il Grido del Populo, Avanti!*, and *L'Ordine Nuovo.*

His theoretical vision, as it unfolds in these working-class publications from 1914 to 1921, ranges through a broad spectrum of issues: popular culture, working-class education, the Russian revolution, the politics of the PSI (Italian Socialist Party) and the CGL (General Confederation of Labor), the political significance of workers' councils, technology and Taylorism, the failures of the *Risorgimento,* colonialism and the *Mezzogiorno,* the class basis of the fascist reaction, and the creation of the PCI (Italian Communist Party). Indeed, much of the political and social theory elaborated more fully in the *Prison Notebooks* finds its initial articulation in these journalistic articles. Most important, given the discussion in Chapters 1 and 2, Gramsci outlines the political rationale and technical basis for creating a genuinely socialist "organization of production" out of workers' councils and a democratic revolutionary party.

Gramsci's writings from the "Biennio Rosso" period most importantly document his changing assessment of the roles to be played by workers' councils and mass parties in an Italian socialist revolution. By adhering to the Marxism "which is eternal, which represents the continuation of German and Italian idealism," Gramsci derogates the "false" Marxist principles he saw being advanced by the PSI and CGL on culture, history, and education as "contaminated by positivistic and naturalist encrustations." [5] His thinking accentuates the importance of popular politics for altering mass consciousness, which falsely accepts notions of culture as undigested factual knowledge, history as dehumanized natural process, and education as mechanical conditioning. Because of his more complex and sophisticated methods of analysis, Gramsci could criticize those apolitical men directly, especially those in the fold of the PSI and the CGL, who viewed history as if "events are hatched off-stage in the shadows; unchecked hands weave the fabric of collective life—and the masses of citizens know nothing." [6] His political theories and activist journalism combat the uncritical thinking—both mechanistic Marxism and positivistic liberalism—that permits the political fortunes of the working class to be "manipulated in the interests of narrow horizons, of the immediate ends of small groups of activities—and the mass of citizens know nothing." [7]

Gramsci's "Philosophy of Praxis"

To escape the economistic sociology of the Second International Marxists, Gramsci adopted Labriola's understanding of labor *in toto* in order to redefine the real subjects of history, antagonistic social classes formed in the social relations of labor, for Marxist philosophy. For Labriola, the "vulgar expounders of Marxism," or Engels, Kautsky, and Plekhanov, had robbed historical materialism of its "imminent philosophy and reduced it to a simple way of deducing changes in the historical conditions from changes in the economic conditions." [8] From this condition, it was a short hop into the mechanical materialism of Stalinist Marxism-Leninism. To recover the philosophical core of Marxism, then, Labriola returned to the concept of labor, because he believed that only labor or praxis can ground the sociality and historicity of men. The historical creation of human beings is the practical history of labor. The techniques of social relations, in turn, must be adapted closely to the constantly changing character of technology.

Consequently, Labriola's notion of praxis enabled Gramsci to escape the Second International's concern with "objective conditions" as well as Croce's "speculative historicism," which evades the role of politics in history in favor of "philosophy." Gramsci's appeal to an absolute historicism, or his own vision of a Hegelian Marxism, in turn, lets him specify the workings of history by referring to the politics of antagonistic social relations and indicating how philosophy and history are expressed by men in politics. Here, he adopts and respecifies the most progressive dimensions of Marx's method of political economy, discussed in Chapters 1 and 2. Gramsci transcends economism by resorting to human subjectivity, or political praxis, "a concept of imminence designating 'the ensemble of social relations in which real men move and function' as the only one capable of grounding idealist subjectivity anew as the 'subjectivity of a social group.' " [9]

Being capable of short-circuiting its philosophical reabsorption by mainstream mechanical Marxism and by retaining class struggles in its analysis, Gramsci's "absolute historicism," as a method, cues one to concentrate on the mediations of philosophy and history in praxis. Gramsci's own Marxist thinking, or what he calls "the philosophy of praxis," Paggi agrees, identifies theory and politics through "the concrete study of past history, and the current activity of creating new history." [10] Yet, it adduces no formal method or scientific codex of fixed methodological rules for directing activity. Instead of reducing historical materialism to another staid interpretative canon of deterministic causal relations between the "base" and "superstructure," Gramsci's philosophy of praxis stresses that formation of collective wills, engaged in creative human action, can resolve the tensions of competing social classes. [11]

Gramsci's dialectic is not reducible to the "materialist dialectics" of Bukharin or Plekhanov, which accentuate material cause and effect in historical and political processes. Rather, Gramsci elevates the dialectic from its role as "a sub-species of formal logic" for the Second International to "the very marrow of historiography and the science of politics." [12] The dialectic captures the continual tensions of opposing social forces whose theoretical mediation can be adduced only through interweaving history, economics, and politics into an organic whole. The dialectic, then, succeeds in giving access to "the *unity, specificity,* and *concreteness* of social phenomena by organically relating the otherwise separate and juxtaposed individual constituent elements." [13] Posed in this fashion, Paggi correctly describes how the philosophy of praxis transcends the linear causation of base-superstructure relations. Gramsci investigates how economic and political history mingle with technology in ensembles of "base" and "superstructural" elements, opening spaces for ethicopolitical action.

Gramsci's scientific problematic, then, "is not a question of 'discovering' a metaphysical law of 'determinism' or even of establishing a 'general' law of causality"; on the contrary, "it is a question of bringing out how in historical evolution relatively permanent forces are constituted which operate with a certain regularity and automatism." [14] The concept of hegemony embodies Gramsci's solution to this question. In the present, the ethicopolitical subject, or the working-class party, must constitute its cultural and political hegemony to create and institutionalize its revolutionary social relations. Moreover, only a correct analysis of all forces active in the present historical period—political, social, and military forces—can provide the mobilized class subject with the guidance necessary for rising to ascendancy. Therefore, in contemporary politics, the working classes, which seek "in turn to become a State" [15] and which are guided by the organic intellectuals trained in their ranks, form a new historical subject—a workers' party—in order to gain hegemony. The science of politics and society aims at translating the subjectivity of this class force into a worldview, or new culture.

On the question of cultural hegemony, some seem to interpret the cultural perpetuation of the bourgeois ethicopolitical moment in merely instrumental terms. Cultural hegemony equals "how the ruling classes control the media and education." [16] To control the means of education and indoctrination allows a class—either the bourgeoisie or potentially the proletariat—to establish and maintain its hegemonic position. In this reading, "Gramsci's life-long efforts to 'educate' the working class away from 'militancy,' and to train a new working class elite" [17] constitutes counterhegemonic struggle. The Gramscian "philosophy of praxis" in this scheme is reduced to the inculcation of bourgeois managerial and technical skills in the working classes. Instead of forging a new creative consciousness for popular political emancipation, counterhegemonic strategies are seen as *accommodating* the workers to the rigors of bourgeois culture.

Gramsci, we are told, "did not despise 'bourgeois' culture; on the contrary, he sought to diffuse it." [18] To be sure, Gramsci did encourage the diffusion of bourgeois culture to discipline and to educate the workers. He did so, however, to encourage their special elaboration of a *new* autonomous cultural project that could direct and fulfill their collective political liberation. Education in bourgeois culture was intended to smash the proletarian's *inner imprisonment* by providing him with the discipline, knowledge, and values to build "the mentality of a creator of history." [19] Yet, this treatment portrays counterhegemonic education as creating the "mentality" of bourgeois managers or technocrats. Here Gramsci sees the revolutionary movement, working to "educate" the workers to wield their powers "reasonably," because "they needed to develop technical and managerial skills, they needed to be better educated generally, above all they needed self-confidence and ability to take a broader, long-term view of their own interests." [20]

Proletarian self-emancipation becomes the ability "to absorb and 'dominate' bourgeois culture," while cultural hegemony is instrumentalized as "the knowledge and self-confidence needed to run society." [21] Clark's account, for example, does not convey the richness of Gramsci's designs for transcending bourgeois culture in order to create an unprecedented autonomous working-class culture. Cultural hegemony and its imposition in the name of the proletariat simply becomes the replacement of the bourgeoisie in their bourgeois institutions. As Clark maintains, "the working class could not take over unless it produced its own technicians, experts, managers, and leaders. Communists must be serious, skilled, disciplined, responsible men, men who could inspire confidence in their ability to manage the economy successfully." [22] A communist, however, in this sort of analysis appears to be a "historically compromised" PCI bureaucrat rather than the revolutionary organic intellectual that Gramsci saw as propounding a new, proletarian, cultural hegemony.

Gramsci's theory of the party outlines the ideal operation of the working-class educational state *in nuce*. Through the party, the " 'national-popular collective will' joins with an 'intellectual and moral reform,' " [23] enabling the historical subject to alter the existing historical bloc and its hegemonic influences. For Gramsci, the party is not a technical apparatus consisting of an elite vanguard to be used for imposing "enlightenment" on the masses. Rather, it must be direct and must educate the masses to attain self-leadership and personal responsibility in political activity: "The Communist Party is the instrument and historical form of the process of inner liberation through which the worker is transformed from *executor* to *initiator,* from *mass* to *leader* to *guide,* from brawn to brain to purpose." [24] It must, to a very significant extent, serve as a central element in a new organization of production suitable for managing a socialist and, then, a communist system of production. In fulfilling this ethicopolitical role, the party should create a new worldview and popular culture during the transition as it sets out Marxist science as a framework for the new hegemonic culture. Yet, this cultural role does not imply a centralist bureaucratic system of statist economic production and consumption, which truly has little to do with socialism.

The Strategy of Workers' Councils

Before Gramsci fully developed his idea of the working-class party, he first explored the possibilities of workers' councils as revolutionary agencies. To prompt the working class to realize "that events should be seen to be the intelligent work of men, and not the products of chance, of fatality," [25] Gramsci asserts that the mediation of a new popular culture, based upon active class will, can be discovered in the workers' council. Such a new popular culture would not be based on useless factual or intellectual knowledge. For Gramsci, "culture is something quite different. It is organization, discipline of one's inner self, a coming to terms with one's own personality; it is the attainment of a higher awareness, with the aid of which one succeeds in understanding one's own historical value, one's own function in life, one's own rights and obligations." [26]

Gramsci's commitment to enact this kind of ethical culture as political practice, through the mediation of the workers' councils, has several derivations. Frustrated by the parliamentary strategy of the PSI, Gramsci's vision of the PSI as a party committing suicide through its electoral struggles with the bourgeois parties initially prevented him from appreciating its significant strengths as well as its *potential* for playing a more decisive mass political role. Instead, he turned for his political inspiration to the *commissione interne,* established prior to the war by the workers' syndicates in the automobile plants around Turin. His initial faith in their potential as revolutionary political mediations, in turn, swelled immensely with each new report he received on the Russian revolution.

The living nucleus of the Russian revolution, he believed, was the *soviet.* That is, "the Soviets were the basic organizations to be integrated and developed, and the Bolsheviks became the government party precisely because they maintained that State power should rest upon and be controlled by the Soviets." [27] The flashes and fragments of news on the Russian revolution suggested that the Russian working classes were making their own historical destiny and culture through the organization of soviets, rather than through the bureaucratic machinations of political parties. Consequently, in those days prior to "war communism," Gramsci held that "the Russian revolution is the triumph of freedom; its organization is based on spontaneity, not on the dictates of a 'hero' who imposes himself through violence. It is a continuous and systematic elevation of a people, following the lines of a hierarchy, and creating for itself one by one the organs that the new social life demands." [28]

To advance and elevate the Italian working class systematically, Gramsci resolved to create the organs that the new social life demanded from within the workplace; from the *commissione interne* would emerge the revolutionary *consigli di fabbrica*. Fiori notes that Gramsci had studied the

> Russian experiment with "Soviets", or councils, and the development of the factory and farm councils into which the workers and peasants had organized themselves. And he asked himself: "Is there in Italy anything, any working-class institution, which one might compare to the Soviets, anything of the same nature? . . . Is there any germ, any first wish or tendency in the direction of government by Soviets here in Italy, in Turin?" The answer was yes. "There does exist in Italy, in Turin, an embryonic form of worker government: the internal committees." [29]

Potentially, Gramsci saw that the party must "become an anti-state that is prepared to take over from the bourgeoisie all its social functions as ruling class," but the factory councils were to impart to "each individual a clear, precise, rationally acquired conviction that the only feasible road to individual and social well-being is via political and social organization." [30]

Prior to the setbacks of 1919 and 1920, the workers' councils incarnated the essence of a consciousness-changing proletarian movement for Gramsci. The party was, at best, a secondary adjunct to the primary struggle for self-determination in the workplace. The communists offered nothing of real value unless they revealed "among the masses a capacity, the beginnings of a new life, the aspiration to create new institutions and the historical drive to renew human society from the roots upwards." [31] The communists as a group probed "capacities" and prodded "aspirations," but it was for the *workers,* organizing their *own* councils in their *own* particular factories, to renew society from the roots upwards. Hence the political imagination of a communist party did not forge a "liberation of spirit, the establishment of a new moral order." [32] On the contrary, such transformations were laid at the doorstep of human labor in the realm of necessity:

> The development of heavy industry has created the conditions for the working class to acquire an awareness of its own historical autonomy: an awareness of the possibility of constructing, through its own ordered and disciplined work, a new system of economic and juridical relations based on the special function performed by the working class in the life of the world.[33]

The councils, unlike the existing working-class unions or parties, could induce the workers to redefine themselves as *producers,* as historical agents, instead of as *commodities,* as mechanical objects. Being based upon the everyday practices of the shop floor, Gramsci firmly believed the councils would give "workers direct responsibility for production, provide them with an incentive to improve their work, instill a conscious and voluntary discipline, and create a producer's mentality—the mentality of a creator of history." [34]

In his account, however, Clark consistently evaluates Gramsci as an ardent "productivist." At many junctures, one may rightly wonder whether Clark is discussing Antonio Gramsci or Gino Olivetti, the secretary-general of the General Confederation of Industry.[35] As "Americanism and Fordism" openly demonstrates, Gramsci saw benefits in Taylorism and scientific management as *means* for attaining his ultimate ethical and political ends. Clark, however, fails to draw this crucial fine distinction in Gramsci's gingerly explored but eventual acceptance of Taylorism. Instead, Gramsci is seen as adopting scientific management as an expedient strategy that serves the political and managerial interests of the *Ordine Nuovo* circle's "true" constituency, namely, the "skilled engineering workers—the labor aristocracy of the time." [36] Even though Gramsci's interest in workers' councils had "moral grounds—it rescues men from serfdom," for Clark, Gramsci mainly backed the councils out of "productivist" motives or on "economic grounds—it alone can produce a sober, disciplined, industrious skilled labor force." [37]

Still, Gramsci did not, in fact, simply accept Taylorism to realize his "productivist" dreams. He admittedly welcomed the disciplinary rhythms of Taylorism, but only inasmuch as they promised as a set of social techniques to lead to a new social psychology, or, in his own words, a new "psycho-physical nexus." [38] Taylorism, for Gramsci, appeared as "the biggest collective effort to date to create, with unprecedented speed, and with a consciousness of purpose unmatched in history, a new type of worker and of man." [39] Although he undoubtedly was wrong on this insight, Gramsci considered Taylorism as a revolutionary means for creating and preserving an autonomous proletarian culture rooted in the totality of the work process. This new social psychology imposed by the workers themselves would "simply have the purpose of preserving, outside of work, a certain psycho-physical equilibrium which prevents the physiological collapse of the worker, exhausted by the new method of production"; moreover, when employed by existing forms of capitalism to control the working classes, "this equilibrium can only be something purely external and mechanical." [40]

Yet, Gramsci believed that in the hands of a working-class movement, scientific management could become an emancipatory force. He asserts, "It can become internalized if it is proposed by the worker himself, and not imposed from the outside, if it is proposed by a new form of society, with appropriate and original methods." [41] Gramsci failed to elaborate upon which technical "methods" would be the *most* appropriate and original, but the critical point is that Taylorism was embraced not as a management goal but rather as a revolutionary technological opportunity for creating a new kind of social individual. He constantly attended to the political dimension of Taylorism, seeking its possible contributions to a new organization of production as well as its potential flaws as a system of social relations. He did not embrace Taylorism, as Lenin did, as a means of shifting the management of superefficient modes of production—complete with superalienation and superexploitation—from the bourgeois entrepreneur to the party bureaucrat. Seeing the revolutionary possibilities in Italy's emergent neotechnical modes of production, he sought to outline the best set of social relations suitable for turning its promise to his revolutionary purposes.

Many studies fail to mark this important dimension in Gramsci's thinking. Consequently, Gramsci is depicted as a committed "productivist" who saw the politics of the workers' councils not as an emancipation of consciousness, but rather as the modern *rational* organization of labor. Clark claims:

> Gramsci's theories cannot be understood unless this aspect is stressed. Taylorism and the Factory Councils were linked. Rational factory organization would promote a sense of participation in collective effort, and the Factory Councils themselves could be defined as an attempt to make "subjective" what was given "objectively," to make workers fully aware of the complexities of industrial production and factory organization.[42]

The workers' "awareness," in turn, of the "complexities" involved in modern industrial production should lead them to "advocate and incarnate hard work, skills, discipline—the traditional 'worker-aristocratic' virtues; and they were designed to overcome the useless insurrectionism, the mindless rioting and striking, which were in Gramsci's view characteristic of the Italian Left, and which would inevitably lead to defeat." [43] Both Taylorism and Marxism, in Clark's opinion, are nothing more than a late-industrial methodism in Gramsci's political calculations, for "through them, Italian workers would abandon their facile spontaneous revolts and their traditional 'subversivism,' and learn to take a broader, more 'modern' view." [44]

This approach reduces Gramsci's considerable *political imagination* to mere PCI *administrative blueprints*. Overcoming "useless" insurrectionism, abandoning traditional "subversivism," forsaking "mindless" striking, adopting "worker-aristocratic" virtues, and learning to take a "modern" view all point toward the policies of the post-World War II PCI. Such ideas about Gramsci's "productivism" lead some to interject an orthodox Taylorism into Gramsci's "philosophy of praxis," which more closely fits the discursive representation of Gramsci by the present-day Italian Communist Party. It ignores, however, Gramsci's own vision of Communist politics, which should reveal to the workers "the beginnings of a new life, the aspiration to create new institutions and the historical drive to renew human society from the roots upwards." [45] Such aspirations often require insurrectionism, subversivism, and spontaneity, but these practices do not necessarily "inevitably lead to defeat." [46] The workers' councils, by the same token, were not backed by Gramsci out of *productivist* motives—to train better workers, to discipline the shop floor, or to raise productivity.[47] The councils, to Gramsci, either before the factory occupations or after his rise to the PCI's leadership, were to be *ethicopolitical* mediations of a new collective individuality—raising industrial output levels and individual unit productivity would be the *by-product* and not the overarching *goal* of council communism. A truly communist organization of production also would be the keystone in new emancipatory social relations. In his analysis of modern industry, Gramsci constantly was searching for the right ethicopolitical organization to match to its revolutionary technical potential.

For the most part, Gramsci's trust in the discipline of the workplace to forge a common consciousness among the urban working class proved to be quite naive. Workers' councils did create an awareness of autonomy, the possibility of a new social system, and the mentality of historical creators. Yet, in the conjunctural moment, these hard-won possibilities could not be translated politically into autonomy, a new society, or historical transformation. The exceptional character of the heavily industrialized Turin region, the considerable strength of the large industrialists, and the resistance of the PSI and CGL to the council communists all combined to entrap Gramsci's theoretical designs in a cage of harsh political realities. Leading up to the events of 1920, Gramsci held that "the Factory Council is the model of the proletarian state." [48] The outcome of the 1920 strike and factory occupations, nevertheless, bore the model out as one of confused indecision. Without an overarching political program, the working class, when mobilized in the councils, soon "found itself trapped and imprisoned in a system of watertight compartments, bewildered, disillusioned, exposed to all manner of anarchoid temptations." [49] Instead of forming "a collective personality, a collective soul, a collective will," [50] the councils at various plants indulged in "factory egoism," while at many sites "ordered and disciplined work" failed to form a "producer's mentality" and the workers simply deserted en masse.

In the councils, Gramsci asserted, "the will of the masses is what is stated in an organic and durable fashion, constructing each day a new cell of the working-class psychology, of the new social organization." [51] Unfortunately, the new social organizations were neither organic nor durable expressions of mass will, because the masses on their own could not direct their will or realize their capacity. Ultimately, as Premier Giolitti mediated a compromise between the workers and the industrialists, Gramsci admitted "the mistake of believing that only the masses can achieve the communist revolution." [52] In the early days of the occupation, Gramsci observed that the workers could "rely on no one but themselves" in the creation of their own history. Sadly, this fact turned out to be the workers' major problem. [53] When cornered in the immediacy of their particular factories, their "disciplined labor relations" gave them no sense of collective action or class strategy. The old disorganization rather than a new organization of production ensued. "Every factory looked to its own defenses, like a militia. There was no co-ordination," as Gramsci later conceded, "there was no communist party." [54]

The exigencies of political struggle during 1919 and 1920, then, forced Gramsci to reevaluate the role of the party. As he had recognized before with regard to unions, in councils alone "the working class is not organized into forms which accord with its real historical structure, and is not mobilized into a formation that is ceaselessly adapting itself to the laws governing the inner process of real historical development of the class itself." [55] In recognizing this, however, Gramsci does not embrace an elitist-vanguard party model. On the contrary, he maintains his faith in mass-popular organization and simply substitutes his vision of a highly politicized popular party for the workers' councils in his schema. A mass-based and popularly organized party would perform all of the social and educational duties of the councils, while at the same time solving the considerable political problems of the council organization.

The Party: Views from
Gramsci, Tasca, and Bordiga

In Gramsci's early journalistic writings, the party increasingly gains definition as the working-class pedagogical state *in nuce*. It roots itself in the entire working class because every effective party is a class party mediating the *totality* of its particular class relations. The party embodies, in Gramsci's view, "the vigilant revolutionary consciousness of the whole of the exploited class . . . so that it may win their permanent trust and thus become their guide and intellect." [56] The party, acting as a guide or class intellect, frees the working class from its own immediacy, the passion and spontaneity of living the already existing culture. The party serves as the political mediation for smashing open the grip of immediacy, for escaping the past, and for creating a new culture. At first, Gramsci believed that the discipline of the workplace, assisted by council organization, would achieve these very same results. In fact, the masses alone, even when aided by workers' councils, only reproduce the immediate relations of everyday living while striving to induce political change; hence the party must be formed as an educational agent to prefigure the goal of, and the means for, transcending the existing culture.

The Gramscian party represents the political and intellectual mediation of the concrete, objective situation—what is—and the ideal subjective conditions—what could be—put into popularly comprehensible political practice. Through the party, Gramsci asserts, the worker can overcome the appearance that "he is intellectually lazy; he cannot and does not wish to look beyond his immediate horizon, so he lacks criteria in his choice of leaders and allows himself to be easily taken in by promises. He likes to believe he can get what he wants without making a great effort himself or thinking too much." [57] As the working-class pedagogical state *in nuce*, the party anticipates the transformative changes of popular culture, giving the workers access to their collective essence:

> The worker takes his place in the Communist Party and there "discovers" and "invents" original ways of living, collaborates "consciously" in the world's activity, thinks, foresees, becomes responsible, becomes an organizer rather than someone who is organized and feels he forms a vanguard that pushes ahead and draws the masses of the people after it.[58]

Factory councils may spark this change, in addition to laying the concrete basis for working-class administration of the economy and industries after the transition. Still, Gramsci realizes that the party would fully transform and guide the working class.

To eliminate completely the "inner imprisonment" of working-class culture, the Communist party should renew and redirect the consciousness of economic objects to reveal their ultimate potential as ethicopolitical subjects in the prefigurative party-state. For Gramsci, "as the Communist Party is formed, a seed of liberty is planted that will sprout to its full height only after the workers' State has organized the requisite material conditions." [59] After the factory occupation failures in 1920, Gramsci forsakes the workers' councils as the ultimate source of an emergent revolution. Instead, he develops this vision of a new type of party, which the PSI *should* have become as an advocate of the working class's proletarian movement. However, it *could not* become this kind of agency because of its parliamentary adventures. The new Communist party had to become this kind of pedagogical force to sustain the *proletarian* movement after 1920 as a *revolutionary* movement.

For the most part, Gramsci's newspaper articles adequately document the "attempt to hammer out, in intimate relations with mass proletarian practice in Turin, a theory of specific organizational forms capable of harnessing the full revolutionary potential of the class and representing the embryos of a future soviet State in Italy." [60] Unfortunately, some still make an effort to vindicate the "correctness" of Bordiga's vanguardism and Tasca's frontism over the "mistakes made" by Gramsci's council communism.[61] Such proponents of Bordiga and Tasca argue that Gramsci theoretically failed "to grasp the essential role of the revolutionary party in centralizing the struggle against the existing order and organizing the insurrectionary seizure of power." [62] In fact, these arguments actually further demonstrate the greater sophistication of Gramsci's notions of both the party and the councils over those of Bordiga and Tasca, particularly given the complete failures in Eastern Europe and the USSR of the bureaucratic centralist party that these ideas inspired.

Bordiga's pragmatic pastiche of electoral abstentionism, party vanguardism, and party manipulation of the workers' councils sharply contrasts with Tasca's orthodox trade-union strategies. Prior to the revolutionary transition, Bordiga takes an instrumental tack on unions and councils; these structures are useful to the Communist party, which "needs organs in which it can operate." [63] Following the revolution, unions and councils would become the party's conduits for industrial administration. Gramsci divorces councils from unions as they represent two distinct forms of struggle for two different goals. Unions encourage a false class consciousness based upon a "commodity mentality" struggling for higher wages, while councils center upon the organization of production and the workplace.

Tasca, on the other hand, unites the two struggles, "since the 'council' is nothing but the expression of trade-union activity at the workplace and the union is the master body grouping the councils by productive sector, co-ordinating and disciplining their action." [64] For Tasca, the structural question is simple: "The council is the cellular unit of a whole—the trade union." [65] Councils and unions engage in the same battle for Tasca. Hence his revolutionary formula, especially after the 1920 occupations, was to restore and strengthen the trade unions to organize and coordinate the working-class movement. "No cause would be more worthy of hazarding all the forces of the proletariat," he concludes, than a revolution provoked "on the elementary terrain of trade union freedom." [66] Gramsci reacted negatively to this weak inspiration, contending that Tasca's orthodox trade-unionist tactics vitiated both council and party practices in returning to a false bureaucratic discipline, "which means giving a factory codification to relations between exploiter and exploited." [67]

Bordiga's vision of the party, the workers' councils, and the unions varied immensely from both Gramsci's and Tasca's. Bordiga's elitist-vanguard party, which grows straight out of Lenin's *What Is to Be Done?*, is attractive to a great many students of Italian politics, including Quintin Hoare and Gwyn Williams,[68] because of its simple project: "the elaboration of a consciousness, a political culture, in the *leaders,* through a more serious study of the problems of the revolution, with fewer distractions from spurious electoral, parliamentary, and minimalist activities." [69] In a two-pronged attack on his rivals, Bordiga asserted that Gramsci and Tasca both lacked the "proper" party perspective. "The forging of a sound and healthy revolutionary movement in Italy," Bordiga claimed, "will never be accomplished by advancing new organs modelled on future forms, like factory councils or soviets—just as it was an illusion to believe that the revolutionary spirit could be salvaged from reformism by importing it into the unions, seen as the nuclei of the future society." [70] Here, Gramsci's vision of the party surpasses Bordiga's uncritical acceptance of the Leninist precedents. Instead of modeling revolutionary organization on its future forms, like Gramsci's notion of both the party and, in part, the councils, Bordiga would create the future by reproducing the political past only under the enlightened aegis of the party vanguard.

The dismal catastrophe of the factory councils movement in Italy cannot be attributed solely to Gramsci and the *Ordine Nuovo* circle. Such "subjective" factors, as Clark argues, had their serious theoretical and practical failings, but they did not cause the failure. On the contrary, the "objective" conditions—Turin's exceptional industrial development, sectarian struggles within the PSI, inadequate working-class training, and "factory egoism"—are the more likely culprits behind the factory councils' eventual collapse. That the *Ordine Nuovo* figures did not effectively "organize and discipline shop-floor militancy" is quite true. Similarly, the fact that the circle itself, as Tasca's defection to the trade-unionist cause and the antifascist front indicates, often was at desperate odds with itself. Hence its members and followers "could be easily diverted into 'reformist' channels." [71] This analysis greatly improves upon claims attributing failure to the lack of a disciplined vanguard party capable of springing into action to seize the day for the Italian proletariat.

Clark's well-documented history, more completely than many other works, records the richness of Gramsci's theoretical project in relation to the social and political upheavals that struck Italy during the decade after its belated entry into World War I. Still, he falls short of appreciating the full import of Gramsci's Marxism, "the one that never dies, the continuation of Italian and German idealist thought." [72] Instead of a Leninized Gramsci wending his way from Hegelian error toward an eventual acknowledgment of Bordiga, Clark introduces a Togliattian Gramsci—one who backs councils as the "right" kind of institutionalized consensus building, who renounces "useless" insurrectionism, who plans the managerial training of workers through self-management, and who smugly embraces Gino Olivetti's "productivist" future. Instead of using Taylorism as political technique to extend the autonomous project of the philosophy of praxis as part of a new "psycho-physical nexus," Clark's Gramsci reduces the philosophy of praxis to efficient but proletarian scientific management. And instead of reading the lessons of the Comintern period back into the "Biennio Rosso," Clark projects the teachings of the *Via Italiana* back into the *Ordinovista* Gramsci. This new generation of criticism pictures Gramsci as a structural reformist who would spread bourgeois expertise, rather than as a Jacobin vanguardist who should build the party. This shift in emphasis perhaps represents some form of progressive evolution, yet it also is an unlikely position for asserting that Gramsci's revolution was one that "failed."

Plainly, more recent attempts by many to "Bordiganize" Gramsci, because of *his* failure to understand the "revolutionary party," seem ill considered. In fact, it appears that it was Bordiga who failed to understand clearly the role of the party. Gramsci immediately realized that Bordiga's party vanguardism would be self-defeating in that it relies on the crude reflection upon existing political appearances by an enlightened leadership. The masses were to be led passively into the working-class state by Bordigan leaders. Yet Gramsci knew that such a vision of the Italian political future would only reproduce the elitist-centralized organization of the past except for its "working-class" leadership. The Gramscian image of the party had little to do with such crude beliefs. Rather, it prefiguratively produces its own revolutionary popular practices in the process of changing the present into the future. The Gramscian party is historical *essence* transformed into popular practice, not existing *appearance* turned to bureaucratic manipulation. The party planned out by Gramsci after 1920 is the pedagogical state *in nuce*, not the apparatchik state *in nuce*. It should create what is not yet—the popular working-class state—not in contradiction to, but out of what has been—the history, culture, and politics of the working class.

Despite Gramsci's high hopes for the party as a pedagogical state *in nuce*, he also was deeply aware of the increasing tendencies toward technocratic domination within bureaucratic formations, such as modern states or mass political parties. He notes that traditional humanistic education increasingly is being displaced by the rise of specialized professional training. In the workings of different bureaucracies, more specifically,

> it may also be observed that deliberative bodies tend to an ever-increasing extent to distinguish their activity into two "organic" aspects: into the deliberative activity which is their essence, and into technical-cultural activity in which the questions upon which they have to take decisions are first examined by experts and analyzed scientifically. This latter activity has already created a whole bureaucratic body, with a new structure; for apart from the specialized departments of experts who prepare the technical material for the deliberative bodies, a second body of functionaries is created—more or less disinterested "volunteers," selected variously from industry, from the banks, from finance houses.[73]

Such dynamics in favor of technocratic process, Gramsci notes, grow out of the differentiation and particularization of knowledge:

> One must bear in mind the developing tendency for every practical activity to create for itself its own specialized school, just as every intellectual available tends to create for itself cultural associations of its own; the latter take on the function of post-scholastic institutions, specialized in organizing the conditions in which it is possible to keep abreast of whatever progress is being made in the given scientific field.[74]

The professionalization of knowledge production, as well as the specialization in its interpretation and application, lies at the root of modern technocratic power in large private and public bureaucracies. For Gramsci,

> this is one of the mechanisms by means of which the career bureaucracy eventually came to control the democratic regimes and parliaments; now the mechanism is being organically extended, and is absorbing into its sphere the great specialists of private enterprise, which thus comes to control both regimes and bureaucracies. What is involved is a necessary, organic development which tends to integrate the personnel specialized in the technique of politics with personnel specialized in the concrete problems of administering the essential practical activities of the great and complex national societies of today. Hence every attempt to exorcise these tendencies from the outside produces no result other than moralistic sermons and rhetorical lamentations.[75]

Nonetheless, in this fusion of bureaucratic growth and knowledge development, a new type of power—resting with a stratum of technocratic/bureaucratic functionaries—arises in any complex modern society, challenging the traditional conditions of political rule.

Consequently, Gramsci foresaw the necessity of completely rethinking the working-class party and its means of exerting control. With regard to the nature of modern political power, he argues:

> The question is thus raised of modifying the training of technical-political personnel, completing their culture in accordance with the new necessities, and of creating specialized functionaries of a new kind, who as a body will complement deliberative activity. The traditional type of political "leader," prepared only for formal-juridical activities, is becoming anachronistic and represents a danger for the life of the State: the leader must have that minimum of general technical culture which will permit him, if not to "create" autonomously the correct solution, at least to know how to adjudicate between the solutions put forward by the experts, and hence to choose the correct one from the "synthetic" viewpoint of political technique.[76]

The emergence of these technocratic discourses out of the eclipse of traditional leadership plainly has a major influence upon the administration of modern states, as Chapters 5 and 6 will illustrate in regard to contemporary American society and Chapters 8 and 9 will indicate about the developing countries.

Gramsci's concern, however, was how to avoid the vanguardist dictatorship latent in these trends, while eliciting the most democratic and culturally sensitive participation of the workers in mass revolutionary organizations. His response was to prefigure the posttransitional state in the transitional struggle by cultivating a wide range of new organic intellectuals among the workers to work for themselves against vanguard elitism and for popular democracy. Prefigurative party struggle would succeed because it fuses and mediates the irrational past—mass culture—with the rational future—party culture—in the process of forming the future, mediating mass-popular activity with pedagogical-party guidance through sophisticated "organic intellectuals." Gramsci, like many Western Marxists after World War I, made "extremely serious mistakes"[77] in his tactics during the "Biennio Rosso" with regard to the party question. Yet, he soon recognized the problem and adduced his own corrections by elaborating his own unique vision of the new communist party needed in Italy. Any attempt to "Bordiganize" or "Leninize" Gramsci adds nothing and, in fact, only takes away much from this very sophisticated concept of the Gramscian party.

Conclusions

In his early political writings, Gramsci demonstrates the scope of his insight into Italian political realities as he foreshadows the advent of fascism by reading its origins out of Italy's relations of production in the 1920s. While the events of national politics spilled into the eddy of the "Biennio Rosso," two channels opened for their further movement—one into a predatory fascist regime based upon the northern industrial cartels and the southern "landowners," and the other into a communist-led socialist revolution. Gramsci notes that "communism is the response of the working class to reaction," [78] as Giolitti's administration prompted many among the petty bourgeois and bourgeois classes to clamor for a man on a white horse to restore order and discipline in Italy.

In Gramsci's analysis, fascism always existed in Italy as the "outgrowth of the disastrous economic conditions to which capitalism has reduced the Italian people; it is an outgrowth of the nationalist illusions and opportunist delusions of a State that can no longer guarantee food, clothing and housing for the population. Reaction is the attempt to wriggle out of the situation by means of a new war." [79] The industrialized north's inability to impose its hegemony on the *Mezzogiorno* blocked Italy's limited "bourgeois revolution." Politically impotent, the bourgeoisie tolerated the Catholic church, the southern landowners, and the petty bourgeois urban functionaries of the small southern cities as they all perpetuated the privileges of the feudal regime.

Even under these conditions this ruling bloc could not make ends meet in either the state or the economy. Consequently, the urban petty bourgeoisie and their northern industrial backers turned to fascism—or, as Gramsci labels them, "the Monkey-People"—in order to maintain the interests of landed property and large industry by embarking upon wars in the Adriatic and Africa. "Having ruined Parliament, the petty bourgeoisie is currently ruining the bourgeois state," Gramsci also accurately realized. "The Monkey-People make news, not history. They leave their mark in newspapers, but provide no material for books." [80] In destroying the last vestiges of the bourgeois state, the fascists also eradicated the communist working-class movement in the 1920s as their last serious political rivals. Although he eventually was defeated, Gramsci made history in resisting the fascists' usurpation of Italian history in the 1920s and 1930s. He proposed, in turn, new political designs for a truly socialized organization of production, which would resurface in Italian critical thinking after World War II to cope with the emerging high technologies of twentieth-century industry.

Notes

1. Giuseppi Fiori, *Antonio Gramsci: Life of a Revolutionary* (New York: Schocken, 1970), 104. For additional discussion, see Walter Adamson, *Hegemony and Revolution: A Study of Antonio Gramsci's Political and Cultural Theory* (Berkeley: University of California Press, 1980); Christine Buci-Glucksmann, *Gramsci and the State* (London: Lawrence & Wishart, 1980); John A. Davis, ed., *Gramsci and Italy's Passive Revolution* (London: Croom Helm, 1979); James Joll, *Gramsci* (London: Fontana, 1977); Anne Showstack Sassoon, ed., *Approaches to Gramsci* (London: Writers & Readers Publishing Cooperative, 1982); and Paolo Spriano, *Antonio Gramsci and the Party: The Prison Years* (London: Lawrence & Wishart, 1979).

2. Fiori, *Antonio Gramsci,* 104.

3. See Antonio Gramsci, *Selections from Political Writings (1910-1920),* with additional texts by Bordiga and Tasca, ed. by Quintin Hoare (London: Lawrence & Wishart, 1977); and Antonio Gramsci, *History, Philosophy and Culture in the Young Gramsci,* ed. by Pedro Cavalcanti and Paul Piccone (St. Louis: Telos, 1975).

4. Gramsci, *Political Writings,* xiii.

5. Ibid., 34.

6. Ibid., 17.

7. Ibid.

8. Arturo Labriola, *Socialism and Philosophy,* trans. by Ernest Untermann (Chicago: C. H. Kerr, 1907), 77-78.

9. Leonardo Paggi, "Gramsci's General Theory of Marxism," *Telos* 33 (Fall 1977), 36.

10. Ibid., 42.

11. For further discussion along similar lines, see Carl Boggs, *Gramsci's Marxism* (London: Pluto, 1976), 21-35. Also see Paul Piccone, *Italian Marxism* (Berkeley: University of California Press, 1983), 1-43.

12. Antonio Gramsci, *Selections from the Prison Notebooks,* trans. by Quintin Hoare and Geoffrey Nowell Smith (New York: International, 1971), 435.

13. Paggi, "Gramsci's General Theory," 44.

14. Gramsci, *Prison Notebooks,* 412.

15. Ibid., 381.

16. Martin Clark, *Antonio Gramsci and the Revolution That Failed* (New Haven, CT: Yale University Press, 1977), 2.

17. Ibid., 6.

18. Ibid., 53.

19. Gramsci, *Political Writings,* 101.

20. Clark, *Antonio Gramsci,* 6.

21. Ibid., 223.

22. Ibid.

23. Gramsci, *Prison Notebooks,* 133. It is doubtful that Gramsci was even exposed to Leninism as a system until 1922. Up to that time, most of his information on Lenin and

Bolshevism was drawn secondhand from newspapers, socialist journals, and his own personal correspondence. Still, as Fiori records, Gramsci admitted to possibly "being misled by my ignorance of sources" in his efforts to understand the workings of "Leninism" in the Soviet Union. Fiori, *Antonio Gramsci,* 166. With regard to the Bolsheviks, Gramsci saw the philosophy of praxis being put to its fullest use in his "The Revolution Against Capital." He states: "The Bolsheviks repudiate Karl Marx, they affirm with the testimony of explicit action, with achieved conquests, that the canons of historical materialism are not so unyielding as one would think or as one has thought.... The Bolsheviks are not 'Marxists'.... They live the Marxist thought that never dies, which is the continuation of Italian and German idealistic thought." Gramsci, *History, Philosophy and Culture," 124.* In keeping with this line of thought, Gramsci's writing in 1925-1926 also supports Lenin by presenting the "Bolshevization" of the communist parties as a continuation of Lenin's "realization" of Marxist science. Obviously, both positions reflect Gramsci's misinformation on the finer points of Leninism as much as they embody Gramsci's unique vision of the Soviet experience.

24. Gramsci, *Political Writings,* 333.

25. Ibid., 18.

26. Ibid., 11.

27. Ibid., 53.

28. Ibid., 54.

29. Fiori, *Antonio Gramsci,* 119.

30. Ibid., 58.

31. Ibid., 172.

32. Ibid., 30.

33. Ibid., 172-173.

34. Ibid., 101.

35. For additional discussion, see Franklin Adler, "Factory Councils, Gramsci and the Industrialists," *Telos* 31 (Spring 1977), 67-90.

36. Clark, *Antonio Gramsci,* 7.

37. Ibid., 11-12.

38. Gramsci, *Prison Notebooks,* 302.

39. Ibid.

40. Ibid., 303.

41. Ibid.

42. Clark, *Antonio Gramsci,* 70.

43. Ibid.

44. Ibid., 71.

45. Gramsci, *Political Writings,* 172.

46. Clark, *Antonio Gramsci,* 70.

47. See Sergio Bologna, "Class Composition and the Theory of the Party at the Origin of the Workers-Council Movement," *Telos* 13 (Fall 1972), 427. Bologna reviews how German workers' councils served as the reserve of highly skilled workers who harbored "productivist" visions for their council activities. Also see Piccone, *Italian Marxism,* 191-194.

48. Ibid., 100.

49. Ibid., 157.

50. Ibid., 345.

51. Ibid., 175.

52. Ibid., 351.

53. Ibid., 345.

54. From *L'Ordine Nuovo,* October 9, 1920, quoted in Gwyn Williams, *Proletarian Order: Antonio Gramsci, Factory Councils, and the Origins of Communism in Italy, 1911-1921* (London: Pluto, 1975), 253.

55. Gramsci, *Political Writings,* 98-99.

56. Ibid., 141.

57. Ibid., 333.
58. Ibid., 333.
59. Ibid.
60. Ibid., xiv.
61. Ibid., xv.
62. Ibid.
63. Ibid., 214.
64. Ibid., 252.
65. Ibid.
66. Ibid., 259.
67. Ibid., 258.
68. See Quintin Hoare and Geoffrey Nowell Smith, "Introduction," *Selections from the Prison Notebooks of Antonio Gramsci* (New York: International, 1971), xxv-lxxxvii. Also see Gwyn Williams, *Proletarian Order*, 253.
69. Gramsci, *Political Writings*, 232-233.
70. Ibid., 232.
71. Clark, *Antonio Gramsci*, 72.
72. Ibid., 51.
73. Gramsci, *Prison Notebooks*, 27.
74. Ibid.
75. Ibid., 27-28.
76. Ibid., 28.
77. Ibid., xiv. With respect to Gramsci's eventual rapprochement with Bordiga and the abstentionist faction of the PSI, Clark correctly observes that it was merely a marriage of convenience, in which Gramsci gained free rein in Piedmont in exchange for his acceptance of Bordiga's preeminence outside of the heavily industrialized northern province. Ultimately, he saw the formation of the PCI under Bordiga's leadership and its subsequent failure to attract many of the PSI's working-class members as a tremendous disaster for working-class organization in Italy. Indeed, the Livorno split was seen by Gramsci as the "greatest triumph of reaction." Clark, *Antonio Gramsci*, 209.
78. Clark, *Antonio Gramsci*, 355.
79. Ibid., 353.
80. Ibid., 374.

PART III

Instrumental Reason
and Popular Revolution

4

The Dialectics of
Social Critique in Rousseau:
On Nature and Society

Critics of Rousseau often suggest that his political and social theories are a purely eighteenth-century project. Rousseau, of course, can be read that way, particularly if this is the critic's rhetorical intent. However, I would argue that his theoretical work must not be buried in the historical confines of only one phase in the development of modern critical discourse.[1] To offer an alternative interpretive perspective, Rousseau also can be viewed as a very contemporary social critic inasmuch as he worked at an important juncture in the development of instrumental reason within modern industrial society. In describing the increasing alienation and reification of everyday life during the stages of primitive accumulation and manufacture as industrial capitalism developed in Europe, Rousseau's critical discourse asks many of the same questions about domination, Enlightenment philosophy, and radical change raised by twentieth-century critical social theorists.[2] His project arguably represents the first thorough critique of the cultural domination in the scientific worldview, the false consciousness engendered by commodity fetishism, and the one-dimensionality of everyday life implicit in the then rising, but now dominant, "Enlightenment schema." [3]

Rousseau's theoretical work, then, historically presages and currently complements Marxian political economy, which was discussed in Chapters 1, 2, and 3, and critical social theory, which will be addressed more extensively in Chapters 5 and 6. When Rousseau records that in his writings, "I demolished the pitiful lies of mankind; I dared to expose their nature in all its nakedness, to follow the progress of time and of things which have disfigured this nature; and, comparing the man, as man has made him [*l'homme de l'homme*], with the natural man [*l'homme naturel*], I showed him, in his pretended perfection, the true source of his misery," [4] he should not be seen as a misguided utopian. Instead, his critical analysis of progress constitutes a penetrating appraisal of the alienation and anomie inherent in modern industrial life.

Like Marx's critique of political economy, which was discussed in Chapters 1 and 2, Rousseau's project does not stop at a mere critique. In understanding his world, Rousseau also seeks to change it. However, unlike Marx, he is deeply distrustful of the transformative potential of modern technology, seeing it as the cause of humankind's ruin. Like Marcuse, who will be considered in Chapter 5, he reasserts the importance of human consciousness and action by stressing how men might escape or forestall the dehumanization of modern life through participatory politics and correct education. In Rousseau's terms, the nature of men has developed even greater disfigurations with the greater "progress of time and of things" since the late eighteenth century. And his theoretical judgments on creating an emancipatory society through meaningful political participation and effective civic education retain considerable value for present-day social theory and political practice.

Rousseau discusses the social conflicts inherent in a society divided between the rich and the poor. Unlike the orthodox Marxist schema, however, which trusts the inevitable workings of the forces of production to change the consciousness of the poor to oppose the rich, Rousseau underscores the "primacy of politics" in prefiguring an emancipatory society to reconstitute social relations without artificial divisions between rich and poor, ruler and ruled, strong and weak. In this chapter, then, I will reconsider several important but often ignored relationships within the body of Rousseau's political and social theory, illustrating how critically significant Rousseau's "sad and great system" [5] remains both for his own time and in the present day.

The System of Rousseau's Thought

Rousseau's critics continually refuse to regard him as a systematic thinker. Shklar submits that Rousseau's project does not possess "great logical rigor or systematic exposition," [6] and Talmon contends that

Rousseau failed to link his thoughts with any "universal system." [7] On these points, however, many of Rousseau's critics seem to ignore the larger picture. His critics all too often are easily seduced—like Cassirer, for example—by Fichte's notion that "the kind of philosophy a man chooses depends upon the kind of man he is. For a philosophic system is no piece of dead furniture one can acquire and discard at will. It is animated with the spirit of the man who possesses it." [8] Unfortunately, Rousseau's mercurial spirit then becomes the critic's pretext for viewing his thought as unsystematic, confused, and contradictory. In this vein, Cassirer concludes that "Rousseau tried in vain to subject his life to any rule or to organize it in accordance with any plan. He moved constantly from one extreme to the other, and in the end life eluded him in contradictory impulses." [9]

Because Rousseau's personal life was fraught with contradictory impulses, it is often alleged that his philosophies were an intellectual compensation that, more often than not, proved to be confused and unsystematic. Given its continuing interpretation as a confused and unsystematic project, Rousseau's thought is alleged to have been "the envious dream of a tormented paranoiac." [10] Shklar sees his thought as reflecting a "profound need for self-vindication." [11] McManners judges Rousseau's critique as verging on a "pathological obsession," [12] and Crocker considers Rousseau's theories as the shallow rationalizations of "infantile dependency" and an "authoritarian personality." [13] Indeed, Crocker completes Fichte's logic in contending that Rousseau's "personality conflicts are projected onto the written page." [14]

Yet, in the last analysis, these discursive reductions of Rousseau's critical philosophy into an example of abnormal psychology does Rousseau, and the critical enterprise, a severe injustice. Because of such criticism, Rousseau often is dismissed, in ad hoc and ad hominem arguments, as a primitivist, a totalitarian, or an authoritarian. Rousseau's peculiar personal spirit, of course, does animate his political and social theory. This spirit, however, is not necessarily that of an emotionalist, irrationalist, or psychotic. Other discursive possibilities also are quite plausible. Actually, in his work, we can see the animus of a systematic social critic intent upon forging an epic political theory to confront the social troubles of his time. His *First Discourse* and *Second Discourse* accurately identify the systemic crises in eighteenth-century European society. The unquestioning and eager pursuit of positive science and the rapid improvement in industrial technology are seen as giving rise to a new and dangerous relation between men and Nature as well as between men and men.

When armed with the outlooks of the developing arts and sciences of the Enlightenment, Rousseau argues that men increasingly relate to each other and to Nature as reified *manipulable objects* rather than as autonomous *active subjects*. Consequently, men objectify Nature as "natural resources" and objectify themselves and each other as "human resources" that can be technically organized, as objects, to serve each individual's utility and interests. Ultimately, each individual's interests are to gain more power, wealth, and status; however, only a few succeed in gaining these different privileges, and their success entails vast inequalities in power, wealth, and status for everyone else. Even though these social struggles have occurred throughout history, modern science and technology vastly accelerate the process by improving society's ability to produce wealth. In turn, the alienation of men from Nature, from each other, and from themselves as full active subjects greatly increases as men seek better to serve and improve their utilitarian interests.

The increase of wealth to the level of destructive luxury on a grand scale and the concomitant addition of power and status to the wealthy culminates in greater tyranny over the weak, the poor, and the lowly. When men lived closer to Nature and to each other, prior to the advancement in the sciences and technical arts, Rousseau suggests that their consciousness was more virtuous, more humanly subjective, and more equal. Technical progress, however, leads to massive urbanization and an "artificial" urban way of life. It also leads to a secularization in human values and consciousness, which entails less virtue. Likewise, technical advancement, economic development, and urbanization necessitate an undesirable differentiation of labor and privilege. The whole man, as an active subject, is socially decomposed into various demeaning roles and false statuses that further aggravate the condition of social inequality.

In the social interactions of the new urban order, "to be and to seem" for men become two different things. The active subject's natural mode of being is negated by the passive object's social mode of being, as a false social personality forms from a faith in positive science, an acceptance of economic utility, and a fetishization of socially defined commodities. Obviously, seeing that social existence determines socially defined individual consciousness, Rousseau scathingly criticizes the "Enlightenment schema" of social existence as the systemic error in modern society responsible for the corruption of man-as-human-subject. To reconstitute human consciousness and to arrest its social corruption, Rousseau advocates that human existence be altered either through intense personal education or through active collective politics based upon participation by all human subjects instead of the domination of underdeveloped human objects as the weak, the poor, and the lowly are dominated by the powerful, the rich, and the notable.

Rousseau's discursive project can be seen as a dialectical philosophy of antagonistic totalities. Like critical social theory, Rousseau seeks to reconstitute society as a concrete totality of fully humane subjects through the mediation of political activity. To combat the "antinomies of bourgeois thought," [15] which originate in the practical arts and rationalist science of the Enlightenment, Rousseau proposes a participatory political community whose very structure and functioning requires the fusion of passive human objects and active human subjects to succeed: Men as citizens can be reunited in a virtuous social order, fusing together the antinomies of emerging bourgeois society—natural essence/social appearance, powerful sovereign/weak subject, thought/praxis, freedom/necessity, nature/society, laborer/owner, and equality/inequality. By urging men to act as subjects, building a self-created world to serve as the conscious form of a free and equal community, Rousseau feels that men can regain their natural virtue through political action. Moreover, they might escape their growing passivity as objects forced to live in the artificial one-dimensional world of the modern Enlightenment.

The radical critique of the *First* and *Second Discourses*, then, determines how the false totality of "enlightenment" encourages theoretical and practical antitheses of subject and object. As the sciences and technical arts progress, human inequality, once only an episodically experienced condition in primitive societies, becomes a hegemonic social relation that can be escaped only if one becomes a correctly educated man or an active citizen-subject.[16] The self-consciousness of the weak, the poor, and the lowly as *natural men* in juxtaposition to their existence as *social men* becomes Rousseau's theoretical mediation for changing praxis. Once the passive unequal members of society sense within themselves a subjectivity comparable to that of Nature, then Rousseau suggests that they will form a sovereign, or identical subject-object, to reconstitute themselves as citizens of virtue.

Such a theoretical schema does not seem to be the product of a confused and unsystematic mind. The brief overview outlined above suggests that Rousseau's political imagination is strongly systematic. His critics, since Voltaire, have found him to suffer from "pathological obsession" undoubtedly because of his insistence upon finding man's progressive *perfection*, which his critics usually embrace in their own beliefs, to be the ultimate cause of his *imperfection*. To claim, and to argue persuasively, that man's pretended civilization in modern times is, in fact, the highest form of human barbarism clearly might lead some to consider Rousseau a "tormented paranoiac." Still, he advances his arguments in a convincing and systematic fashion, while he presages similar arguments made in the twentieth century by critical social theory. The systematicity of his project also can be seen by rereading the internal relations of Rousseau's conceptual structures.

In characterizing his own work, Rousseau consciously regarded himself as a "painter of nature and the historian of the human heart." [17] He felt that his critical reconsiderations of man's transition from *l'homme naturel* to *l'homme de l'homme* formed the basis of a "sad and great system, the fruit of a sincere examination of the nature of man, of his faculties and of his destiny." [18] While Rousseau recognized the conflicts within his own life, he also saw his major works as "inseparable and together form[ing] a single whole." [19] The testimony of his letters and the overall organization of his ideas support his own claims of systematicity: "I wrote on diverse subjects, but always with the same principles; always the same teaching, the same belief, the same maxims, and, if you prefer, the same opinions." [20]

Nonetheless, more than Rousseau's own word guarantees the systematic quality of his theoretical project. His writings do compose a systematic exposition that continually returns to the same teachings: how man was constituted in Nature, how Nature gave way to the false consciousness of society, and how man might reconstitute his social consciousness to recapture the providential order and virtue of Nature. Moreover, these teachings all turn upon the same conceptual group of internal relations between Nature and society, natural man and social man, equality and inequality as Rousseau develops his thoughts in his texts. The *Discourse on the Arts and Sciences* vindicates the importance of Nature in molding man's original constitution and determining his primitive condition. It additionally pinpoints the destructive role played by the "contagion of useless knowledge" [21] on a human existence "adorned only by the hands of nature." [22] The *Discourse on the Origin of Inequality* explicates the course of man's historical perfection of imperfection as modern society's false consciousness works "to adorn our wit and corrupt our judgment." [23]

The loss of human subjectivity encouraged by the division of labor and property is shown as the source of "that fatal inequality introduced among men by the difference of talents and the cheapening of virtue." [24]

At the same time, however, the *Discourse on Political Economy* and *The Social Contract*, respectively, balance the *First* and *Second Discourses*, in both tone and detail, by illustrating how a self-created civic order might emerge from the corrupt social order of the modern commercial lifeworld. To remedy the collective vice of historical development and the false consciousness of corrupted judgment rooted in "the perfection of individuals" and "the decrepitness of the species," [25] Rousseau offers the practical corrective of participatory politics. He states, "I saw that everything depends in a radical way upon politics." [26] Therefore, political participation becomes the mediation for the collective regeneration of the "enlightened" society's corrupted individuals.

During most of his life, Rousseau plainly suffered from intense inner turmoil and personal anguish. This fact undoubtedly is most obvious in his attitudes about women and their role in public life. It presumes far too much, however, to regard this "unhappy consciousness" as some kind of psychosis that perverted all of Rousseau's philosophical thinking. Here, the theoretically more informative approach assumes that Rousseau was a "normal" person who was overwhelmed by the "abnormalities" of an irrational age. His own spiritual and intellectual crises, then, reflect the larger cultural contradictions and social crises of the newly "enlightened" age.

Like William Blake, Rousseau felt compelled to create his own system of thought to avoid being permanently enslaved by the corrupted systems of others. Also, like Blake, Shelley, and Wordsworth, Rousseau resisted the spirit of his age—the Enlightenment—because it disenchanted Nature, it objectified human relations, and it substituted the phantom objectivity of positive science, economic utility, and commodity fetishism for the concrete subjectivity of Nature and Divine Providence. Rousseau's critique documents the increasing extent to which this false consciousness gripped eighteenth-century European society as industrialization, rationalization, secularization, and urbanization altered more and more lives. His system marks the first point in the modern era at which the rationalist faith in progress confronted the romantic "unhappy consciousness," as the positive intellectual met the critical critic, and the Enlightenment schema was seen as a dehumanizing one-dimensionality.

Rousseau's Dialectical Method

In *Anti-Dühring*, Frederick Engels notes:

> Already in Rousseau, therefore, we find not only a line of thought which corresponds exactly to the one developed in Marx's *Capital*, but also, in details, a whole series of the same dialectical turns of speech as Marx used: processes which in their nature are antagonistic, contain a contradiction, transformation of one extreme into its opposite; and finally, as the kernel of the whole thing, the negation of the negation.[27]

Of course, many commentators would dismiss this observation because "in 1754 Rousseau was not yet able to speak the Hegelian jargon"; Engels nevertheless maintains that "he was certainly, sixteen years before Hegel was born, deeply bitten with the Hegelian pestilence, dialectics of contradiction." [28] Even though Engels might not be widely regarded as an "eminent" Rousseau scholar, if Rousseau's lines of thought do correspond exactly to the one developed in Marx's *Capital*, then Rousseau's dialectical argument merits further investigation.

Rousseau's dialectic of historical analysis, however, concentrates upon different contradictions from Marx's opposition of the forces and relations of production. Marx lays primary emphasis upon the contradiction between economic forces, the owners and the actual producers in production, while Rousseau accentuates the contradiction of political forces between the rulers and the ruled, the strong and the weak, the notable and the lowly, or the rich and the poor. Marx criticizes the increasing inability of the actual producers to enjoy the products or profits of their own labor given the bourgeoisie's expropriation of their collectively produced surplus value. Rousseau criticizes the unending growth of moral or political inequality as the rulers, the strong, the notable, and the rich turn their power, status, and wealth to their class advantage at the expense of the ruled, the weak, the lowly, and the poor classes. Marx's dialectic gains its greater detail and systematicity by explicating the internal relations of an industrial capitalist society, while Rousseau's dialectic traces the less well-defined exploitative internal relations of societies based on primitive accumulation and manufacture. Nevertheless, the concern for the artificial division of thought and practice into antitheses of subject/object, freedom/necessity, abstract/concrete reality, theoretical/practical activity, and producer/product relations animates Rousseau's thought nearly as much as Marx's.

Rousseau's dialectical method most clearly emerges in his answer to the "most knotty philosophical question" of historical analysis:

> For how is it possible to know the source of inequality among men, without knowing men themselves? And how shall man be able to see himself, such as nature formed him, in spite of all the alterations which a long succession of years and events must have produced in his original constitution, and how shall he be able to distinguish what is his own essence, from what the circumstances he has been in and the progress he has made have added to, or changed in, his primitive condition? [29]

Each advance made by men serves only to obscure further the true essence and concrete nature of the primitive condition, "the more we accumulate new knowledge, the more we deprive ourselves of the means of acquiring the most important of all; and it is, in a manner, by the mere hint of studying man that we have lost the power of knowing him." [30] Rousseau rejects the *philosophes'* doctrines of natural law and right as vacuous sophistications, "for it is no easy task to distinguish between what is natural and what is artificial in the present constitution of man, and to make oneself well acquainted with a state which, if ever it did, does not now, and in all probability never will exist, and of which, notwithstanding, it is absolutely necessary to have just notions to judge properly of our present state." [31] In the last analysis, then, Rousseau's dialectical argument unfolds from these contradictions between Nature and society.

To judge the present situation of *man in society,* a state of endemic inequality, Rousseau analyzes the whole of history and society in terms of *man in Nature* to discover the sources of inequality in social circumstances and progress. Nature enables one to overcome, theoretically and practically, the false relations of society:

> If we consider human society with a calm and disinterested eye, it seems at first sight to show us nothing but the violence of the powerful and the oppression of the weak; the mind is shocked at the cruelty of the one, and equally grieved at the blindness of the other; and as nothing less stable in human life than those exterior relations, which chance produces oftener than wisdom, and which are called weakness or power, poverty or riches, human establishments appear at the first glance like so many castles built upon quicksand; it is only by taking nearer survey of them, and by removing the dust and the sand which surround and disguise the edifice, that we can perceive the unshakable basis upon which it stands, and learn to respect its foundations. Now, without a serious study of man, his natural faculties and

their successive developments, we shall never succeed in making these distinctions, and in separating, in the present constitution of things, what comes from the divine will from what human contrivance has aspired to do.[32]

Rousseau's "nearer survey" of the inequalities of society, then, follows the dialectical unfolding of the "present constitution of things" from man's "natural faculties and their successive development."

Such an analysis becomes the best guide, at the same time, for potentially changing the exploitative "external relations" of human establishments:

> This same study of original man, of his real needs, and of the fundamental principles of his duties, is likewise the only good method we can take, to surmount an infinite number of difficulties concerning the origin of moral inequality, the true foundations of political bodies, the reciprocal rights of their members, and a thousand other similar questions that are as important as they are ill-understood.[33]

Rousseau wishes to ascertain the essential needs and duties of *natural man*, posed as an ideal type of man—individually and collectively—in the natural state, in order to criticize the largely evil and circumstantial needs and duties that multiple inequalities impose on *social man*. In so doing, he aims at propounding both a critical reappraisal of social man and a practical theory of reconstituting, as best one can in the present stage of social development, *natural man* from *social man* as *civic man*. Again, each of these discursive representations of man as an ideal type are encoded with the particular indications of individual action and collective meaning of human beings in each of these global conditions.

Consequently, Rousseau investigates three varying conditions of being of his theoretical man in his hypothetical theory. He first describes natural man as a creation of Nature, or "such as nature formed him" to characterize man as an integral part of the natural totality, as an aspect of Nature's collective subjectivity. Second, he examines man, as part of Nature's providence, "in his original constitution" to understand better how his social perfection has altered this concrete essence. And third, he attempts to reconstruct the probable lifeworld, even if it no longer exists, to account for natural man in "his primitive condition." Taken together, Rousseau then juxtaposes these aspects with their dialectical opposites. Knowing man "such as nature formed him," Rousseau can reveal man "such as society formed him." As the victim of the endemic alienation and oppressive objectifications of cultural perfection, man's "original constitution" suffers from the adoption of superfluous social needs and duties, giving him a new "artificial constitution."

The artifices of the sciences, the technical arts, language, and social conventions, in turn, progressively destroy the simplicity of the "primitive condition" in the corrupt complexity of man's "social condition." Man's essence, or "such as he must have issued from the hands of nature," [34] dialectically develops from an opposite into its opposite, man's appearance, which is "altered in society by the perpetual succession of a thousand causes, by the acquisition of numberless discoveries and errors." [35] Man's faculty of *perfectibility*, "though by slow degrees, draws him out of his original condition," and "produces his discoveries and mistakes, his virtues and his vices, and, in the long run, renders him both his own and nature's tyrant." [36] The antagonistic process of perfectibility brings out from within natural man his opposite, social man, negating the natural condition; still, the opposite of social man lies latent within the social condition ready to negate this corrupted form with a new transformation—a synthesis of man's social discoveries and natural virtues in a new concrete but social totality to create *civic man*.

The analytical goal, then, of Rousseau's dialectic becomes the discovery of a new mediation capable of reconstituting man's corrupted social consciousness. He contends that, "instead of a being always acting from certain and invariable principles, instead of that heavenly and majestic simplicity which its author has impressed upon it," [37] man's consciousness, through sociohistorical progress, devolves into "nothing but the shocking contrast of passion that thinks it reasons, and an understanding grown delirious." [38] Natural man prospered in accord with the "first and most simple operations of the human soul," namely, his inherent sensibilities for interests "in our preservation and welfare" and for "a natural aversion to seeing any other being, but especially any being like ourselves, suffer or perish." [39]

Natural man acted in conformity with these inherent dictates as natural needs and duties, "not so much because he is a reasonable being, as because he is a sensible being." [40] It is, however, man's natural self-love, or *amour de soi*, and his capacity for pity that historical development erodes. As this *amour de soi* changes into *amour-propre*, or selfishness based upon egoistic rational calculation, through the adoption of social conventions and the false need for cultural artifacts, the power for pity atrophies.[41] The key to why man's natural consciousness becomes evilly twisted by "progress" into the corrupt false consciousness of *amour-propre* can be found in the contradiction between "what comes from divine will and what human contrivance has aspired to do." [42]

Divine will, as expressed in natural providence, represents Rousseau's original collective subjectivity or totality, in which and by virtue of which man had virtuous true consciousness. Human contrivance, as elaborated in sociohistorical development, destroys this initial mediation of collective subjectivity by creating a "second state of nature" [43] that gives men a "second nature" of social needs and duties based on selfish reason. The latter state, Rousseau suggests, becomes one of pure alienation: "It is reason that engenders self-love, and reflection that strengthens it; it is reason that makes man shrink into himself; it is reason that makes him keep aloof from everything that can trouble or afflict him; it is philosophy that destroys his connections with other men." [44] Therefore, to comprehend Rousseau's search for new mediations of virtuous collective subjectivity, one must reconstruct his schema of Nature as a subject. It is from Nature's collective subjectivity that man "in his original constitution" emerged and that, in developing socially, his deprivation "in his artificial constitution" was assured.

Rousseau's notions of Nature and society, natural man and social man, and equality and inequality are dialectically interconnected. Unlike all of his contemporaries, Rousseau denies that Nature is nothing but a dead object, a complex aggregate of rational principles, a passive reserve of raw material for human production.[45] Nature, for Rousseau, is itself an active subject—it is both freedom and necessity, producer and product, subject and object. " 'Nature' here," with Rousseau, as for Lukács, "refers to authentic humanity, the true essence of man liberated from the false, mechanizing forms of society: man as a perfected whole who has inwardly overcome, or is in the process of overcoming, the dichotomies of theory and practice, reason and the senses, form and content; man whose tendency to create his own forms does not imply an abstract rationalism which ignores concrete content; man for whom freedom and necessity are identical." [46] Nature is both the actor and the action that wholly creates the totality of reality in the primitive condition of equality for natural man.

Consequently, Rousseau's Nature can be understood best as an active subject, or as "Providence," while natural man and his natural condition in the state of natural equality might be comprehended best as the subject's action, or as "providence." The state of society, as a state of reason following the natural state of pity, represents an artificial separation of social man from "Providence." Moreover, the advent of inequality in the false conventions of a socially constructed lifeworld represents a concomitant lack of "providence." *Providence* and *providence* are not redundant terms. Nature, or *Providence*, means a free, divinely guided, active subject that forms events through its prescience, loving care, or managing interventions; natural man and natural equality, or *providence*, implies an instance or act of prudent foresight, prescient care, or guiding interventions.[47] Thus Nature teaches men in their primitive condition, the "state of nature," setting man's original constitution in accord with his true needs and duties. Nature's providence, fairly and wisely, guides the lifeworld of natural man and guarantees his moral equality by speaking through man's natural self-love and pity.

Self-love works to preserve the individual, and pity ensures the survival of the species: "It is this pity which, in the state of nature, takes the place of laws, manners, virtue, with this advantage, that no one is tempted to disobey her gentle voice." [48] Man partakes of Nature's providence as an integral part of its form and content, its freedom and necessity, its objectivity and subjectivity. The *Second Discourse* and, in part, *Emile* illustrate the qualities of the natural man and his natural equality fashioned by the agency of Nature. Still, it is necessary to discuss briefly how social inequality arose through "human contrivance" in society to supersede destructively Nature's providential design.

Throughout his theoretical project, Rousseau dismisses the thesis of natural, ascribed equality—that is, an equal endowment of abilities at birth. He accepts that Nature has established men such that they vary widely in their individual abilities, faculties, health, intelligence, and strength. Natural inequality, however, is acceptable because Nature ensures that no man gains undue advantage in the natural condition from natural inequalities. For man in his primitive state,

> it was the consequence of a very wise providence, that the faculties, which he potentially enjoyed, were not to develop themselves, except in proportions as there offered occasions to exercise them, lest they should be superfluous or troublesome to him when he did not want them, or tardy and useless when he did. He had in his instinct alone everything requisite to live in a state of nature; in his cultivated reason he has barely what is necessary to live in a state of society.[49]

Nature carefully constituted human nature to conform to and to perform in a lifeworld framed entirely by natural providence. Man, potentially, is both pitying and egoistic, sensible and reasonable, uncommunicative and communicative, passive and active, feral and sociable.

In the primitive condition, natural man largely conforms to the dictates of Nature, which bid him to follow the "voice of the human heart" speaking to his natural needs and duties. Yet, eventually, natural distastes and the passing of time invoke circumstances in which man is forced to become sociable, active, communicative, reasonable, and egoistic, alienating him from Nature's providence. Reason and social conventions, as they develop, encourage men vainly to pursue society's artificially defined "privileges" such as wealth, power, honors, and status. Equity, balance, and proportionate allocation of these "privileges" are impossible to obtain. Social convention necessarily excludes those who lack the natural faculties—skill, genius, beauty, strength, or guile—that merit privilege. In other words, a majority of the population becomes the victim of inequalities enforced by the strong, the beautiful, and the skillful. Nature no longer ensures that the strong will pity the weak, that the beautiful will have empathy for the plain, that the skillful will not harm the unskilled. The diverse qualities intrinsic to natural man are constrained by social selection and historical perfection to constitute a false "second nature" of artificial needs and duties.

Rousseau vividly describes the alienation and dehumanization that follow from developing into the highest state of society:

> Behold then all of our faculties developed; our memory and imagination at work; egotism involved; reason rendered active; and the mind almost arrived at the utmost bounds of that perfection it is capable of. Behold all of our natural qualities put in motion; the rank and lot of every man established, not only as to the amount of property and the power of serving or hurting others, but likewise as to the genius, beauty, strength or skill, merits or talents; and as these were the only qualities which could command respect, it was found necessary to have or at least to affect them. It became to the interest of men to appear what they were really not. To be and to seem become two very different things, and from this distinction sprang haughty pomp and deceitful knavery, and all the vices which form their train. On the other hand, man, heretofore free and independent, was now, in consequence of a multitude of new needs, brought into subjection, as it were, to all nature, and especially to his fellows, whose slave in some sense he became, even by becoming their master; if rich, he stood in need of their services, if poor,

of their assistance; even mediocrity itself could not enable him to do without them. He must therefore have been continually at work to interest them in his happiness, and make them, if not really, at least apparently find their advantage in laboring for his: this rendered him sly and artful in his dealings with others, and laid him under the necessity of using ill all those whom he stood in need of, as often as he could not awe them into compliance and did not find it in his interest to be useful to them.[50]

Natural man, who was once free by being part of Nature, becomes unfree in society as social artifice works to dominate Nature. By accepting new social needs and duties, social man becomes something he really is not and generates a false objectivity that robs him of his true essence.

As man increasingly turns into an object of false desires and status manipulated by other equally false human objects, tremendous vice follows as alienation lays social man "under the necessity of using ill all those whom he stood in need of . . . to be useful to him." Furthermore, once man has been perfected, he must and can only remain in the social condition—the natural state and its providential equality are lost and inaccessible once social man divorces himself from the collective subjectivity of Nature. The invention of the technical arts and the rise of property combine in the practice of social man to negate the providential action of Nature as Nature increasingly becomes, for the property-seeking and technically oriented social man, a dead object to be exploited and appropriated for individual advantage. "Equality vanished; property was introduced; labor became necessary; and the boundless forests became smiling fields, which had to be watered with human sweat, and in which slavery and misery were soon seen to sprout out and grow in harvests." [51]

Man "in his original constitution" flourished in a "primitive condition" of equality; man "in his artificial constitution" suffers in a "social condition" of inequality. Equality engendered by Nature is an instance of prudent foresight or care produced by a prescient collective subject in which natural man partakes in both producer and product. Nature creates moral equality in the premoral state by assuring an impartial treatment for all human beings, despite their individual diversity, in the collective enjoyment of Nature's bounty. All naturally have equal "title to and access in" the common estate of Nature's benefits. As long as no artificial "human contrivance" exalts a few human abilities over all others, Nature enforces an impartial providence of equality. "But even if nature in the distribution of her gifts should really affect all of the preferences that are imputed to her, what advantage could the most favored derive from her partiality, to the prejudice of others in a state of things which admits hardly any kind of relation between them?" [52]

In Nature, human beings are naturally "unequal," but the mediation of Providence prevents this "inequality" from leading to any evil or corruption. In society, on the other hand, men are naturally and socially "unequal." Lacking the mediation of Providence, their condition increasingly devolves into the corruptions of inequality in power, status, and wealth. Nature, as a collective subject, constructs the total governance of natural man, ensuring impartial equity in every cost and benefit, and each being has equal access to and enjoyment of Nature's offerings. Society, as a collection of individual objects alienated from their true essence, effects a partial association that guarantees the ultrapartial inequality in all the benefits and costs of social life, and all men gain only unequal access and unequal shares of scarce social privileges and limited individual property in addition to losing their natural freedom.

Having tentatively answered the "most knotty philosophical question" of history, namely, the sources and the circumstances of the origin of social inequality, Rousseau demonstrates the contradictions leading from the transformation of opposites into opposites. The social man, through the mediation of artificial human contrivances, unfolds from within natural man to negate the concreteness of the natural situation. In doing so, the new external relations of social man also annihilate the providential internal relations of Nature's guidance of men. In making his argument, Rousseau establishes the thesis of alienated social man, while at the same time detailing its antithesis in the authentic humanity of natural man. Man as part of the second state of nature effaces Nature's providence with a second nature of technical artifice and social property.

Social man, nonetheless, contains the potential for generating his virtuous opposite from the enslavement of society's *amour-propre*. Man may not return to Nature, nor can he ever again fully realize himself as a participant of Her collective subjectivity. Yet, he may reconstitute himself, through the mediation of correctly conscious political action, as a participant in a new collective subject to redeem his equality and freedom, but in the social state. The civic consciousness can negate social consciousness, and as long as it remains "everywhere tacitly admitted and recognized, . . . each man regains his original rights and recovers his natural liberty, while losing the conventional liberty for which he renounced it." [53]

Social man's corrupted consciousness, defined by the reifications of technical artifice and the fetishism of property, can be supplanted by the mediation of a political collective subject that creates true consciousness and virtuous freedom. Clearly, Rousseau presents Nature in his discursive system as the model for such a collective subject. Man is born free, as a participant of Nature's providence. Yet everywhere he is in chains, as a victim of society's artificially produced inequality. Consequently, Nature suggests a correct consciousness of society's inequalities for both masters and slaves. "Many a one believes himself the master of others," Rousseau argues, "and yet he is a greater slave than they." [54]

Still, the social inequalities instituted by the masters create numerous classes of slaves: the weak, the poor, the ruled, and the lowly. As slaves, they "lose everything in their bonds, even the desire to escape from them." [55] Hence the slaves suffer under the masters, or the strong, the rich, the rulers, and the notable, usurpation of their natural rights to equality as the master classes transform power into right and obedience into duty. Yet, for Rousseau, "might does not make right, and we are bound to obey none but lawful authority," [56] which the social state largely lacks because of its illegitimate division of property, status, and power. The right to slavery and the duty of slaves "is invalid, not only because it is illegitimate, but because it is absurd and meaningless." [57] The natural rights to equality and freedom "are derived from the nature of things, and are founded on reason," [58] so, to redeem himself, social man must overcome the artificial inequalities of the social condition by finding "a form of association which may defend and protect with the whole force of the community the person and property of every associate, and by means of which each, coalescing with all, may nevertheless obey only himself, and remain as free as before." [59]

The means of smashing society's false needs, then, comes with the masters and the slaves all "coalescing with all," which abrogates the false contract of the masters and the slaves based on exploitative external relations in favor of a civic contract, "everywhere tacitly admitted and recognized," in the civic consciousness. Each associate of the community gives himself up entirely "with all his rights" to the whole community, and thereby constitutes a new collective subject: "Forthwith, instead of the individual personalities of all the contracting parties, this act of association produces a moral and collective body, which is composed of as many members as the assembly has voices, and which receives from this same act its unity, its common self (*moi*), its life, and its will." [60]

By so doing, social man constitutes a new collective subject capable of regenerating man's authentic humanity. Through a *civic* mediation, man again can bridge the dichotomies of theory and practice, object and subject, freedom and necessity, producer and product, abstract and concrete reality as a sovereign-citizen, ruler-ruled. "Each of us puts in common his person and his whole power under the supreme direction of the general will; and in return we receive every member as an indivisible part of the whole," which, Rousseau reports, "is called by its members *State* when it is passive, *sovereign* when it is active, *power* when compared to similar bodies. With regard to the associates, they take collectively the name of *people*, and are called individually *citizens*, as participating in the sovereign power, and *subjects*, as subjected to the laws of the State." [61] Once established, the sovereign mediates the workings of the General Will; the civic collective subject or public person, the producer and the product, the abstract and concrete totality, the object and the subject of civic man's true consciousness. The sovereign, with its General Will, taps the true concrete essence of man's humanity, hence it "is always everything that it ought to be" and it constantly tends "to equality" [62] in its unerring omniscience.

Having studied the needs and duties of *natural man*, Rousseau detects the possibility of the General Will acting as a providential force ensuring the virtue, freedom, and equality of *civic man* as this new communal being negates the inequality of the *social man's* lifeworld. The General Will annihilates the false objectivity of social man in "an admirable union of interest and justice, which gives to the deliberations of the community a spirit of equity that seems to disappear in the discussion of any private affair, for want of a common interest to unite and identify the ruling principle of the judge with that of the party." [63]

As civic men compose their self-created political lifeworld and recapture their authentic humanity as part of this collective political subject, they produce and are the product of moral equality: "Every act of sovereignty, that is, every authentic act of the general will, binds or favors equally all the citizens; so that the sovereign knows only the body of the nation, and distinguishes none of those who compose it." [64] The civic man's own practice fuses together abstract and concrete reality, theory and practice, producer and product, form and content, freedom and necessity as he serves as both sovereign and citizen, active ruler and passive subject, political subject and political object in the workings of the General Will.

By underwriting "moral freedom, which alone renders man truly master of himself" and realizing an "altering of man's constitution," [65] the General Will allows man truly to enjoy the advantages of social living without the abuses and degradation of inequality: "His faculties are exercised and developed; his ideas are expanded; his feelings ennobled; his whole soul is exalted." [66] The selfishness fostered by alienation and reification is negated by the sovereign-citizen's sense of civic justice. The General Will of the sovereign, the civic collective subject, acts as Providence for civic man and assures a more providential order of equality.

As long as the General Will develops from the civic state, it can assure impartial equity in every cost and benefit, and provides each being with equal access and enjoyment of the civic state. Should men's particular wills reassert themselves, the General Will would dissipate into the more corrupt social condition once again. Hence the citizenry must remain vigilant, self-reliant, and virtuous to encourage the survival of their collective subjectivity, "intimately united in the hearts of the citizens, made, as it were, only one single body," [67] mediated through popular political participation. This vigilance is critical in order to preserve pluralism and difference among the citizenry. Rousseau's vision of personal subjectivity plainly made it difficult for him to see "civic virtue" destroying individual autonomy and particularity. On the contrary, he saw man's technical and social perfection as truly pernicious disruptive forces, eliminating personal difference and social plurality.

At this juncture, Rousseau's schema closely parallels the logic developed in Marx's *Capital*. The thesis of natural man serves as the critique for ascertaining how his sublimated antithesis, social man, represented a deterioration of man's essence. Ultimately, however, the original thesis and its corrupted antithesis merge themselves, through the mediation of correct education or participatory politics, into the synthesis of civic man. *The Social Contract*, the *Discourse on Political Economy*, and, in part, the *Letter to d'Alembert* all sketch the outlines of the "civic constitution" of man, "such as the polity would form him," and as he would be in the "civic condition." Rousseau's schema for documenting the history of the human heart dialectically unfolds by the change of opposites into opposites from opposites. Each stage of human activity unfolds from within its opposite and each is destroyed by the other's creation. Rousseau's narrative of this historical process develops dialectically and systematically.

Rousseau's Antibourgeois Critique

While Engels perceptively pinpoints Rousseau's dialectical qualities, he also unfairly and incorrectly tags Rousseau as an exponent of "bourgeois equality." Plattner, for example, asserts that "Jean-Jacques Rousseau was the first great *modern* critic of bourgeois society. . . . He opposed bourgeois society in the name of the very principles to which it itself appealed—freedom and equality. Rousseau was the first political philosopher to attack bourgeois society from the left." [68] Still, in following Marx, Engels groups Rousseau along with the *philosophes* and other advocates of natural rights and reason:

> This kingdom of reason was nothing more than the idealized kingdom of the bourgeoisie; that this eternal Right found its realization in bourgeois justice; that this equality reduced itself to bourgeois equality before the law; that bourgeois property was proclaimed as one of the essential rights of man; and that the government of reason, the Contract Social of Rousseau, came into being, and only could come into being, as a democratic bourgeois republic.[69]

Elements in Rousseau allow one to draw such conclusions. Even so, Engels recognizes that Rousseau is quite unlike "the great thinkers of the eighteenth century," because he does "go beyond the limits imposed upon them by their epoch." [70] Rousseau, in fact, continually incurred the invectives of his more "bourgeois" contemporaries for his very unorthodox antibourgeois critique. Indeed, Rousseau takes great pains, throughout his theoretical project, to argue against conventional "bourgeois" notions of justice, property, legality, and natural reason as he contrasts them to his critical standards of the collective subjectivity of Nature and the General Will.

Rousseau's "social man" living in the "social condition" with "his artificial constitution" is, in fact, bourgeois man. Rousseau's natural and civic man, therefore, can be seen as radical critiques and alternative visions of the bourgeois lifeworld that Rousseau saw emerging in the eighteenth century. This point becomes clear in reexamining his notions of Nature, property, and the political contract.

Beginning with Bacon, and leading through Descartes, Leibniz, and Newton, the new forms of the "bourgeois" intellect sought a structure of scientific logic and formal reason capable of ensuring "the calculability of the world." [71] In reducing Nature to nothing but a rational design, a calculable mechanism, and a dead object, bourgeois thought gained the power, through the mediation of science and technical arts, to manipulate Nature and society exploitatively for the advantage of the enterprising, wealthy, propertied, and powerful. The "idealized kingdom of the bourgeoisie" ultimately turns "nature into mere objectivity," [72] robbing both Nature and humanity of subjectivity, which reduces them to different classes of objects suited to different purposes as objective materials.

As objective materials, both natural resources and human beings increasingly become trapped in reified definitions as objects, as things, as commodity-forms; in turn, the commodity-form reinforces the bourgeois forms of life based upon the market, the commodity, and rational calculation. Here, men and Nature fall victims to the phantom objectivity of the commodity-form as "it became to the interest of men to appear what they were not," [73] namely, commodity-objects and calculating particular wills, as "man, heretofore free and independent, was not, in consequence of a multitude of new needs, brought into subjection" [74] by these reifications of bourgeois commodity fetishism. The bourgeois *philosophe* armed with Enlightenment rationalism objectified Nature and then naturalized humanity, as La Mettrie's and Helvetius's notion of "man as machine," in fact, illustrates.

Rousseau, on the other hand, remained critical of these notions. In contradiction, he sought to subjectify Nature and, by doing so, to rehumanize humanity through the General Will, virtuous legislation, and an active educated conscience. The bourgeois vision of Nature—which codifies the formal laws "which nature imposes upon herself" rather than the active subjective principles "which she prescribes" [75] to realize virtue— follows from the "contagion of useless knowledge" [76] created by the arts and sciences. All of the Enlightenment's bourgeois mechanistic accounts never caused him to "doubt for a moment the existence of a beneficent Providence." [77] His "first principle" was "that a will moves the universe and animates nature." [78] Nature is not Newton's efficient dead machine, nor is it Hobbes's random bodies in motion; rather, Nature is the physical and moral embodiment of a moral subject.

Rousseau declares that "the right of property is the most sacred of all rights of citizenship." [79] He does not proclaim, however, bourgeois property to be an essential right of man. Rousseau agrees that property must be the foundation of the civic state given the social evolution of man, yet he affirms this point only to guarantee that "every one should be maintained in the peaceful possession of what belongs to him." [80] Unlike the majority of bourgeois intellectuals of his age, Rousseau does not support the philosophy of possessive and acquisitive individualism. Man has a right to possess what he needs and uses, but he does not have a right to the unlimited pursuit of individual property to satiate his particular will. The Hobbesian or Lockeian "social contract" that equally entitles every man to "life, liberty, and the pursuit of property," in Rousseau's eyes, only serves the interests of the rich to the detriment of the poor.

The bourgeois self-interest in property and its accumulation clearly constituted one of the Enlightenment's first articles of faith. Yet, for Rousseau, bourgeois property rights "fixed for ever the laws of property and inequality; changed an artful usurpation into an irrevocable right; and for the benefit of a few ambitious individuals subjected the rest of mankind to perpetual labor, servitude, and misery." [81] According to liberal bourgeois theory, the individual pursuit of each man's self-interested utility both created and added to the collective interest and general prosperity of the entire state. Rousseau, however, radically criticizes this fetishization of property and the particular wills of individuals as a false consciousness generated out of artificial external relations—"society no longer offers . . . anything but an assemblage of artificial men and factitious passions, which are the work of all these new relations." [82]

Property, then, for Rousseau, is a social right to be or not to be affirmed by the decisions of the sovereign, "for the State, with regard to its members, is owner of all their property by the social contract, which, in the State, serves as the basis of all rights." [83] Unlike the Anglo-Saxon contract theorists, who cast property as an inalienable, God-given, natural right, Rousseau dismissed such rights as a usurpation enforced by the coercive power of the strong, the rich, the powerful, and the notable. This radical critique of class privilege is followed, in turn, by Rousseau's affirmation of the communal right to control the individual use, ownership, and alienation of property: "The right which every individual has over his own property is always subordinate to the right which the community has over all." [84] Actually, the essential bourgeois "right" to property, for Rousseau, is the privilege to acquire and control property because of one's greater strength, power, wealth, status, or guile.

Rousseau's right to property "is an obvious inference from the general will" in that it allows the community to provide "for the public wants" while "keeping within narrow bounds the personal interest which so isolates the individual that the State is enfeebled by his power." [85] Instead of granting the citizenry an unlimited right to acquire new property, Rousseau's civic constitution would take measures ensuring that "the goods of family should go as little out of it and be as little alienated as possible." [86] Otherwise, the continual quest for new property would erode the General Will by exciting the citizenry's particular wills. Such "markets" provide no substitute for the sovereign's dictates:

> Nothing is more fatal to morality and to the Republic than the continual shifting of rank and fortune among the citizens: such charges are both proof and the source of a thousand disorders, and overturn and confound everything; for those who were brought up to one thing find themselves destined for another; and neither those who rise nor those who fall are able to assume the rules of conduct, or to possess themselves of the qualifications requisite for their new condition, still less to discharge the duties it entails.[87]

A full-blown bourgeois notion of property with citizenship defined in terms of possessive individualism, then, is not the keystone of Rousseau's political and social theory.

In a certain sense, the bourgeois notion of the political contract aimed to guarantee human equality before the law as well as to found a government of reason. The social or political contract served this bourgeois vein of thought as the public writ incorporating the citizen's commonwealth. Each citizen, by its proviso, gained the right individually to pursue, as a particular will or as part of a corporate will of all, his economic life, his legal liberties, and his right to property, confident that the state will provide a common judge and base of authority for his redress should he incur any wrong. Nature's name is invoked only as the bourgeois intellect's legitimation of each man's right to accumulate property. The state of nature also serves as a legal fiction to explain why the bourgeois citizen needs government to protect his accumulated wealth from the lowly poor. "The philosophers," Rousseau argues,

> attribute to man in that state the ideas of justice and injustice without troubling to prove that he really must have had such ideas, or even that such ideas were useful to him: others have spoken of the natural right of every man to keep what belongs to him, without letting us know what they mean by the word *belong*, to others, without further ceremony ascribing to the strongest an authority over the weakest, have immediately brought government into being, without thinking of the time requisite for men to form any notice of the things signified by the words authority and government. All of them . . . have transferred to the state of nature ideas picked up in the bosom of society.[88]

On the other hand, Rousseau attacks the bourgeois social contract as an evil mystification that "provides a powerful protection for the immense possessions of the rich, and hardly leaves the poor man in quiet possession of the cottage he builds with his own hands." [89] Indeed, when dealing with the state of nature and the social contract, the bourgeois thinkers "in speaking of savages . . . have described citizens," [90] and, from Rousseau's vantage, when speaking of bourgeois citizens, they actually describe sophisticated savages. The terms of the bourgeois social contract enacted by the rich to subdue the poor, Rousseau observes, "may be summed up in a few words: 'You have need of me, because I am rich and you are poor. We will therefore come to an agreement. I will permit you to have the honor of serving me, on condition that you bestow on me the little you have left, in return for the pains I shall take to command you.' " [91]

Rousseau's thought radically attacks these class-based mystifications for making a "democratic bourgeois republic." Rousseau's opposition to "bourgeois equality" is clearly drawn in the *Discourse on Political Economy*:

> Are now all the advantages of society for the rich and powerful? Are not all lucrative posts in their hands? Are not all privileges and exemptions reserved for them alone? Is not the public authority always on their side? If a man of eminence robs his creditors, or is guilty of other knaveries, is he not always assured of impunity? Are not the assaults, acts of violence, assassinations and even murders committed by the great, matters that are hushed up in a few months, and of which nothing more is thought? But if a great man himself is robbed or insulted, the whole police force is immediately in motion, and woe even to innocent persons who chance to be suspected. If he has to pass through any dangerous road, the country is up in arms to escort him. If the axle-tree of his chaise breaks, everybody flies to his assistance. If there is a noise at his door, he speaks but a word, and all is silent. If he is incommoded by the crowd, he waves his hand and every one makes way. If his coach is met on the road by a wagon, his servants are ready to beat the driver's brains out, and fifty honest pedestrians going quietly about their business had better be knocked on the head than an idle jackanapes be delayed in his coach.

These differential rights of the poor laborers and rich owners, then, are stiffly attacked by Rousseau:

> Yet all this respect costs him not a farthing; it is the rich man's right, and not what he buys with his wealth. How different is the case of the poor man! The more humanity owes him, the more society denies him. Every door is shut against him, even when he has right to its being opened: and if ever he

obtains justice, it is with much greater difficulty than others obtain favors. If the militia is to be raised or the highway to be mended, he is always given the preference; he always bears the burden which his richer neighbor has influence enough to get exempted from. On the least accident that happens to him, everybody avoids him: if his cart be overturned in the road, so far is he from receiving any assistance, that he is lucky if he does not get horse-whipped by the impudent lackeys of some young duke: in a word, all gratuitous assistance is denied to the poor when they need it, just because they cannot pay for it.[92]

Rousseau does not uncritically uphold bourgeois equality before the law. He advances the law, as an expression of the sovereign's General Will, to smash bourgeois equality, as a reflection of the bourgeois will of all and its use of law to entrench falsely defined class privileges.

Rousseau's conception of the political contract criticizes the injustices of bourgeois compacts. As expressions of particular class wills, they tend naturally toward preferences and privileges, whereas the General Will works toward true equality. "Under bad governments," the equality of bourgeois legal right "is only apparent and illusory; it serves only to keep the poor in their misery and the rich in their usurpations." [93] The sovereign's General Will "substitutes a moral and lawful equality for the physical inequality which nature imposed upon men, so that, although unequal in strength or intellect, they all become equal by convention and legal right." [94] Furthermore, the correct consciousness, embodied in his ideal civic man's moral needs and political duties, eventually would guarantee that "they all have something, and none of them has too much." [95]

As an enemy of positive science, economic utility, commodity fetishism, and the individual alienation engendered by the bourgeois lifeworld, Rousseau hardly advances the interests of "the idealized kingdom of the bourgeoisie: a democratic bourgeois republic." On the contrary, Rousseau is a powerful antibourgeois critic whose work initiates the radical critique of the bourgeois "Enlightenment schema." Of course, his intense concern for the poor, the powerless, the ruled, and the lowly does not even verge upon an identification with industrial workers. In an age devoted to economies of primitive accumulation and of manufacture, the proletariat did not yet exist in great numbers during Rousseau's lifetime. Nonetheless, Rousseau accurately assessed the rising bourgeoisie classes' theory and practice with regard to Nature, property, and the political contract during his time.

Rousseau's Critical Consciousness

The essential basis of Rousseau's epic theory of participatory politics remains his revitalization of a new critical consciousness. Social man can be redeemed from his present unhappy state only by changing human consciousness from its false adherence to the particular will of individuals to a correct conformity to the General Will. "All is well as it comes from the hands of the Author of things, everything degenerates in the hands of man." [96] The social condition almost wholly poisons the human consciousness with an existence based on reified social relations and alienation. Collective participation, then, as part of the civic collective subject, is both the product and the producer of this new form of virtuous living.

The natural inner voice of conscience suffocates in the particular will's excitation by false social needs:

> This universal desire of reputation, of honors, of preference, with which we are all devoured, exercises and compares our talents and forces; how much it excites and multiplies our passions; and, by creating an universal competition, rivalry, or rather enmity among men, how many disappointments, successes, and catastrophes of every kind it daily causes among the innumerable aspirants whom it engages in the same competition. [97]

Human beings are trapped in "an assemblage of artificial men and factitious passions, which are the work of all these new relations." [98] As a result, inauthentic being leads to a kind of "false consciousness."

> Everything being reduced to appearances, becomes mere art and mummery; honor, friendship, virtue, and often vice itself, of which we at last learn the secret of boasting; how, in short, ever asking others what we are, and never daring to ask ourselves, in the midst of so much philosophy, humanity, and politeness, and such sublime moral codes, we have nothing but a deceitful and frivolous exterior, honor without virtue, reason without wisdom, and pleasure without happiness. . . . it is merely the spirit of society, and the inequalities which society engenders, that thus change and transform all our natural inclinations. [99]

Man's alienation from himself, from others, and from Nature, which is caused by the external relations of social artifice and convention, is "the real source of all those differences." Indeed, the natural man "lives within himself, whereas social man, constantly outside himself, knows only how to live in the opinion of others; and it is, if I may say so, merely from their judgment of him that he derives the consciousness of his own existence." [100]

Rousseau therefore recommends the formation of a new collective subject to mediate the concrete authenticity of virtuous living. The sovereign's General Will performs this essential task for "the voice of the people is in fact the voice of God." [101] And, as the voice of God, the sovereign's will mediates the providential design of virtue in the civic state. The sovereign-citizen's own self-activity, then, introduces and enforces virtue in his consciousness; "every man is virtuous when his particular will is in all things conformable to the general will, and we voluntarily will what is willed by those whom we love." [102] The General Will resurrects man's essence in the artificial world of external relations to destroy the pseudoconcrete "will of all" arising from the false individual particular wills. Each man, as sovereign, constitutes the authority that reconstitutes each man, as subject, with a correct consciousness based on the equality, freedom, and virtue created by the civic collective subject. "The general will is always for the common good." [103] It "penetrates into a man's inmost being, and concerns itself no less with his will than with his actions"; for the civic man, "it is needful only to act justly, to be certain of following the general will," [104] for it recreates and redeems his corrupt social consciousness as it grows up in "the hearts of the citizens."

Rousseau does not resort to institution building and to grand legislation simply for their own sake or merely to improve the operations of society as it currently exists. Rather, he turns to the vision of the legislator and to the authority of the sovereign's General Will in order to reconstitute social existence and, by doing so, wholly to change men's consciousness. As the sovereign-citizens create their civic collective subject, their corrupted false consciousness changes: "We cannot doubt that they will learn to cherish one another mutually as brothers, to will nothing contrary to the will of society, to substitute the actions of men and citizens for the futile and vain babbling of sophists, and to become in time defenders and fathers of the country of which they will have been so long the children." [105] Because of the General Will, it is not too late "to lead us out of ourselves when once the human ego, concentrated in our hearts, has acquired that contemptible activity which absorbs all virtue and constitutes the life and being of little minds." [106] Knowing the regenerative powers of the civic totality, social man can gain critical consciousness of his own plight and act decisively to escape from it through collective participatory political action. "If you would have the general will accomplished," Rousseau asserts, "bring all the particular wills into conformity with it; in other words, as virtue is nothing more than this conformity of the particular wills with the general will, establish the reign of virtue." [107] What matters most is "to think rightly rather than to know much." [108] Thinking rightly, or correct consciousness, however, can come only from conquering social alienation and reification through the mediation of collective subjectivity as the "voice of God" speaks again to civic man's conscience and heart through the "people's" collective action.

Conclusion

This chapter has argued that Rousseau is a systematic, dialectical, and antibourgeois social critic. Many of the social problems and cultural crises that Rousseau assailed in his political and social theory continue to plague society today. Moreover, their ongoing development has led to even greater alienation and reification along with a concomitant loss of freedom and equality. Rousseau's arguments, then, can be of great value in understanding the powerlessness and inequalities characteristic of modern life.

Rousseau's project points toward the revitalization of smaller-scale, face-to-face social relations to mediate society's emancipation from the alienation of modernization. He sees such more intimate social groups reconstituting man's moral consciousness and redressing the inequalities caused by complex social institutions. Progress in the scientific and industrial arts is mainly responsible for these corrupting social trends; hence Rousseau recommends that social production be reorganized on a smaller and more human scale. Only an existence lived close to the providence of Nature and through man's own whole self-activity in total cooperation with his fellows can engender a correct consciousness. Rousseau's belief in the primacy of politics for correcting false consciousness provides a discursive and practical model for participatory theorists in the present day. Political participation can serve as both the political end of and cultural means for improving the individual's virtue, freedom, and equality, because it generates a new collective subjectivity among the participants, drawing out the best of their authentic being.[109]

Rousseau, unlike Marx, does not trust in the further machinations of history to provoke a general crisis to change the human condition. Such a stance only entrenches more deeply the alienation and reification intrinsic to society's false external relations. Like Gramsci and Marcuse, Rousseau holds that the emancipatory society can become reality only through political action taken by the citizenry as sovereign-citizens, who create their own civic totality without the repressive antinomies of social inequalities. By uniting the antitheses of ruler/ruled in the sovereign's General Will, the civic state also might bridge the antitheses of strong/weak, rich/poor, notable/lowly, theory/practice, laborer/owner, and freedom/necessity. Once technical artifice and false social conventions are controlled, the artificial inequalities of society also can be limited or constrained by the participatory reign of virtue. Rousseau's systematic critical theory stands for the rehumanization of a dehumanized modern lifeworld as well as for the real humanizing of Nature rather than the artificial naturalizing of man. As Miller contends, Rousseau remains a radical visionary of democratic emancipation:

> Seeking a glimpse of a worldly redemption, he allowed himself to imagine a civilized freedom, a state of lasting happiness, a true democracy. By recording what he saw, he gave his images space, he made his ideas endure. Through the city he thus so vividly summoned, he engendered a new way of thinking, a new way of acting, and, above all, a new way of feeling. By conveying all this through his books, he performed the political duty he could never discharge in practice. His virtue was in writing, his courage in communicating a fantasy. By dreaming of himself as an ideal citizen of a Geneva that never was, he interpreted the world anew.[110]

For these reasons, Rousseau's critical theories are a fresh and still unfulfilled radical project. In many ways, Rousseau's project remains very much active today. Political ideas as diverse as Bookchin's "post-scarcity anarchism" or Barber's "strong democracy" directly tie back from the present into Rousseau's critique of the Enlightenment as well as his vision of civic virtue in a democratic community.[111] And, as Chapters 5 and 6 illustrate, Marcuse and contemporary critical theorists continue much of Rousseau's radical project in their own responsive critiques of instrumental reason, contemporary economic crises, and social revolution.

Notes

1. Rousseau's critics all too often connect his thoughts to starkly unrelated problems and themes without heeding Rousseau's own advice to his readers: "Learn my vocabulary better, my good friend, if you want us to understand each other. Believe me, my terms rarely have their usual meaning." Quoted in Stephen Ellenburg, *Rousseau's Political Philosophy: An Interpretation from Within* (Ithaca, NY: Cornell University Press, 1976), 24.

2. Like many contemporary critical theorists, Rousseau concerns himself with a critique of science and of the industrial worldview in order to appraise the alienation, reification, and dehumanization of modern everyday life. He also relies upon a dialectical mode of argument both to criticize the problems of social relations and to develop the points of his project's arguments. And, like the critical theorists, Rousseau seeks to create a new emancipated condition for persons caught up in the dehumanization of a technological society based upon capitalistic economic relations. For more on this topic, see William H. Blanchard, *Rousseau and the Spirit of Revolt: A Psychological Study* (Ann Arbor: University of Michigan Press, 1967); N. J. H. Dent, *Rousseau: Introduction to His Psychological, Social, and Political Theory* (New York: Blackwell, 1989); Edward Duffy, *Rousseau in England: The Context for Shelley's Critique of the Enlightenment* (Berkeley: University of California Press, 1979); Hilail Gildin, *Rousseau's Social Contract: The Design of the Argument* (Chicago: University of Chicago Press, 1983); Ronald Grimsley, *Rousseau and the Religious Quest* (Oxford: Clarendon, 1968); Joan McDonald, *Rousseau and the French Revolution, 1762-1791* (London: Athlone, 1965); James Miller, *Rousseau: Dreamer of Democracy* (New Haven, CT: Yale University Press, 1984); Andrzej Rapaczynski, *Nature and Politics: Liberalism in the Philosophies of Hobbes, Locke and Rousseau* (Ithaca, NY: Cornell University Press, 1987); Kennedy F. Roche, *Rousseau: Stoic and Romantic* (London: Methuen, 1974); and Joel Schwartz, *The Sexual Politics of Jean-Jacques Rousseau* (Chicago: University of Chicago Press, 1984).

3. The term *Enlightenment schema* refers to the notions developed on this subject by Horkheimer and Adorno in *The Dialectic of Enlightenment*. Succinctly stated, they characterize the schema as a paradoxical stage in modern cultural history: "The program of the Enlightenment was the disenchantment of the world; the dissolution of myths and the substitution of knowledge for fancy." Max Horkheimer and T. W. Adorno, *The Dialectic of Enlightenment* (New York: Herder & Herder, 1972), 3. Yet, the fulfillment of this program, especially the social consequences of its successes, becomes the main problem for Rousseau's radical critique of modern social existence.

4. Jean-Jacques Rousseau, *The Confessions of Jean Jacques Rousseau* (New York: Walter J. Black, 1960), 401.

5. Mario Einaudi, *The Early Rousseau* (Ithaca, NY: Cornell University Press, 1967), 104.

6. Judith N. Shklar, *Men and Citizens: A Study of Rousseau's Social Theory* (London: Cambridge University Press, 1969), 1.

7. J. L. Talmon, *The Origins of Totalitarian Democracy* (London: Secker & Warburg, 1955), 19.

8. Ernst Cassirer, *Rousseau, Kant and Goethe* (Princeton, NJ: Princeton University Press, 1970), 2.

9. Ibid.

10. Talmon, *Origins of Totalitarian Democracy,* 39.

11. Shklar, *Men and Citizens,* 2.

12. John C. McManners, "The Social Contract and Rousseau's Revolt Against Society," *Hobbes and Rousseau,* ed. by Maurice Cranston and Richard S. Peters (Garden City, NY: Doubleday, 1972), 301.

13. J. Patrick Dobel, "Review of Lester Crocker's *Jean Jacques Rousseau: The Quest and the Prophetic Voice,*" *Western Political Quarterly* 29, no. 3 (September 1976), 476.

14. Ibid. Of course, not all Rousseau scholars take this psychobiographical approach to Rousseau's work. In contrast to this school of thought, see Galvano Della Volpe, *Rousseau and Marx and Other Writings* (London: Lawrence & Wishart, 1978); R. Derathé, *Rousseau et al science politique de son temps* (Paris: Press universitaires de France, 1950), M. Launay, *J. J. Rousseau: écrivain politique, 1712-62* (Cannes: CEL, 1971), and Roger D. Masters, *The Political Philosophy of Rousseau* (Princeton, NJ: Princeton University Press, 1968).

15. The "antinomies of bourgeois thought" are described by Lukács as the conceptual expression of formal, reified modes of thinking in which a passive contemplative duality of

subject and object replaces a dialectical union of subject and object in theory and practice. He observes: "Thus classical philosophy finds itself historically in the paradoxical position that it was concerned to find a philosophy that would mean the end of bourgeois society, and resurrect in thought a humanity destroyed in that society and by it. In the upshot, however, it did not manage to do more than provide a complete intellectual copy and the *a priori* deduction of bourgeois society. It is only the *manner* of this deduction, namely the dialectical method that points beyond bourgeois society. And even in classical philosophy that is only expressed in the form of an unsolved and insoluble antinomy. This antinomy is admittedly the most profound and the most magnificent intellectual expression of those antinomies which lie at the roots of bourgeois society and which are unceasingly produced and reproduced by it—albeit in confused and inferior forms. Hence classical philosophy had nothing but these unresolved antinomies to bequeath to succeeding (bourgeois) generations. The continuation of that course which at least in method started to point the way beyond these limits, namely the dialectical method as the true historical method was reserved for the class which was able to discover within itself on the basis of its life-experience the identical subject-object, the subject of action; the 'we' of the genesis: namely the proletariat." Georg Lukács, *History and Class Consciousness* (Cambridge: MIT Press, 1971), 148-149.

This argument elaborates upon these assertions by speculating that Rousseau was the first modern social critic to overcome them through a dialectical analysis. Of course, from Lukács's perspective, Rousseau fails somewhat because of his reliance upon the classical philosopher's themes and language—virtue, Nature, goodness, commonwealth, citizenship, and patriotism—to make his critique. Nonetheless, if one accepts that the "we of genesis," the subject of action, might be the sovereign-citizen as he acts to become and to create an identical subject-object, then Rousseau's project seems to be an extremely innovative and highly original radical critique.

16. Rousseau's writings provide both a partial and a total solution to the imperfections created by man's sociohistorical condition. In a parallel answer to the social condition, one could become a correctly educated man; and in a total solution for the problematic, one should become an active subject-citizen in a civic state.

As Judith Shklar contends, Rousseau asks social man either to become *men*—living simple self-sufficient lives in rural rustic surroundings—or to become *citizens*—living virtuous interdependent lives by partaking in their sovereignty as civic subjects in a political union. Through the strict discipline of education, men might individually gain a true consciousness of man's real needs and true duties in spite of their society's false consciousness. Yet such an existential quest for authentic being in an inauthentic world allows only for the Pyrrhic conquest of the social lifeworld. By education, only individuals or, at best, families overcome the artificial external relations of the social condition. This sort of limited episodic arrest of alienation is, in a sense, the social condition's equivalent of natural man's inability to communicate his achievements to his fellows. The moral man's achievements cannot be shared widely with his fellows in society; hence in society the art of moral perfection would perish "with the inventor; there was neither education nor improvement; generations succeeded generations to no benefit; and as all constantly set out from the same point, whole centuries rolled on in the rudeness and barbarity of the first age." Jean-Jacques Rousseau, *The Social Contract and the Discourse on the Origin of Inequality,* ed. by Lester G. Crocker (New York: Pocket Books, 1967), 209.

Society's corrupt state becomes a second state of nature, and in this second nature, the race would grow old but man would remain a child in moral terms. The partial solution, then, of correctly educating men in the tranquil household cannot significantly change an entire people. Yet a viable state of true consciousness will succeed only if the entire people is changed. In fact, "the educational experiments, advocated by Rousseau in *Emile*, of withdrawing children from the common life of every day and bringing them up in the country, have turned out to be futile, since no success can attend an attempt to estrange people from the laws of the world," because, as Hegel observes, the collective consciousness and external relations of society will "gain mastery of those outlying regions." Georg Hegel, *The Philosophy of Right* (London: Oxford University Press, 1967), 261. Consequently, Hegel seems to judge correctly that the total solution of political action remains social man's best hope: "It is only by becoming a citizen of a good state that the individual first comes into his right." Ibid., 261-262. Social man's total redemption from the "rudeness and barbarity" of the social condition flows from his constitution of a new collective subject, equal to that of Nature, by means of collective political action.

17. Shklar, *Men and Citizens,* 1.

18. Einaudi, *The Early Rousseau,* 103.

19. Rousseau, *Letters to Malesherbes* (January 1762; P, I, 1136), quoted in Ellenburg, *Rousseau's Political Philosophy,* 13.

20. Rousseau, *Letter to Beaumont* (March 1763; P, IV, 928), quoted in Ellenburg, *Rousseau's Political Philosophy,* 13.

21. Jean-Jacques Rousseau, *The Social Contract and Discourses,* ed. by G. D. H. Cole (New York: E. P. Dutton, 1906), 152.

22. Ibid., 164.

23. Ibid., 166.

24. Ibid., 168.

25. Rousseau, *The Social Contract* (Crocker ed.), 220.

26. Einaudi, *The Early Rousseau,* 153.

27. Frederick Engels, *Anti-Dühring: Herr Eugen Dühring's Revolution in Science* (Moscow: Progress, 1969), 167.

28. Ibid.

29. Rousseau, *The Social Contract* (Crocker ed.), 167.

30. Ibid., 168.

31. Ibid., 169. As Rousseau notes, by dealing with Nature in this fashion, "we shall not be obliged to make man a philosopher before he is a man." Ibid., 171-172.

32. Ibid., 173.

33. Ibid., 172.

34. Ibid., 179.

35. Ibid., 167.

36. Ibid., 188.

37. Ibid., 168.

38. Ibid.

39. Ibid., 171.

40. Ibid., 172.

41. Rousseau contrasts the two types of self-regard in this fashion: "We must not confuse selfishness with self-love; they are two very distinct passions both in their nature and in their effects. Self-love is a natural sentiment, which inclines every animal to look to his own preservation, and which, guided in man by reason and qualified by pity, is productive of humanity and virtue. Selfishness is but a relative and factitious sentiment, engendered in society, which inclines every individual to set a greater value upon himself than upon any other man, which inspires men with all the mischief they do to each other, and is the true source of what we call honor." Ibid., 256.

42. Ibid., 173.

43. Ibid., 242-244.

44. Ibid., 203.

45. Lukács, *History and Class Consciousness,* 136.

46. Ibid.

47. A return to Rousseau's texts affirms this important point:

> "And how shall man be able to see himself, such as nature formed him." (Crocker ed., 167)

> "to know man as constituted by nature" (Ibid., 167)

"one which a I call natural, or physical inequality, because it is established by nature" (Ibid., 175)

"Nature treats them exactly in the same manner." (Ibid., 175)

"the simple, uniform and solitary way of life prescribed to us by nature" (Ibid., 183)

"allowing that nature intended" (Ibid., 183)

"Nature speaks to all animals, and beasts obey her voice." (Ibid., 187)

"for we cannot desire or fear anything, but in consequence of the ideas we have of it, or of the simple impulses of nature" (Ibid., 187)

"The progress of the mind has everywhere kept pace exactly with the wants to which nature had left the inhabitants exposed." (Ibid., 187)

"as if nature thus meant to make all things equal" (Ibid., 187)

"What these origins may have been, we may at least infer from the little care which nature has taken to bring men together by mutual wants . . . how little she has done towards making them sociable, and how little she has contributed to anything which they themselves have done to become so." (Ibid., 198)

These examples indicate how Rousseau presents Nature as a caring subject. In this respect, Rousseau's construction of Nature accords with the classical and Renaissance sense of Nature as an active persona. For Rousseau, then, Nature forms, Nature constitutes, Nature establishes, Nature treats, Nature prescribes, Nature speaks, Nature leaves, and Nature contributes.

48. Ibid., 204.

49. Ibid., 199.

50. Ibid., 224.

51. Ibid., 220.

52. Ibid., 209.

53. Ibid., 18.

54. Ibid., 7.

55. Ibid., 9.

56. Ibid., 15.

57. Ibid.

58. Ibid.

59. Ibid., 17-18.

60. Ibid., 19. Rousseau concisely summarizes this assertion by claiming: "These clauses, rightly understood, are reducible to one only, viz., the total alienation to the whole community of each associate with all his rights; for, in the first place, since each gives himself up entirely, the conditions being equal for all, no one has any interest in making them burdensome to others.

"Further, the alienation being made without reserve, the union is as perfect as it can be, and an individual associate can no longer claim anything; for, if any rights were left to individuals, since there would be no common superior who could judge between them and the public, each, being on some point his own judge, would soon claim to be so on all; the state of nature would still subsist, and the association would necessarily become tyrannical or useless.

"In short, each giving himself to all, gives himself to nobody; and as there is not one associate over whom we do not acquire the same rights which we concede to him over ourselves, we gain the equivalent of all that we lose, and more power to preserve what we have." Ibid., 18.

61. Ibid., 18-19.

62. Ibid., 21, 27.

63. Ibid., 34.

64. Ibid. Of course, "law" for Rousseau is nothing but the concretized will of the sovereign-citizen that serves as the foundation of the state's activities: "But when the whole

people decree concerning the whole people, they consider themselves alone; and if a relation is then constituted, it is between the whole object under one point of view and the whole object under another point of view, without any division of all. Then the matter respecting which they decree is general like the will that decrees. It is this act that I call a law." Ibid., 39.

65. Ibid., 43.

66. Ibid., 22.

67. Jean-Jacques Rousseau, *Politics and the Arts: Letter to D'Alembert on the Theatre* (Glencoe, IL: Free Press, 1960), 67.

68. See Marc F. Plattner, *Rousseau's State of Nature* (DeKalb: Northern Illinois University Press, 1979), 3; and Engels, *Anti-Dühring*, 407.

69. Frederick Engels, "Socialism: Utopian and Scientific," *The Marx-Engels Reader,* ed. by Robert C. Tucker (New York: Norton, 1972), 606. To some extent, Engels here is misusing Rousseau's ideas for his own purposes. Engels's observation, of course, follows from Marx's characterization of Rousseau as an advocate of abstract subjectivity in his "On the Jewish Question." That is, "the abstract notion of political man is well formulated by Rousseau," in Marx's analysis, and Rousseau's "political emancipation" is a reduction of man, on the one hand, to a member of civil society, an "*independent* and *egoistic* individual, and on the other hand, to a *citizen*, to a moral person." Robert C. Tucker, ed., *The Marx-Engels Reader* (2nd ed.) (New York: Norton, 1978), 46. Plainly, Rousseau does develop a complex philosophy of the subject. Yet, his basic dissatisfaction with bourgeois subjectivity is the same as Marx's, namely, "Man in his *most intimate* reality, in civil society, is a profane being. Here, where he appears both to himself and to others as a real individual he is an *illusory* phenomenon. In the state, on the contract, where he is regarded as a species-being, man is the imaginary member of an imaginary sovereignty, divested of his real, individual life, and infused with an unreal universality." See Karl Marx, "On the Jewish Question," *The Marx-Engels Reader,* ed. by Robert C. Tucker (New York: Norton, 1972), 34.

Rousseau's project is aimed at overcoming man's "illusory" and "profane" being in civil society and his "imaginary sovereignty" in the state by reconstituting civic life and citizenship in the workings of the new sovereign of the social contract. Rousseau's critique would undoubtedly move him to endorse Marx's assertion about human emancipation becoming complete only "when the real, individual man has absorbed into himself the abstract citizen; when as an individual man, in his everyday life, in his work, and in his relationships, he has become a *species-being* and when he has recognized and organized his own powers (*forces propres*) as *social* powers so that he no longer separates this social power from himself as *political* power." Marx, "On the Jewish Question," 46. The desire to overcome this division and revitalize an original "species being" is certainly at the root of Rousseau's critical intentions.

70. Ibid.

71. Horkheimer and Adorno, *Dialectic of Enlightenment,* 7.

72. Ibid., 9.

73. Rousseau, *The Social Contract* (Crocker ed.), 224.

74. Ibid.

75. Ibid., 170.

76. Rousseau, *The Social Contract* (Cole ed.), 152. While the bourgeois "kingdom of reason" laid great emphasis on progress in the arts and sciences, Rousseau questions "what a number of wrong paths present themselves in the investigation of the sciences." Ibid., 157. In answer, he notes, "Astronomy was born of superstition, eloquence of ambition, hatred, falsehood, and flattery; geometry of avarice; physics of idle curiosity; and even moral philosophy of human pride." Ibid., 158. Moreover, "their evil origin is, indeed, but too plainly reproduced in their objects." Ibid., 159. The technical reification engendered in social man's life by the objectification of nature, in Rousseau's ultimate analysis, corrupts everyone's consciousness as "there prevails in modern manners a servile and deceptive conformity; so that one would think every mind had been cast in the same mould." Ibid., 149.

77. Einaudi, *The Early Rousseau,* 205.

78. Jean-Jacques Rousseau, *The Creed of a Priest of Savoy* (2nd. ed.) (New York: Ungar, 1957), 13-14.

79. Rousseau, *The Social Contract* (Cole ed.), 311.

80. Ibid., 320.

81. Ibid., 228.

82. Ibid., 244.

83. Ibid., 24.

84. Ibid., 26.

85. Ibid., 311.

86. Ibid., 312.

87. Ibid., 313.

88. Rousseau, *The Social Contract* (Crocker ed.), 110.

89. Rousseau, *The Social Contract* (Cole ed.), 322.

90. Rousseau, *The Social Contract* (Crocker ed.), 110.

91. Rousseau, *The Social Contract* (Cole ed.), 323-324.

92. Ibid.

93. Rousseau, *The Social Contract* (Crocker ed.), 26.

94. Ibid.

95. Ibid.

96. Einaudi, *The Early Rousseau,* 3.

97. Rousseau, *The Social Contract* (Crocker ed.), 240.

98. Ibid., 244.

99. Ibid., 245.

100. Ibid.

101. Rousseau, *The Social Contract* (Cole ed.), 291.

102. Ibid., 301.

103. Ibid., 291.

104. Ibid., 297.

105. Ibid., 309.

106. Ibid., 308.

107. Ibid., 298.

108. Einaudi, *The Early Rousseau,* 66.

109. Rousseau's major problem in taking this stance, of course, is his denial of political and economic rights to women. For additional discussion of this major contradiction, see Schwartz, *Sexual Politics of Jean-Jacques Rousseau.* Also see Joan B. Landes, *Women and the Public Sphere in the Age of the French Revolution* (Ithaca, NY: Cornell University Press, 1988), 66-89; and Jean Bethke Elshtain, *Public Man, Private Woman: Women in Social and Political Thought* (Princeton, NJ: Princeton University Press, 1981).

110. Miller, *Rousseau: Dreamer of Democracy,* 210.

111. See Murray Bookchin, *Post-Scarcity Anarchism* (Montreal: Black Rose, 1986); and Benjamin Barber, *Strong Democracy: Participatory Politics for a New Age* (Berkeley: University of California Press, 1984).

5

A Phenomenological/Freudian Marxism?
Marcuse's Critique of
Advanced Industrial Society

Like Rousseau's philosophical and literary career, Herbert Marcuse's lifework encompasses a critical historical era. During Marcuse's lifetime, the most dynamic elements of entrepreneurial capitalism combined with the administrative designs of the modern service state, which reconstituted classical capitalist forms of social production as state-corporate capitalism. Marcuse, in the political context of Weimar Germany and, later, post-New Deal America, immediately discerned the essential problems posed by this historical transformation for Marxist theory, namely, that the *proletarian class in itself* fails to constitute itself as a *revolutionary class for itself.* With the rise of the corporate culture industries and the administrative welfare state in the 1920s and 1930s, Marcuse saw a basic change developing out of what were hitherto antagonistic class relations.[1] With this change, Marcuse argued that "the development of mature capitalism shows a long-range trend toward class collaboration rather than class struggle, toward national and international division rather than solidarity of the proletariat in advanced industrial countries."[2] Marcuse traced the roots of this failure to the new uses that mature capitalism had for scientific-technical rationality, particularly in the new forms of social control and domination inherent in the productive capabilities of modern technics, which assumed the attributes of "one-dimensionality."

Marcuse's critical discourse maintained that Marxism, as the practical science of *proletarian* revolution,[3] had to face "the task of redefining the conception of the transition to socialism and of the strategy in this

128

period" [4] as the historical qualities of entrepreneurial/*class* societies faded into the one-dimensionality of state-corporate/*mass* society. In the phase of liberal entrepreneurial capitalism, the working classes represented the negative, transcendent opposition to the established bourgeois order. Yet the advent of fascism in Europe and consumerism in North America shifted these forces into new alignments after World War I. As the affluence of state-corporate production increasingly compromised the workers with consumer goods, mass culture, and welfare benefits, much of this class-based negativity—rooted in the practical experience of *labor*—dissipated. Marcuse argued that almost all class-derived culture disappears in the age of mass consumption as the classes themselves, both bourgeoisie and proletarian,[5] are atomized merely into masses of individuals by the reifying domination of the technological apparatus.

Like the other major figures of the Frankfurt school, Marcuse redefined the problematic of making the socialist transition by recasting Marxism as *critical theory*, or as "Marxism" *without* the proletariat.[6] In order to render late capitalism more comprehensible while retaining the essential precepts of Marxism, the major figures of the Frankfurt school returned to their *non-Marxist* philosophical and scientific training in aesthetics, phenomenology, psychology, or sociology in order to continue the *Marxist* tradition. By making this theoretical leap, Marcuse greatly extended the critical scope of Marxism as he artfully interwove aspects of Schiller's aesthetics, Marx's political economy, Husserl's phenomenology, Heidegger's existential analysis, and Freud's metapsychology into a new political theory to reveal the possibilities of emancipation for state-corporate mass societies.

Still, this new political theory is not without its serious problems. Marcuse's search for new organic sources of negativity in late capitalism led directly from classical Marxism to a new discourse based upon a phenomenological critique of technological rationality and to a psychoanalytic theory of history. His inventive combination of these disparate frameworks, as "immanent critique," resulted in some serious misrepresentations both of present-day political realities and of their emancipatory possibilities. In the last analysis, Marcuse perhaps proved insufficiently critical of technological rationality as he attributed its domination largely to its misuse by exploitative groups. By the same token, he concluded his critique of modern technological society mistakenly by rooting his emancipatory politics and his theory of negative collective subjectivity in the organic instinctual energies of each human individual as he displaced Marx's model of production with his own reading of Freud's analysis of reproduction. In seeking to replace the historical negativity of the identical subject-object of *labor*, or the proletariat, Marcuse resorts to an equally problematic solution, namely, the naturalistic, presocial, and prehistorical collective subjectivity—the identical subject-object of *pleasure*, or the individual's and the human species' erotic instincts.

Given these issues, this chapter explores this basic question: How convincing and practical is Marcuse's "immanent critique" of advanced industrial society? And, granted its foundations in a phenomenological treatment of technological rationality as well as a psychoanalytic philosophy of history, why is Marcuse's emancipatory politics so problematic?

Marcuse's Phenomenological/Freudian Marxism

Marcuse resorted to Heideggerian phenomenology and Freudian psychoanalysis in order to *rehistoricize* Marxism and its dialectic of history.[7] Indeed, his first published theoretical analysis, "Contributions to a Phenomenology of Historical Materialism" (1928), outlined a philosophical merger of Marxism and Heideggerian phenomenology. Likewise, his first major work published after World War II in the United States was his Freudian-inspired *Eros and Civilization* (1956). Given the alternative and largely ahistorical versions of "Marxist" analysis available to him at that time, his attempt to ground Marxism in phenomenology was an inventive step. The Social Democratic school of positivized Marxist science and the increasingly apologistic forms of Marxism-Leninism, created after 1928 in the USSR, essentially ignored the constantly changing historicity of political events.[8] Unfortunately, despite his phenomenological innovations, much of Marcuse's argument also reproduces the basically ahistorical ontological approach to the material environment taken by Heidegger.

Unlike Husserl, who identified the *Lebenswelt* with the always changing forms of material human praxis associated with the productive base, Heidegger approached the *Lebenswelt* as the immediate world of everyday existence as *Umwelt* or *Mitwelt*, or simply the given immediate environment with no clear connections to the more determinate economic base.[9] Marcuse recognizes some of these limits. He also largely follows, however, this Heideggerian usage. And, in turn, Marcuse defines "the material content of historicity" [10] not in terms of the developing material praxis of the productive base, but rather as "the concrete shared social world" [11] of everyday given immediacy. Consequently, Marcuse never conceptually taps deeply into the more political, historical, and cultural essence of the notion of *Lebenswelt*. As Piccone and Delfini have observed, "This is fatal, since the base is always seen as static and, although he [Marcuse] can offer a strikingly accurate analysis of *phenomenal* reality he never succeeds in penetrating into its essential structure, which is necessarily precategorical." [12]

Marcuse, of course, went beyond Heideggerian phenomenology as he sought a more solid foundation for his thinking, first in Hegel and then later in Freud. [13] Nonetheless, this phenomenological interlude clouds Marcuse's notions of technological rationality. [14] Marcuse's view of technical reason unfolds as a preexisting environment of things and thoughts that remains stuck in the already disclosed and objectified modes of everyday life. Scientific-technical rationality and its apparatus so deeply threaten men in their everyday living because, in Marcuse's thinking, technological reason "works as an *a priori*—it predetermines experience, it *projects* the direction of the transformation of nature, it organizes the whole." [15] And, in doing so, technology essentially effaces the tension between subject and object, destroying the mediation of objective reason and reality. [16] Because concrete reality is approached as a given system of instrumentalities, "metaphysical 'being-as-such' gives way to 'being-instrument,' " [17] and it "appears to be deprived of its logos, or rather its logos appears to be deprived of all reality, a logical form without any substance." [18] Technical reason, to Marcuse, then, is a priori instrumental control and organization that transforms both man and Nature into reified entities, wholly fungible to both technical domination and political manipulation.

For Marcuse, as scientific technics become the universal form of material production in contemporary industrial civilization, it projects an entire culture, it predetermines psychic forms, and it organizes the whole political structure—the technological a priori becomes a political a priori as "pure instrumentality, without finality, has become a universal means of domination." [19] Technological rationality, somewhat like Heidegger's *Dasein*, often emerges as an automatically actuating totality that envelops all subjects as objects and transforms material objects into technical subjects. Marcuse's essentially static view of the historical base prevents him from discerning many of the actual historical conditions or concrete political alliances that are behind the use of technological production as domination. Instead, all history is domination, while technological domination is simply the logical form of domination for advanced industrial civilization. Negativity and otherness, almost necessarily, cannot come from *within* the apparatus. To break the hold of technological reason, Marcuse relies on wholly external sources of negativity, or the "Outsider," and upon a politics of subversive transformation "from without.' " [20]

In advanced science, Marcuse maintains that philosophy no longer infuses scientific-technical reasoning with an essential logic, a *telos*. Therefore, the notion of an inwardly rational objective being crumbles in the abstract mechanics of operationalistic physical-mathematical structures. For Marcuse, technological reasoning allows "no nature or human reality left to represent a substantial *cosmos*," therefore, "technology, strictly speaking, has taken the place of ontology." [21] To subvert this false ontology in an attempt to discover a hitherto undetected source of objective reason, Marcuse plunges into an entirely new sphere of being, namely, into the deepest instinctual levels of man's somatic-psychic being. [22] Although he originally took up the study of Freud and psychoanalysis, in part, to explain why the European working classes had lapsed into political passivity, [23] Marcuse soon detected the critical, negative dimension of Freudian analysis that might be mobilized as a critique of advanced industrial society.

Unable to resurrect a historical-philosophical mediation of critical objective reason from the one-dimensional docility of the late capitalist proletariat, Marcuse reevaluated Freudian metapsychology, hoping to uncover an inward *telos* of being, and a potentially negative collective subjectivity, capable of toppling the technological order of domination. Even though the full outlines of his intentions do not emerge until 1955 with his *Eros and Civilization*, Marcuse, by 1938, in his "On Hedonism," recognized that inasmuch as technological reason fails to satisfy all the psychic needs, somatic wants, and emotional capacities of the individual, "this idea of reason implicitly contains the sacrifice of the individual." [24]

By preforming the individual ego to attain a distorted and repressive form of happiness in commodity consumption, the technological apparatus forces the "moment of resignation and approbation" [25] upon the pacified members of modern consumer society. A social guilt feeling is introjected into every individual and, in turn, this introjected *performance principle* enforces the current regimen of dedicated labor and limited recreational pleasure. To sustain the existing status quo, the workers exchange their docility for limited material pleasures that are accessible through commodity consumption to even the lowest wage earner. Real hedonism, then, despite its commitment to personal satisfaction in an impoverished social world, contains for Marcuse, "in an abstract and undeveloped form, the demand for the freedom of the individual"[26] fully actualized in the material realm of everyday life. And, insofar as it rebels against the domination of technologically rational labor and pleasure, hedonism "is linked with the interest of critical theory."[27]

In doing critical theory, or Marxist analysis without the prospect of the predicted proletarian revolution, Marcuse grounds his critique of late capitalism upon "individuals," especially in their "ontogenetic" growth as repressed individuals, which ironically recapitulates the "phylogenetic" development of repressive civilization from the primal horde to the stage of civilized society.[28] To provide a vision of emancipation for individuals under late capitalism, Marcuse goes beyond the collective subjectivity of *praxis* as the political negation of the capitalist conditions of production, which would enable the historical liberation of the working classes. Instead, he establishes *Eros*, or the primal energies of the life instincts, as the negation of advanced technological production and as the inner logic behind political emancipation. In late capitalism, for example, he argues that "the unpurified, unrationalized release of sexual relationships would be the strongest release of enjoyment as such and the total devaluation of labor for its own sake. No human being could tolerate the tension between labor as valuable in itself and the freedom of enjoyment. The dreariness and injustice of work conditions would penetrate explosively the consciousness of individuals and make impossible their peaceful subordination to the social system."[29]

In Freud's metapsychology, and despite its apparently transhistorical and scientistic categories, Marcuse discovered *his* historicization of Marxism to deal with the political challenges of advanced industrial society. Freud's theory of the instincts serves as his historical-philosophical mediation of critical objective reason. Marcuse portrays *Eros*, or the will to gratification, increasingly unfolding through the greater material productivity of modern technics as the negation of *Logos*, the modern logic of domination, which now is an outmoded fetter on the further historical development of society. Marcuse takes *Eros*, as the essence and *telos* of being, as the negative otherness of technological rationality, "the Logos of domination—commanding, mastering, directing reason, to which man and nature are to be subjected."[30] As reality principles, technical reason, or "the traditional ontology is contested: against the conception of being in terms of *Logos* rises the conception of being in alogical terms: will and joy. This counter-trend strives to formulate its own Logos: the logic of gratification."[31]

Marcuse mediates his vision of critical objective reason with a notion of emancipatory collective subjectivity derived not from *class*, or the identical subject-object of labor/*praxis*, but rather from biological *genus*, or the identical subject-object of pleasure/*Eros*.[32] Unfortunately, as an essentially biologistic notion—albeit layered with phenomenological historicity—*Eros* appears to be an ahistorical mediation of essential being. Indeed, *Eros*—as an organic, unchanging, structural aspect of the human animal's biological makeup—is actually nothing but the *most* static base imaginable for understanding the structures of man's historical development.

Marcuse largely fails to demonstrate the necessity of how freedom would be obtained by liberating the life instincts. In spite of the fact that modern technics seems to be completing the material preconditions for erotic freedom, Marcuse sees that the actual enactment of such emancipation is based upon a *decision* or a *choice* to be made by those "active minorities that abhor the concrete shared social world of late capitalist society. As a critical theorist, Marcuse identifies the choices—the "Great Refusal," the emancipation of *Eros*, the acceptance of the "happy consciousness"—but never proves the necessity of their historical determination in advanced industrial society. Much like Heidegger's phenomenological existentialism, Marcuse's critical theory projects an unfettered realm of historical possibilities merely to be chosen over the almost wholly overdetermined existential present.

Therefore, Marcuse largely remains boxed in between two one-dimensional abstractions, the *reality* of technological domination and the *possibility* of emancipated *Eros*, which robs the dialectical logic of its most important category—*actuality*. Actuality should fuse these two abstract categories into a single concrete totality, or a unity of potentiality in reality that can develop by virtue of the inherent contradictions of the *possible* in the *real*. By failing to ground his possible choices in any actual determinate historical necessity, Marcuse cannot emancipate the integrated majority—the Insiders—from the exploitation of late capitalist societies. Thus, in his political theory, the Outsiders, or the nonintegrated "active minorities" that he sees surviving in the academic community, the racial ghettos, or the Third World, emerge as agents of social change, because they have made their existential choice to resist technological rationality or because they have never been entirely integrated into the fold of scientific-technological domination.

Marcuse on Technics and Technology

Marcuse's notion of technological rationality first arises in "Some Social Implications of Modern Technology," published in 1941.[33] Here, Marcuse sketches out many of the core themes of *One-Dimensional Man.* Basically, he contrasts "technological rationality" (or the social mode of reason prevailing under state-corporate capitalism) and "individual rationality" (the liberal-bourgeois individual mode of economic reasoning common to the stage of entrepreneurial capitalism) and with "critical rationality" (the progressive individual critique of technological reality that seeks to realize fully the emancipatory productive potential of technical reason). Obviously, with the demise of entrepreneurial capitalism, individual rationality—with its inherent assumptions of individual autonomy, critical self-reflection, and informed self-interest—becomes increasingly "irrational." The state's intervention into corporate management destroys the objective foundations of individual rationality, as the open market and autonomous civil society are brought under centralized bureaucratic control, through economic planning in the public and private spheres.

Confronted by this planned organization of cultural, economic, political, and social life, Marcuse argues that the individual must adapt and adjust his hitherto critical capacities to match this technically enforced conformity. Having destroyed the material bases of individual freedom, technological rationality strives to efface the possibility of psychic freedom as well. Marcuse notes:

> The apparatus to which the individual is to adjust and adapt himself is so rational that individual protest and liberation appear not only as hopeless but as utterly irrational. The system of life created by modern industry is defined in terms of expediency, convenience and efficiency. Reason, once defined in these terms, becomes equivalent to an activity which perpetuates this world. Rational behavior becomes identical with a matter-of-factness which teaches reasonable submissiveness and thus guarantees getting along in the prevailing order.[34]

During the era of entrepreneurial capitalism, rational behavior represented a more negative, critical, or oppositional mode of being as the bourgeois individual struggled against the antiquated institutions and ideas of feudal tradition.

However, once it becomes embedded as the norm of everyday life in technological artifacts, technological reason embodies the social premises of individual submission, passive contemplation, and collectively dictated group interest.[35] Modern individuals, then, acquire needs for expediency, convenience, and efficiency that reproduce the essential qualities of the repressive economic, political, and social structures that prevent their emancipation. In other words, for Marcuse,

> technology and technics applied in the economic process are more than ever before instruments of social and political control. The satisfaction of needs (material and intellectual) takes place through scientific organization of work, scientific management, and the scientific imposition of attitudes and behavior patterns, which operate beyond and outside the work process and precondition the individuals in accord with the dominant social interests.[36]

Hence Marcuse suggests that man's increasing command over Nature through technology necessarily results in a greatly increased ability to dominate human nature. The two spheres are intimately connected inasmuch as the complex technical control implicit in technology demands that men exercise greater discipline over their own labor and patterns of consumption.[37] By preconditioning the behavioral patterns of individuals, Marcuse sees technological reason introjecting its technical demands into each person's somatic-psychic constitution, which "becomes the psychological basis of a *threefold domination*: first, domination over one's self, over one's nature, over the sensual drives that want only pleasure and gratification; second, domination of the labor achieved by such disciplined and controlled individuals; and third, domination of outward Nature, science, and technology." [38]

Still, for Marcuse, this mode of domination can be overcome as it "is not the eternal opposite of freedom, but rather its presupposition." [39] Technological domination, however, serves as the presupposition of technological emancipation through Marcuse's "cunning of technological reason." Marcuse, then, contends that the technological apparatus, which enforces this repressiveness in the forms of everyday life, in fact, actually constitutes its own negation in simply expanding its own technical operations.[40] The increasing "technification of domination undermines the foundation of domination" [41] in such a way that "a 'threefold freedom'— moral, political, and intellectual—emerges from the work of domination." [42] By ordering man's somatic-psychic instincts rationally and in elaborating the material preconditions of freedom technically, Marcuse argues that technological rationality—despite its present repressive functioning—also contains the new possibilities for human emancipation from outmoded instinctual repression, from socially necessary labor, and from the false domination of scientific-technical reason. Given this analysis and critique of technical reason, it is necessary to investigate more closely the implications of Marcuse's understanding of technological rationality to determine how it embodies domination and emancipation in the same moment.

Technology as Such and Historicized Technology

Marcuse suggests that technics and technology can be defined by approaching technology analytically in two distinct senses—as *technology as such* and as *historicized technology*. First, technology as such is presented by Marcuse as being intrinsically neutral and a priori instrumentalistic. It is a pure functional form "which can be bent to practically all ends." [43] As an essentially neutral framework of scientific methods, technology as such embodies "neither a telos itself nor is it structured toward a telos." [44] Instead of grounding itself in *Logos*, the essential structure of being, technology as such incarnates itself as *Ratio*, or as the subjective reason "of pure calculability and predictability." [45] Obviously, the mediation of technology as such emerges with the science of nature and, in doing so, *Ratio*—while remaining substantively neutral—becomes methodologically instrumentalistic.

Even though technology as such is "instrumentality which lends itself to all purposes and ends—instrumentality *per se*, 'in itself,' " [46] it also "develops under the technological *a priori* which projects nature as *potential instrumentality*, stuff of control and organization." [47] In other words, *technology as such* merely denotes a hypothetical system of structured physical-mathematical propositions, whose *potential* instrumentalism merely effects their logical and theoretical closure. This aspect emerges as a crucial point in that Marcuse argues that all technology as such is a priori organized as an instrumental system, which, as pure *Ratio*, necessarily approaches nature as the stuff of organization and control. Yet, it does so only *potentially* or *hypothetically* as a wholly *theoretical* structure. While technology as such is necessarily instrumentalistic as a theoretical method, it is only contingently instrumentalistic, according to Marcuse, as substantive practice.

Marcuse maintains that technological rationality's contingent instrumentalism follows from technology's second sense, namely, that of historicized technology. At a certain historical juncture, substantively neutral and potentially instrumental *technology as such* merged with a *specific* practical application of its method in a particular social and historical context. Hence technology as such assumes as its own the concrete practical ends of human subjects as *historicized technology*. Of course, in actual practice, this fusion of potential means and actual ends in historicized technology occurred as the European bourgeoisie began to conquer Nature through manufacture and industrial production.[48] Once historicized within this given social universe, then, the *potential* instrumentalism of technology as such, theoretical reason, becomes *actual* technological instrumentalization, practical reason. And, Marcuse maintains, as the historicized means of fulfilling bourgeois-entrepreneurial ends, "the principles of modern science were *a priori* structured in such a way that they could serve as conceptual instruments for a universe of self-propelling, productive control; theoretical operationalism came to correspond to practical operationalism." [49] What is more, "the scientific method which led to the ever-more-effective domination of nature thus came to provide the pure concepts as well as the instrumentalities for the ever-more-effective domination of man by man *through* the domination of nature. Theoretical reason, remaining pure and neutral, entered into the service of practical reason." [50]

At the same time, the *Ratio* of technology as such comes to obliterate any sense of *Logos* beyond that projected within the subjective practice of technological production. With its historicization, then, *Ratio*, which was originally neutral in substance and methodologically instrumentalistic, becomes substantively instrumentalistic in bourgeois society as a major element in the *Logos* of capitalistic technological domination. Yet, its manipulative technical activity is hidden behind its alleged methodological neutrality. Although it is denied by the "technological veil" that mystifies the historical class interests embodied in *historicized technology*, Marcuse discerns that "in the construction of the technological reality, there is no such thing as a purely rational scientific order; the process of technological rationality is a political process." [51] Historicized technology produces the material comforts that underlie the rising standards of industrial living. But, as history unfolds toward advanced industrial society, the forms of domination not only extend "through technology but *as* technology," [52] as technological rationality "determines *a priori* the product of the apparatus as well as the operations of servicing and extending it." [53]

In this political universe, Marcuse concludes, historicized technology

> also provides the great rationalization of the unfreedom of man and demonstrates the "technical" impossibility of being autonomous, of determining one's own life. For this unfreedom appears neither as irrational nor as political, but rather as submission to the technical apparatus which enlarges the comforts of life and increases the productivity of labor. Technological rationality thus protects rather than cancels the legitimacy of domination and the instrumentalist horizon of reason opens on a rationally totalitarian society.[54]

Theoretical reason as practical reason, then, subverts the autonomous sphere of human "interaction" in subjugating it to the dictates of technological "work." [55] Instead of effecting a "humanization" of progress[56] and the liberation of "culture," [57] technological rationality amplifies the technification of domination and the repressiveness of civilization.

In drawing this distinction, Marcuse distinguishes the two aspects of modern technological reason. He demonstrates the "*internal* instrumentalist character" [58] of technical reason, as a *potential* in technology as such and as a *reality* in the modern social forms of historicized technology. In all advanced industrial societies, Marcuse suggests that technology functions as domination, yet it does so *only* by virtue of its present *historical* utilization. "The hypothetical system of forms and functions [or technology as such] becomes dependent on another system—a pre-established universe of ends [or the calculative *Ratio* of industrial capitalism], in which and *for* which it develops." [59]

What appeared extraneous, foreign to the theoretical project, shows forth as part of its very structure (methods and concepts); "pure objectivity reveals as object for a subjectivity which provides the *telos*, the ends [or, now, the historicized technology embedded in the state-corporate apparatus]." [60] In other words, the *false* historicization of technology under the class-biased forms of advanced industrial production, and not any essential quality of it as such, emerges as the fetter upon liberation. For Marcuse, if the pure neutrality of technology as such could be reclaimed and recombined with a new source of revolutionary social subjectivity, like *Eros* and its liberated life instincts, then a humane technological society might emerge from the false totality of one-dimensional society.

Here, Marcuse projects the emancipatory potentialities held within contemporary political reality by asserting that technological reason can be overcome not through its abolition, but rather through its reorganization to satisfy the objective reason of the liberated life instincts. By eliminating technically the need for human labor from the technological apparatus, Marcuse sees individuals possibly living a new life, or an "existence in free time on the basis of fulfilled vital needs," [61] as automation replaces human labor. With this development, "the very structure of human existence would be altered; the individual would be liberated from the work world's imposing upon him alien needs and alien possibilities." [62] Therefore, individuals could freely exert their autonomy and satisfy their own unique individual needs.

Here, Marcuse's analysis discovers an escape from the present inauthentic being of advanced technology that leads into an authentic being based upon a *rehabilitated* technology. In keeping with the "cunning of technological reason," the false historicization of technology via increasing automation and productivity is unceasingly tending toward its own negation. Once again, Marcuse reveals himself to be working from the premise of a *static* productive base; indeed, the advanced technological base must remain fixed because it "might release individual energy into a yet uncharted realm of freedom beyond necessity." [63]

The biological genus of individuals seeking emancipation must not destroy the technical apparatus. Instead, individuals must accept the state-corporate apparatus, while redirecting and reorganizing its technics to satisfy individual needs, for "such control would not prevent individual autonomy, but rather make it possible." [64] Unable to transform men's being by reconstituting the *Dasein* of technical reason, Marcuse accepts its overwhelming power and urges a collective adaptation to it as an emancipatory strategy for realizing man's inner instinctual *Sein*. "In other words," Marcuse states, "the completion of the technological reality would be not only the prerequisite, but also the rationale for *transcending* the technological reality." [65]

Problems in Marcuse's Strategies

Two problematic issues arise from Marcuse's characterization of technological rationality.[66] First, he seems to misjudge technology as such as being only *potentially* and *hypothetically* an instrumentalizing system.

Second, he wrongly accepts the given objectifications of modern technological reason, or modern productive technics, as projecting, even at least in part, the realm of liberating possibilities. Marcuse works within the preestablished technics of advanced industrial society—largely because of their unprecedented productive capacities—rather than discovering the practical-theoretical necessity for going beyond these technics into new forms of more humane, appropriate technics. Although he is aware of these problems, I would argue that Marcuse's analysis and critique of modern technological rationality ultimately dissatisfies because he is insufficiently critical of their implications for his theoretical project.

Marcuse takes an analytical misstep as he distinguishes *technology as such* from *historicized technology* in that both aspects of technological reason are wholly historical. Neither technology as such nor historicized technology is either substantively neutral or merely methodologically instrumentalist. On the contrary, the intention of total control and organization, be it control of Nature, society, or humanity, is an inescapable component of all technical activity per se. The values of efficiency, calculability, manipulability, and predictability, or the essential qualities of *Ratio*, may have arisen in the historically specific social context of early industrial bourgeois capitalism. And these "class values" may reproduce some of the traits and qualities of that historical moment as *Ratio* unfolds the totality of modern technological rationality.

Nevertheless, these techniques and their operation, once discovered and put into effective technical practice, are equally productive in *any* sociohistorical moment for *any* historical subject. The domination that Marcuse traces in technological rationality back to the group interests of historical subjects, in fact, arises as a necessary part of technology per se.[67] The efficiency, the calculability, the manipulability, and the predictability projected by and for technical reasoning are *necessary* factors that must function in this fashion if technical activity and rationality are to function productively.

Obviously, Marcuse draws the "as such" versus "historicized" distinction in order to preserve an element of "purity and neutrality" in technical reason, which would allow an emancipatory subject to "rehistoricize" technological activity under the horizon of a new *Logos*, namely, that of *Eros* and the liberated life instincts. At the same moment, this resistant "as such" element also serves as the immanent critique of the present technological rationality historicized as the practical reason of late capitalism. In practice, however, technical reasoning can operate only as technical reason by virtue of its intrinsic *Logos* whether it is "historicized" in Asiatic society, late feudalism, entrepreneurial capitalism, advanced industrial society, or Marcuse's socialist utopia, the only *Logos* that enacts the theoretical and practical utility of technical reason is *Ratio*.

This argument is one of Marcuse's shortcomings. He attempts to indicate how technology as such does not contain any inherent domination by illustrating how it became dominating only as its use renounced philosophy and historicized itself as the means of narrow class-derived practical ends. In fact, however, technology is technically effective *only* to the degree that its practices renounce outmoded philosophical frameworks, leaving its genesis under a certain class interest an *inessential* moment of its domination. No form of philosophy will or can improve upon the technical propositions of scientific-technological reason as it now functions; philosophical foundations or additions would be only window dressing or useless brakes on technical productivity. Marcuse's critical theory is no exception to this inescapable fact.

Technology as such and historicized technology are, in truth, *both* historicized modes of technology. The domination intrinsic to historicized technology is equally inherent to technology as such. Likewise, Marcuse has not foretold and cannot adequately foretell exactly what a "liberating" technology would do. He also cannot establish how it would operate differently from current technological activity, while at the same time maintaining productivity. As Shapiro observes, "If Marxism regards science as a mere instrument of the bourgeoisie, then it must be able to say, for example, what a non-bourgeois physics would be like, or a specifically socialistic technology. However, no Marxist has been able to do this; nor is the problem solved by Marcuse's suggestion of aesthetic rationality as a higher form of reason." [68] In all fairness to Marcuse, his notion of aesthetic reason[69] and its "play impulse," which are drawn from Schiller's desire to render "reason into the sensuous" and "sensuousness into rationality," [70] serve as the vehicle of technical liberation. These shifts may define a "higher" form of reason, but it is not a higher form of *technical reason*. Clearly, Marcuse is caught in an unavoidable contradiction. To enjoy the abundant productivity of modern technology, one *must* accept and do what technological rationality dictates. Yet, to foretell the values of an emancipatory socialist utopia, which apparently presupposes advanced industrial affluence, Marcuse also *must* reject and deny the inherent logic of modern technological rationality.

Furthermore, Marcuse immerses himself in a similar set of contradictions when he uncritically accepts the given technical objectification of modern technological reason, or advanced industrial technics, as an integral part of human emancipation. Obviously, as was true of technology as such, Marcuse portrays technics, or the material-mechanical objectifications of technological reason, as *neutral*. For Marcuse, "the machine is indifferent toward the social uses to which it is put, provided those uses remain within its technical capabilities." [71] Therefore, "the machinery of the technological universe is 'as such' indifferent towards political ends—it can revolutionize or retard a society. An electronic computer can serve equally a capitalist or socialist administration; a cyclotron can be an equally efficient tool for a war party or a peace party." [72] As long as he regards technics as *neutral*, Marcuse can integrate them unproblematically into his transition-period program for the realization of the socialist utopia.

Inasmuch as advanced industrial technology has become *in itself* a form of social control, and to the degree that domination extends itself not through technology but *as* technology, Marcuse once again has misplaced his bets. Technics do not simply serve restrictive social forms. Technics, much to the contrary, come to embody and incarnate social repression and domination in their very material structure, an argument made in Chapter 1 about Mumford and Marx. An electronic computer indeed can serve a capitalist or a socialist administration equally well, yet the two administrations may constitute different forms of domination. Consequently, the computer, as Marcuse understands it, can incarnate the qualities of domination in its material makeup: centralized control of information, restricted flows of information, concentrated use of capital, monopolization of expertise, hierarchical command of knowledge, and the efficient processing of politically useful knowledge. Marcuse's strategy for the socialist transition would be aborted, necessarily, by the frozen alienation, the dead domination, and the objectified reification embodied in the technics of late capitalism.

Marcuse, nonetheless, contends that

if the completion of the technological project involves a break with the prevailing technological rationality, the break in turn depends on the continued existence of the technical base itself. For it is this base which has rendered possible the satisfaction of needs and the reduction of toil—it remains the very base of all forms of human freedom. The qualitative change rather lies in the reconstruction of this base—that is, in its development with a view of different ends.[73]

Simply stated, nothing could be further from the truth. Here, Marcuse slips into Lenin's tracks. Using the old base apparatus to pursue new ends while promising to rebuild the base to attain these ends is one of the major fallacies in organizing the transition to socialist emancipation. It does not work. If a genuine break with technological domination is to succeed, then Marcuse must discard this static vision of technics, and the technical base must be reconstituted *first*, as a precondition of the transition, if only to liberate the human individual from the reified somatic-psychic constitution that functionally interlocks with it.[74] Otherwise, the domination of late capitalist technological reason would reappear through the daily use of its unreconstituted technics, which are impregnated with its repressive alienation. As Shapiro notes, "The technical object is communication per se, and the world of technical objects becomes the medium of intersubjectivity." [75] Every technical entity, each mechanical process, all instrumental procedures once taken uncritically into the processes of Marcuse's socialist transition inexorably would reproduce the culture, the psychology, and the values of their inhumane social origins, unless they wholly were reorganized to serve the purposes and ends of liberated individuals in the emancipatory socialist utopia.

In the last analysis, Marcuse plainly proves uncritical of the corrupted one-dimensional subjectivity embodied in each of his supposedly neutral and pure technics-objects—a point already disputed in Chapters 1 and 2. The machine is *never* wholly indifferent to the social or political uses to which it is put. In fact, the cultural, political, and social uses of technics, especially late capitalist technics, necessarily are incarnated in the material makeup and practical operation of all technics-objects. This uncritical inattentiveness to technics, as well as his unsuccessful attempt to salvage modern technical reason from its historical forms of domination, renders Marcuse's critique of technological rationality both unconvincing as a political analysis and impractical as a revolutionary program.

Although Marcuse clings to his "cunning of technological reason" to presage the demise of advanced industrial society, at the same time he relies on the Outsider for the "subjective factor" to revolutionize mass consciousness and to indicate the emancipatory political possibilities for attaining the forms of liberation intrinsic to large capitalist productivity. However, as Chapter 6 suggests, most of these "Outsiders" now are "Insiders." The "cunning of technological reason" remains a contingency, never becoming a necessity. Unable to connect its negativity with the productive activity of the material base, Marcuse's critique again emerges only as an existential choice, an individual act, that denies the inauthenticity of technological existence by projecting the possibility of reorganizing its material features into the technical basis of an authentically free humane existence for the genus of human individuals. Yet the full meaning of Marcuse's emancipatory politics cannot be appreciated without a brief discussion of its metapsychological aspects, which seek to ground the necessity for revolution in an alternative form of negativity only to meet many of the troublesome contradictions that stymied Marcuse's notions of technics and technology.

Marcuse's Critical Metapsychology

Blocked by the overwhelming alienation embedded in technologically rational late capitalism, Marcuse realizes that "the critical analysis of this society calls for new categories: moral, political, aesthetic," [76] which he immediately creates from the Freudian theory of instincts. Essentially, Marcuse asserts that human beings subject their organic pleasure-seeking life instincts to the rigors of social organization and external authority as they struggle to build civilization. Beginning with the authority of the primal father and extending into advanced forms of civilization, men repress their need for immediate satisfaction under the pleasure principle in order to restrain satisfaction as part of their social reality principle.[77] Phylogenetically, as an animal genus, this historical unfolding of repression, restraint, and discipline enters the biological constitution of men, historicizing their somatic-psychic functioning. Moreover, this social psychology also becomes the design for individual psychology as each individual's ontogenesis retraces sociohistorical repression in the person's own maturation.[78] The human struggle against freedom or pleasure, then, "reproduces itself in the psyche of man, as the self-repression of the repressed individual, and his self-repression in turn sustains his masters and their institutions," [79] as the continuation of human civilization.

Scarcity, and the struggle against Nature for socially exploitable wealth, indicates to men that the pleasure principle provides an inadequate guarantee for ensuring adequate levels of productivity and toil. Hence to conquer scarcity finally, men submit to the designs of a demanding reality principle, the *performance principle*, which instrumentalizes economic and social activity as competitive economic performances for the social means of production. So repressive are these tasks that "men do not live their own lives but perform pre-established functions" [80] within the objectified totality of material civilization. Thus the needs of society and the individual collapse into the extension of the increasingly rationalized industrial and social structures. By subordinating the individual's labor, the social structures assure productivity and affluence, which in turn "fulfills the needs and faculties of the individuals." [81]

"For the vast majority of the population," however, Marcuse sees their labor as leading to surplus repression and personal alienation as "the scope and mode of satisfaction are determined by their own labor; but their labor is work for an apparatus which they do not control, which operates as an independent power to which individuals must submit if they want to live." [82] And, to question the continued operation of such an apparently progressive and benevolent social order becomes, under the modern regimen of administered consciousness, the ultimate individual derangement. The increasingly productive *rationalization* of domination in a sociological sense, then, more concretely "rationalizes" in a psychological sense the continued social repression of individual needs and desires. [83]

Marcuse's critical metapsychology, however, turns the tables on this repressive reality principle. According to the "instinctual values" of the life instincts, individual acts of rebellion against social restraints are not irrational in a really rational world, but rather the rationality of technical civilization has become irrational and unreal. The very success of the performance principle in conquering scarcity annihilates the necessary pretext of *Ananke*, or the representation of man's conscious struggle for existence, that historically legitimated this reality principle's discipline. [84] The apparatus survives, nevertheless, by fostering unproductive labor and superfluous consumption that satisfy the individual needs of modern man. Confronted only by such prepackaged passive personalities among the working masses, in all advanced industrial societies "the authorities are hardly forced to justify their dominion. They deliver the goods; they satisfy the sexual and the aggressive energy of their subjects." [85]

Still, Marcuse maintains that this system, with "its sweeping rationality, which propels efficiency and growth, is itself irrational," [86] inasmuch as its false consciousness fetters and violates the essential values, the instinctual morality, and the necessary emancipation of *Eros*. The *Ananke*-inspired repression, historicized as part of men's biological makeup, "is subject to change if the fundamental conditions that caused the instincts to acquire this nature have changed." [87] *Eros*, as the somatic-psychic force that remains essentially free from the oppression of the modern reality principle, then, emerges as *the* source of new moral, political, and aesthetic consciousness for realizing freedom within the spheres of advanced technological living.

Having failed to indicate how the essence of freedom lies in the necessity of technologically rational labor, Marcuse seeks to uncover the transcendent freedom beyond necessity in the liberation of the life instincts from the sociobiological necessity of instinctual repression. The archaic sublimation of erotic energies, in juxtaposition to the current conquest of scarcity, has indeed become *archaic*. In fact, these erotic energies can be seen, once again, as the essence of being and as the realm of transcendent human freedom, which "is the possibility, even necessity, of going beyond, negating every given situation in existence." [88]

As a critical theorist, or a Marxist who basically has dispensed with the uncooperative proletariat, Marcuse still retains his attachment to a teleological philosophy of history, which serves as a theory of the progressive unfolding of being. Living in a period that witnessed the rise of fascism in Europe, the advent of bureaucratic socialism in the Soviet Union, and the consolidation of state-corporate capitalism in North America, Marcuse renounced a more conventional Marxist philosophy of history that portrays the collective subjectivity of working-class *praxis* as the negation of mature capitalism. Instead, Marcuse established the transcendence of freedom beyond necessity in *Eros* as part of each individual's biological constitution.

Yet, this synthesis of Freud's metapsychology and a Marxian philosophy of history poses serious problems for Marcuse's theoretical project. A convincing, effective philosophy of history presupposes totality, or the completion of the ultimate ends that it presages as historically determined. In Lukács, or earlier with Marx, this theory of the progressive unfolding of being is anchored in the collective subjectivity of class consciousness that gains increasing definition through the dynamic impact of productive *praxis*. In Marcuse's project, however, the historical theory of human beings progressively realizing their essence is rooted in the basically static and only slowly changing organic makeup of human organisms.

Hence Marcuse's metapsychological historical theory *naturalizes* human essence. That is, he biologizes human activity—aesthetic, moral, political praxis—in the organic absolute of *Eros*, which *dehumanizes* and dehistoricizes collective human subjectivity as already attained aspects of every human's genetic inheritance.[89] In so doing, Marcuse also ontologizes Freud's psychoanalytic categories as real social forces that provide "a biological foundation for socialism" [90] as well as a biological critique of all historical social forms, which embody the false objectivity of civilized "second nature." [91]

Marcuse's ontologization of metapsychological concepts, as a theoretical philosophy of history, destroys much of the particularity, the specificity, and the otherness in concrete actuality that might lead to emancipatory social forms. For Marcuse, all historical societies are tainted by domination, despite their occasional enactment of false formal freedoms, inasmuch as the fight against *Ananke* necessitates the repression of *Eros* and the dominance of the death instincts. To negate the one-dimensional, Marcuse unfortunately raises a one-dimensional negation: *Eros* must annihilate the *Logos* of *Ratio* because all forms of its being constitute domination that can be overcome only through qualitatively new freedoms intrinsic to the life instincts.

Marcuse's totalizing perspective robs his analysis of its potential accuracy and utility by merging all existing forms of economic and political needs as *false* needs that express only false freedoms and empty satisfactions. The true needs and ultimate freedoms of the life instincts are *not* the only forms of potential human liberation, and Marcuse seriously weakens the power of his critique by introducing such a one-dimensional negation of sublate one-dimensionality. To claim, like Marx, that all history is domination, as Marcuse does, is to presume its conclusion, its attainment of final closure. But to assume the possibility of historical totalization and *not* attain its totality, as Marcuse also does, is to project a false totality, which distorts all of its own philosophical claims in that it *fails* to attain politically or socially the historical totality that it claims *is necessarily* attainable.

Eros, then, serves as Marcuse's essential being, the absolute true *Logos* that presupposes and implies human liberation. It is seen as holding a truthful being, a morality, and a consciousness within the instinctual energies of the organism. Moreover, *Eros* serves as the mediation that the "active minorities" or the Outsiders must activate as the basis of an emancipatory morality and of revolutionary political solidarity. Marcuse, in fact, asserts:

> This radicalism activates the elementary, organic foundation of morality in the human being. Prior to all ethical behavior in accordance with specific social standards, prior to all ideological expression, morality is a "disposition" of the organism, perhaps rooted in the erotic drive to counter aggressiveness, to create and preserve "ever greater unities" of life. We would then

have, this side of all "values," an instinctual foundation for solidarity among human beings—a solidarity which has been effectively repressed in line with the requirements of class society but which now appears as a precondition for liberation.[92]

Indeed, *Eros* becomes the universal objective reason that Marcuse requires to complete his revolutionary critical project. *Eros* transforms the false consciousness of the Insider (modern mass man, the genus-in-itself) caught in the *Logos* of technical *Ratio* into the true consciousness of the Outsider (emancipated humanity, the genus-for-itself).

Armed with this new sensibility, Marcuse sees men and women escaping from the guilt and repression of the Insider and learning *not* "to identify themselves with the false fathers who have built and tolerated and forgotten the Auschwitzes and Vietnams of history, the torture chambers of all the secular and ecclesiastical inquisitions and interrogations, the ghettos and the monumental temples of the corporations, and who have worshipped the higher culture of this reality," [93] in order to become Outsiders within the technological apparatus, destroying it once and for all. *Eros* for Marcuse, much like *praxis* for the Hegelian Marxists, cmerges as the essential mediation of collective subjectivity that teaches emancipation, as the essential *telos* of autonomous human being, and as the transcendent realm of freedom surfacing from within the structures of repressive necessity.

In the last analysis, however, Marcuse's universal objective reason appears not to be universal, objective, or reasonable. In fact, *Eros* as a prevolitional, preconscious, and prehistorical mode of being seems entirely arational, if not irrational, in that Marcuse directly and wrongly attributes a moral and social content to the biological life instincts. *Eros* allows Marcuse to presuppose the totalizing end of history, but this naturalized, dehumanized, and dehistoricized mode of reason greatly distorts history's ultimate *telos* of play-oriented, pleasure-based, aesthetically principled socialism.

At the same time, Marcuse does not and cannot indicate how this erotic *Logos* will be necessarily realized. Rather, his false totalization of history leaves its enactment to an *individual* choice "under the horizon of *self-determination*—of men and women who assert their freedom, their humanity, in the satisfaction of their vital material needs." [94] And, as an issue of *self-determination*, Marcuse must talk of "if and *when* men and women act" [95] instead of *how* and *why* all persons will necessarily act together to transcend historically repressive social forms to realize the *Logos* of emancipation. To the degree that human liberation remains a contingent individual choice, Marcuse's totalizing theory of history as the necessary realization of erotic freedom remains a false totality that underwrites an unworkable social theory.

Moreover, if certain "cultural needs can 'sink down' into the biology of man," [96] then it would appear that the outcomes of liberated *Eros* would be continually questioned, if only in the short-run transitional future, by the deeply naturalized repressive cultural needs and social values of civilization's domination. Even if the "active minorities" could prod the "integrated majority" into accepting and abiding by the life instincts, the *new* forms of emancipation would seem to require new modes of repression, if only to suppress the historical domination biologized as part of each individual's somatic-psychic constitution. And, if erotic liberation were not challenged by historicized aspects of the human organism, then it would continue to battle with the historicized domination embedded in almost every material artifact not fabricated by persons living in accord with the life instincts.

Ultimately, Marcuse's metapsychological face-lift of Marxism proves to be as weak a critical mediation as his phenomenological reworking of Marx. The critical theory of the instincts and human liberation based upon the biological genus, likewise, points toward an even worse theoretical dead end than the Marxian notion of labor and class liberation. Indeed, in the last analysis, Marcuse presents his critical theory as the utter denial of certain necessity as its theoretical understanding projects "nothing but a chance." Under Marcuse's categories, "the critical theory of society possesses no concepts which could bridge the gap between the present and its future; holding no promise and showing no success, it remains negative. Thus it wants to remain loyal to those who, without hope, have given and give their life to the Great Refusal!" [97]

Conclusion

In the early 1990s, it would appear that Marcuse's political moment has passed. The exhilarating days of New Left revolution, when many (but not most) young radicals worldwide read "Marx, Mao, and Marcuse," have passed into history as largely unsuccessful attempts by disorganized intellectual groups to disrupt and paralyze the state-corporate apparatus. To the extent that Marcuse served as one theoretical guide for some of the political challenges made by the New Left, this failure may seem inevitable. At best, Marcuse's writings appear only to legitimate and rationalize individual acts of rebellion taken by the "active minorities" in loosely organized social movements against the technological apparatus.

Still, these contributions should not be dismissed out of hand as being of little consequence. In its positive moments, such utopian anarchism tied to "the radical act" continues to question technological rationality by building and protecting important free spaces for critical interaction in free schools, alternative technologies, neighborhood co-ops, residential communes, and a participatory political counterculture. In its more negative moments, however, the practice of radical acts has fallen prey to the violent logic of technological domination in anarchistic terrorist groups' attempts to paralyze the apparatus of technological rationality by attacking its human victims, using such ineffective techniques as airline hijacking, political kidnapping, and bombings.[98] For the most part, the state-corporate technological apparatus remains as potent as ever. In both of these political moments, the utopian anarchosocialism that Marcuse partly inspired leaves the apparatus largely untouched and its passive integrated majorities of commodity-consuming individuals basically undisturbed.

Nonetheless, as Chapter 6 suggests, the total co-optation thesis is not entirely accurate. Marcuse once argued that "advanced industrial society is indeed a system of countervaluing powers. But these forces cancel each other out in a higher unification—in the common interest to defend and extend the established position, to combat the historical alternatives, to contain qualitative change. The countervaluing powers do not include those which counter the whole." [99] Actually, the continuing rational operation of advanced capitalist states seems to have presumed the presence of weak but not entirely ineffectual political challenges, "which counter the whole," in order to continue delivering its expected level of goods and services.[100]

In many respects, almost all groups today could be considered to be Insiders or, at least, "candidate" Insiders. Even the revolutionary Outsiders seem to have been integrated into the workings of technological rationality. University students have become salaried members of the middle-class intelligentsia, many racial and ethnic minorities have joined the struggle for middle-class satisfactions, and many formerly revolutionary Third World nations now are seeking full membership in the technological consumer society. As Marcuse concludes, "The world tends to become the stuff of total administration, which absorbs even the administrators. The web of domination has become the web of Reason itself, and this society is fatally entangled in it." [101] Under this horizon, for example, all of Nature in the 1990s is seen as a single system of "physical/economic resources" to be managed optimally by its "human resources" until global warming, nuclear holocaust, or overpopulation explode world society and these "webs of Reason" from within. Thus even these marginal sources of external negativity have been integrated into the advanced technological society during the 1970s and 1980s. Marcuse's initial strategies for overcoming technological rationality by mobilizing these forces of negative collective subjectivity still remain unconvincing.

In fact, the technological apparatus perhaps has only proven its ultimate dominating strengths by absorbing and instrumentalizing selected aspects of the Outsiders' critical programs as a new source of internal control over its operations. The violent advocates of the New Left's emancipatory politics were successfully contained or eradicated by the security forces of the administrative state. However, the more constructive elements of the New Left have been continued even into the present, for example, as the environmental movement, public interest lobbying, grass-roots community organizing, or the alternative technology movement. Even so, these movements, rather than always indicating emancipatory paths out of technological rationality, in fact are frequently serving instead to improve its social functioning and political effectiveness. The web of Reason can accommodate marginal redistributions of purchasing power, institutional access, cultural significance, or ecological constraints to perpetuate its continued functioning. Marcuse's vision of emancipatory politics, then, has stalled as its major political agents have been sidetracked into more moderate pursuits than pushing toward the final transcendence of technological rationality. Yet, in the final analysis, this co-optation is not total. And these surviving spaces for resistance in "artificial negativity" do raise the question of how to resist powerful state and corporate bureaucracies while remaining ensnared within their workings—an issue that will be investigated in greater detail in Chapter 6.

Notes

1. For more discussion, see Daniel Bell, *The Coming of Post-Industrial Society* (New York: Basic Books, 1973); Jürgen Habermas, *Legitimation Crisis* (Boston: Beacon, 1975);

Max Horkheimer, *The Eclipse of Reason* (New York: Seabury, 1974); and Claude Lefort, "What Is Bureaucracy?" *Telos* 22 (Winter 1974-75), 31-65.

2. Herbert Marcuse, *Soviet Marxism: A Critical Analysis* (New York: Vintage, 1961), 4.

3. Although both Antonio Gramsci and Karl Korsch saw Marxism as the practical science and political theory of *proletarian* class revolution, the most articulate formulations of this position are the work of Georg Lukács prior to his "Leninization" and subsequent adoption of orthodox Stalinist Marxism-Leninism. See Georg Lukács, *History and Class Consciousness: Studies in Marxist Dialectics* (Cambridge: MIT Press, 1971) and his *Tactics and Ethics: Political Essays, 1919-1929* (New York: Harper & Row, 1975). See also Antonio Gramsci, "The Philosophy of Praxis," *Prison Notebooks* (New York: International, 1971), 323-472; and Karl Korsch, *Marxism and Philosophy* (New York: Monthly Review Press, 1970).

4. Marcuse, *Soviet Marxism*, 5.

5. As Marcuse observes, this reification of both the class struggle and all class interests entails external and internal counterrevolutions among the working classes: "In advanced capitalist countries, the radicalization of the working classes is counteracted by a socially engineered arrest of consciousness, and by the development and satisfaction of needs which perpetuate the servitude of the exploited." Herbert Marcuse, *One-Dimensional Man: Studies in the Ideology of Advanced Industrial Society* (Boston: Beacon, 1964), 6. This mutation of the potential collective subject, "the workers," into the actual administered object, "the average consumers," marks the start of Marcuse's departure in search of a revolutionary consciousness beyond the bounds of the proletariat as classically defined." He maintains that the working classes are still objectively, or "in-itself," the potential revolutionary subject, but subjectivity, or "for itself," the proletarians have a long way to go. Thus, "without losing its historical role as the basic force of transformation, the working class, in the period of stabilization, assumes a stabilizing, conservative function; and the catalysts of transformation operate 'from without.' " Herbert Marcuse, *An Essay on Liberation* (Boston: Beacon, 1969), 54-55.

6. For further analysis, see Martin Jay, *The Dialectical Imagination: A History of the Frankfurt School and the Institute of Social Research, 1923-1950)* (Boston: Little, Brown, 1973), 41-48. For other discussions of Marcuse's work, see Morton Schoolman, *The Imaginary Witness: The Critical Theory of Herbert Marcuse* (New York: Free Press, 1980); Alain Martineau, *Herbert Marcuse's Utopia* (Montreal: Harvest House, 1986); Alasdair MacIntyre, *Herbert Marcuse: An Exposition and a Polemic* (New York: Viking, 1970); Robert Marks, *The Meaning of Marcuse* (New York: Ballantine, 1979); John Fry, *Marcuse: Dilemma and Liberation* (Atlantic Highlands, NJ: Humanities, 1974); Sidney Lipshires, *Herbert Marcuse: From Marx to Freud and Beyond* (Cambridge, MA: Schenkman, 1974); Barry Katz, *Herbert Marcuse and the Art of Liberation* (London: New Left, 1982); Paul Mattick, *Critique of Marcuse* (New York: Seabury, 1973); Philip Slater, *Origin and Significance of the Frankfurt School* (London: Routledge & Kegan Paul, 1977); Paul Breines, ed., *Critical Interruptions* (New York: Herder & Herder, 1970); Martin Jay, *Marxism and Totality* (Berkeley: University of California Press, 1984); Gad Horowitz, *Regression, Basic and Surplus Repression in Psychoanalytic Theory: Reich, Freud and Marcuse* (Toronto: University of Toronto Press, 1977); and David Held, *Introduction to Critical Theory: Horkheimer to Habermas* (Berkeley: University of California Press, 1980).

7. Marcuse continually chides Heidegger, for example, for his abstract, ahistorical, impractical, and individualistic solutions to the problem of modern man's alienation. See Herbert Marcuse, "A Phenomenology of Historical Materialism," *Telos* 4 (Fall 1969), 17, 18, 21, 22. As Kellner argues, "Marcuse attended to re-examine and develop the Marxian project in order to make it more relevant to the particular situation and problems of the present age. . . . his work is an extremely critical, speculative and idiosyncratic version of Marxism." Douglas Kellner, *Herbert Marcuse and the Crisis of Marxism* (Berkeley: University of California Press, 1984), 5.

8. And, as Marcuse contends, "this omission of historicity by all sciences concerned with the character and the meaning of human existence which approach their subject-matter as 'relevant,' leads to failure." "Thus," in Marcuse's mind, and this underlies his improvements in Heidegger's phenomenology, "if the phenomenological analysis does not take into account actual historicity, it fails to attain a clear view of its object. Moreover, phenomenology cannot restrict itself with the demonstration of the historicity of the object, and subsequently fall back into abstractions. It must always remain very concrete." Marcuse, "Phenomenology of Historical Materialism," 21.

9. For the comparison in detail, see Edmund Husserl, *The Crisis of European Sciences and Transcendental Phenomenology,* trans. by David Carr (Evanston, IL: Northwestern University Press, 1970), 103-189.

10. Marcuse, "Phenomenology of Historical Materialism," 26.

11. Ibid. As Kellner notes, "Heidegger himself makes a distinction between his concept of 'historicity' and 'ontic history,' which banishes the real content of history, real historical crises and problems, from his pure ontological perspective. This flight from concrete history into an ontological realm of Being reveals the dangers of the Heideggerian ontological perspective which at the time had Marcuse at least partially under its seductive sway. Perhaps, in his early essays, Marcuse thought that he could de-mystify Heidegger much as Marx had concretized and reconstructed Hegel." Kellner, *Herbert Marcuse,* 50-51.

12. Paul Piccone and Alexander Delfini, "Herbert Marcuse's Heideggerian Marxism," *Telos* 6 (Fall 1970), 43. For a very succinct but useful treatment of the *Lebenswelt* in Marcuse, see Pier Aldo Rovatti, "Marcuse and *The Crisis of European Sciences," Telos* 2 (Fall 1968), 113-115.

13. Or, from a different perspective, as Piccone and Delfini note, "it is thus not at all surprising that, in his latest works, we find Marcuse hovering in the caverns of the Freudian instinctual substructure with a make-shift Marxist flashlight searching for reality." Piccone and Delfini, "Herbert Marcuse's Heideggerian Marxism," 43.

14. For the philosophical arguments that led Marcuse to drop phenomenology for Freudianism, see Herbert Marcuse, "The Concept of Essence," *Negations: Essays in Critical Theory,* trans. by Jeremy J. Shapiro (Boston: Beacon, 1968); Herbert Marcuse, "On Science and Phenomenology," *Boston Studies in the Philosophy of Science* (vol. 2), ed. by Robert S. Cohen and Marx W. Wartofsky (Boston: Reidel, 1964); and Herbert Marcuse, "The Realm of Freedom and the Realm of Necessity: A Reconsideration," *Praxis* 5, nos. 1-2 (1969). Also see Ben Agger, "The Aesthetic Politics of Herbert Marcuse," *Canadian Forum* 53 (October 1973), 24-30.

15. Marcuse, *One-Dimensional Man,* 152.

16. For an elaboration of the notion of "objective reason," see Horkheimer, *Eclipse of Reason,* 9-12.

17. Marcuse, *One-Dimensional Man,* 52.

18. Herbert Marcuse, "World Without Logos," *Bulletin of Atomic Scientists* 20, no. 1 (January 1964), 25.

19. Ibid., 26.

20. Marcuse, *Essay on Liberation,* 55.

21. Marcuse, "World Without Logos," 25.

22. Basically, the "somatic-psychic constitution" stands for the interface of ontogenetic and phylogenetic repression that binds the human organism through historicized biologistic needs and socially dictated reality principles. Yet none of these rules is consciously acquired by the human individual; rather, the rules are preconsciously and subconsciously embedded in his organic and mental structures as he personally matures. See Herbert Marcuse, "Freedom and Freud's Theory of Instincts," *Five Lectures: Psychoanalysis, Politics, and Utopia,* trans. by Jeremy J. Shapiro and Shierry M. Weber (Boston: Beacon, 1970), 20-22.

23. For an excellent treatment of how Freudian psychology became part of the critique of totalitarian society and working-class depoliticization, see Paul Robinson, *The Freudian Left* (New York: Basic, 1969); and Jay, *The Dialectical Imagination,* 86-113.

24. Herbert Marcuse, "On Hedonism," *Negations,* 159. (This essay originally appeared in *Zeitschrift für Sozialforschung* 7, 1938.)

25. Ibid., 160.

26. Ibid., 162.

27. Ibid.

28. Herbert Marcuse, *Eros and Civilization: A Philosophical Enquiry into Freud* (Boston: Beacon, 1966), 20.

29. Marcuse, "On Hedonism," 187.

30. Marcuse, *Eros and Civilization,* 125.

31. Ibid., 124.

32. As Habermas notes, "Marcuse has a chiliastic trust in a revitalizing dynamic of instincts which works through history, finally breaks with history and leaves it behind as what then will appear a prehistory." Jürgen Habermas, "Psychic Thermidor and the Rebirth of Rebellious Subjectivity," *Berkeley Journal of Sociology* 24-25 (1980), 9. Still, Marcuse's critical theory retains its Marxist forms by becoming the "Marxism" for comprehending modern *mass* society. The class struggle is displaced by the struggle of reality principles for the organization of labor and human instincts. *Eros* supplants the activity of the proletarians, the *Logos* of technical *Ratio* supersedes the passivity of the bourgeoisie. Class, and the identical subject-object of labor, is replaced by genus, or the identical subject-object of pleasure. *Ananke* embodies false consciousness; *Eros* assumes the function of true consciousness. Likewise, alienation is found embedded in the somatic-psychic constitution, and not in the relations of production. And revolutionary transformation follows from the liberation of erotic true consciousness rather than from the proletarians' reconstitution of the relations of production and exchange. While much of the "Marxist" content leaves Marcuse's critical theory, the basic forms and relations of the Marcusean elements retain a strong "Marxist" cast.

33. Herbert Marcuse, "Some Social Implications of Modern Technology," *Studies in Philosophy and Social Sciences* 9 (1941).

34. Ibid., 421.

35. In making this claim, Marcuse extends Marx's notions on the necessary interconnection of production and consumption. Marx argues that "production not only provides the material to satisfy a need, but it also provides the need for the material." The same relations hold true for all modes of production, especially advanced technological production. Again, Marx claims that "production thus produces not only the object of consumption but also the mode of consumption, not only objectively but also subjectively. Production therefore creates the consumer." Hence, "in totally structuring the conditions of everyday modern life, it is not unusual that technology plays a large part in creating consumers who are submissive, passive, and group-interested as long as it continues to supply the needs that it has performed the consumers to prefer." Quotes from Karl Marx, *A Contribution to the Critique of Political Economy,* ed. by Maurice Dobb (Moscow: Progress, 1970), 197.

36. Herbert Marcuse, "Preface to the Vintage Edition 1961," *Soviet Marxism,* xii.

37. For an extensive discussion of the interpenetration of domination over Nature and human nature, see Bruce Brown, *Marx, Freud, and the Critique of Everyday Life: Toward a Permanent Cultural Revolution* (New York: Monthly Review Press, 1973), 70-97; William Leiss, *The Domination of Nature* (Boston: Beacon, 1974), 101-198; and Albrecht Wellmer, *Critical Theory of Society* (New York: Herder & Herder, 1971), 131-139.

38. Marcuse, "Freedom and Freud's Theory," 12.

39. William Leiss, "Appendix; Technological Rationality: Marcuse and His Critics," *The Domination of Nature,* 205.

40. Of course, this "ruse of reason" does not imply that the fastest route to liberation is through the total technologization of life, as some critics have suggested. See, for example, Edward Andrew, "Work and Freedom in Marcuse and Marx," *Canadian Journal of Political Science* 3, no. 2 (June 1970), 241-256. This discussion, in turn, generated a considerable exchange, including William Leiss, "Technological Rationality: Notes on 'Work and Freedom in Marcuse and Marx,' " *Canadian Journal of Political Science* 4, no. 3 (September 1971), 398-404. Also see Morton Schoolman, "Further Reflections on Work, Alienation and Freedom in Marcuse and Marx," *Canadian Journal of Political Science* 6, no. 2 (June 1973), 295-302; Ben Agger, "The Growing Relevance of Marcuse's Dialectic of Individual and Class," *Dialectical Anthropology* 4, no. 2 (July 1979), 135-145; Ben Agger, "Marcuse and Habermas on New Science," *Polity* 9, no. 2 (Winter 1976), 158-181; John Fremstad, "Marcuse: The Dialectics of Hopelessness," *Western Political Quarterly* 30, no. 1 (March 1977), 80-92; and C. Fred Alford, *Science and the Revenge of Nature: Marcuse and Habermas* (Gainesville: University Presses of Florida, 1985).

41. Herbert Marcuse, "The End of Utopia," *Five Lectures,* 66.

42. Leiss, "Appendix," 205.

43. Marcuse, *One-Dimensional Man,* 157.

44. Ibid., 156.

45. Marcuse, "World Without Logos," 25. Here, *Ratio* suggests the artificial character of a projected scientific understanding of the world based on subjectively generated mathematical assumptions and propositions, while *Logos* implies an inherent and necessary structure to the essence of being that is understandable only through the mediations of philosophy.

46. Marcuse, *One-Dimensional Man,* 156.

47. Ibid., 153; emphasis added.

48. Because of this class-based historicization of reason, scientific-technological "observation and experiment, the methodical organization and coordination of data, propositions, and conclusion never proceed in an unstructured, neutral, theoretical space"; to the contrary, "the project of cognition involves operations on objects, or abstractions from objects which occur in a given universe of discourse and action." Marcuse, *One-Dimensional Man,* 157.

49. Ibid., 158.

50. Ibid.

51. Ibid., 168.

52. Ibid., 158.

53. Ibid., xv.

54. Ibid., xvi.

55. For a largely ineffective critique of Marcuse's technological rationality posed in terms of these rather tenuously drawn categories, see Jürgen Habermas, "Technology and Science as 'Ideology,' " *Toward a Rational Society,* trans. by Jeremy J. Shapiro (Boston: Beacon, 1970), 81-122.

56. Marcuse, "Progress and Freud's Theory," *Five Lectures,* 28.

57. Herbert Marcuse, "Remarks on a Redefinition of Culture," *Daedalus* 94, no. 1 (Winter 1965), 192.

58. Marcuse, *One-Dimensional Man,* 156.

59. Clearly, the exclusively historical bases of technological domination have been questioned ardently; see, for example, Rolf Ahlers, "Is Technology Intrinsically Repressive?" *Continuum* 8 (1970), 111-122.

60. Marcuse, *One-Dimensional Man,* 168.

61. Ibid., 231.

62. Ibid., 2.

63. Ibid.

64. Ibid.

65. Ibid., 231.

66. From different perspectives, other observers have also taken Marcuse to task for his inconsistent and ambiguous conceptualizations of technological rationality, especially with regard to its differences during the "early industrial" and "advanced technological" phases of its development. To pursue these arguments, see Hans-Dieter Bahr, *Kritik der "Politischen Technologie"* (Frankfurt: Suhrkamp, 1970); Joachim Bermann, "Technologische Rationalitat und spätkapitalistische Oekonomie," *Antworten auf Herbert Marcuse,* ed. by Jürgen Habermas (Frankfurt: Suhrkamp, 1968); and Claus Offe, "Technik und Eindimensionalitat," *Antworten auf Herbert Marcuse.*

67. Technological domination, then, can be controlled once it is recognized as a necessary aspect of its own successful practice, but it can never be entirely eliminated or expunged from pure technical practice. See Lewis Mumford, "Democratic and Authoritarian Technics," *Technology and Culture,* ed. by Melvin Kranzberg and William H. Davenport (New York: Schocken, 1972).

68. Jeremy J. Shapiro, "The Dialectic of Theory and Practice in the Age of Technological Rationality: Herbert Marcuse and Juergen Habermas," *The Unknown Dimension: European Marxism Since Lenin,* ed. by Dick Howard and Karl E. Klare (New York: Basic, 1972), 292.

69. Marcuse, *Eros and Civilization,* 172-196.

70. Ibid., 187. While under the new horizon of the aesthetic ethos, Marcuse speculates that technique would embody the erotic sensibilities of liberation as artful play: "The liberated consciousness would promote the development of a science and technology free to discover and realize the possibilities of things and men in the protection and gratification of life." Marcuse, *Essay on Liberation,* 24.

71. Marcuse, *One-Dimensional Man,* 155. This rather indefensible position on the inner neutrality of technics, moreover, is present in his 1941 essay as well, where Marcuse holds that "technics hamper individual development only insofar as they are tied to a social apparatus which perpetuates scarcity." Marcuse, "Some Social Implications of Modern Technology," 423.

72. Marcuse, *One-Dimensional Man,* 154.

73. Ibid., 231.

74. For the intimations of how a new dynamically projected social technology connected to the processes of material production might liberate individuals from their alienated somatic-psychic constitution, see Antonio Gramsci's notion of the "psychophysical nexus." Antonio Gramsci, "Americanism and Fordism," *Prison Notebooks,* 302-304. Also see Wilhelm Reich's programs for "Sex-Pol" organizing to subvert the "sexual economy" and the "political economy" of modern mass societies. Wilhelm Reich, "What Is Class Consciousness," *SEX-POL: Essays, 1929-1934* (New York: Random House, 1972), 275-358.

75. Jeremy J. Shapiro, "One-Dimensionality: The Universal Semiotic of Technological Experience," *Critical Interruptions: New Left Perspectives on Herbert Marcuse,* ed. by Paul Breines (New York: Herder & Herder, 1972), 156.

76. Marcuse, *Essay on Liberation,* 7.

77. Marcuse, *Eros and Civilization,* 12.

78. Ibid., 20.

79. Ibid., 16.

80. Ibid., 45.

81. Ibid.

82. Ibid.

83. This *rationalization* of domination at the sociological level, however, leads to a "rationalization" of the death instincts hegemony over the increasingly repressed life instincts at the phylogenetic-biological level. "The performance principle," Marcuse suggests, "enforces an integrated repressive organization of sexuality and of the destruction instinct." Marcuse, *Eros and Civilization,* 131.

84. Ibid.

85. Ibid., xi-xii.

86. Marcuse, *One-Dimensional Man*, xiii.

87. Marcuse, *Eros and Civilization*, 138.

88. Marcuse, "Freedom and Freud's Theory," 23.

89. Marcuse, *Essay on Liberation*, 10.

90. Ibid., 7.

91. Ibid., 11.

92. Marcuse, *Essay on Liberation*, 10.

93. Ibid., 24.

94. Marcuse, "The Left Under the Counter-Revolution," *Counterrevolution and Revolt* (Boston: Beacon, 1972), 18.

95. Marcuse, *Essay on Liberation*, 24-25; emphasis added.

96. Ibid., 10.

97. Marcuse, *One-Dimensional Man*, 257.

98. Marcuse, of course, completely condemned such actions. See Herbert Marcuse, "Murder Is Not a Political Weapon," *New German Critique* 4, no. 3 (1977), 7-8.

99. Marcuse, *One-Dimensional Man*, 51.

100. See, for further discussion, Paul Piccone, "The Changing Function of Critical Theory," *New German Critique* 12 (Fall 1977); and Adolph Reed, Jr., "Black Particularity Reconsidered," *Telos* 37 (Fall 1978).

101. Marcuse, *One-Dimensional Man*, 169.

6

After One-Dimensionality:
Culture and Politics in the
Age of Artificial Negativity

Given the analysis of contemporary technological society advanced by Herbert Marcuse, and in light of the critique presented in Chapter 5, one must ask, What comes after "one-dimensionality"? The thesis of "artificial negativity," as it has been tentatively outlined up to this time, asserts that Marcuse's "one-dimensionality" thesis actually fits a specific period of history. That is, it defines the transition to full monopoly capitalism, which began seriously in the United States during the Great Depression of the 1930s, and this transition was already complete when Marcuse described its workings.[1] After being tested briefly by the Progressives as they dealt with the final crises of entrepreneurial capitalism after the 1890s, the one-dimensional logic of the transition, as Marcuse's work argues, emerged full-blown only with the advent of the New Deal.[2] At this historical juncture, monopoly capital sought "to organize the *entire* society in its interest and image,"[3] through new business marketing strategies and government regulations. Thus the forms of labor, education, entertainment, health care, housing, leisure, transportation, and social welfare increasingly were rationalized to suit bureaucratic/professional agendas. Through the institutional interactions of the culture industry, the interventionist welfare state, and the mass consumption of corporate-produced and -marketed consumer goods, collective capital largely homogenized traditional American society to conform to the post-1945 administrative regime of New Deal liberalism and Cold War internationalism.[4]

In fact, late capitalism so successfully reorganized American society during 1940s and 1950s that, by the 1960s and 1970s, the further extension of corporate capital's institutional rationality proved politically counterproductive and organizationally destructive.[5] Because its own institutional reason totally reconciled the remaining structural contradictions and countervailing forces that initially regulated the state-corporate system from within, by the mid-1960s, the destruction of the system's internal control mechanisms[6] forced the state-corporate social formation to begin "artificially" nurturing its own "negativity." [7] In other words, the attempts to generate "artificial negativity" are some of the administrative regime's own responses to its continuing but changing crises.

The age of "artificial negativity" opens with the political and cultural efforts of small, critical, progressive groups responding to the rationality and legitimacy crises of the 1960s and 1970s *from within* the regime of corporate capital. During the past decade, these progressive sectors, such as many new knowledge-intensive industries, technology-exporting commercial corporations, university intellectuals, and various political activist groups, have sought to counter the one-dimensional logic of instrumental reason still followed by the less progressive elements of state-corporate society, or the capital-intensive, goods-exporting industries, organized labor, and the federal executive, with its many bureaucracies, which together have formed the hegemonic political bloc during the transition to full monopoly capitalism. The state-corporate system, having become *too* systematic for its own continued survival, has experienced significant internal conflict over the last 15 years as the "more" progressive elements of corporate capital have assailed the bureaucratic domination of its "less" progressive elements and the administrative state.

In encouraging the regeneration of contradictions, the revitalization of diversity, and the renewal of antagonism, monopoly capital—whose knowledge-intensive transnational economic base enables it to manage these challenges for its own continued growth—has partially displaced the transitional state-corporate bloc, whose now outmoded bureaucratic program once dissolved contradictions, homogenized diversity, and suppressed antagonisms in traditional society.[8] Still, the battle is far from over as the emergent regime of full monopoly capital, so powerfully implied by the world economy of flexible accumulation managed by blocs of transnational corporations, remains hobbled by the political and structural leftovers of the now obsolete transitional state-corporate system. In the final analysis, then, "artificial negativity" emerges with the cultural alternatives and the political movements *arising from within* state-corporate capitalism, but *directed* against it. These internal challenges to the administrative domination of the transitional system could uncover its unreconciled contradictions, recreate some of its internal political checks and cultural balances, limit its purposive-rational social domination, and allow for the reopening of the public spheres.

Still, one cannot adequately comprehend the struggles surrounding the recent emergence of "artificial negativity" without considering the shifting characteristics of several crucial social spheres from the transitional period up to the present day. Of course, certain critics rightly have suggested that despite its previous theoretical elaborations, "artificial negativity" remains something of a mercurial mystery, the ultimate identity and essential properties of which are most elusive. Thus, in this interpretative discussion, my purposes are to counter such premature, ill-considered criticisms of "artificial negativity" by lending historical concreteness to many of its main tenets, especially with regard to important political and cultural changes in the United States during the last 15 years.

The Transition to One-Dimensionality

Given this posttransition vantage point, the larger scope and structural design of the transitional phase can be seen with greater clarity than in the often aphoristic presentations of the early critical theorists from Adorno to Marcuse. And what is more, this reconsideration of the transition's inner political logic can provide the interpretative clues necessary for the contemporary critical theorist's unraveling of the political problematics of full monopoly capitalism.

The massive expansion of entrepreneurial capitalism within the precapitalist world, which began during the fourteenth and fifteenth centuries, met its inevitable historical limits in the late 1880s and early 1890s.[9] Until that time, entrepreneurial capital achieved its unprecedented transformation of global economic relations by *extending* its rationalizing influences into the comparatively prerational societies of the Western and Southern hemispheres. Yet, as the ink dried on the Treaty of Berlin in 1885, which finalized the European powers' market shares in the last unclaimed regions of precapitalist Africa, and as Frederick Jackson Turner closed the book on further economic expansion on the great North American frontiers in 1890, the world economy was seized by a massive depression, the impact of which finally crumbled the increasingly shaky entrepreneurial-capitalist mode of production.

Having pressed against its historical limits with the extinction of the last precapitalist societies in the colonial periphery, the progressive business, industrial, and intellectual elites of entrepreneurial capital recognized the necessity of transforming capital from its historical mode of interaction—corporate capital based upon intensifying production through new means of technical rationalization guided by scientific research.[10] Hence the social transition from entrepreneurial to monopoly capital demanded the conscious rationalization of capital by means of increased state regulation, the technical reorganization of labor, and the scientific management of all spheres of social interaction by bureaucratic professionals in the "private" and "public" sectors.

In the United States, these needs were recognized and advocated during the Progressive Era by such figures as Herbert Croly in *The Promise of American Life*[11] and Woodrow Wilson in *The New Freedom*,[12] both of whom maintained that Yankee science and government authority could and should be used to place "our businessmen and producers under the stimulation of a constant necessity to be efficient, economic, and enterprising." [13] Thus in 1900 General Electric opened the first corporate industrial laboratory in the United States, where, in the words of a latter-day imitator, "science gets down to business." In 1913-1914, Henry Ford perfected the continuously moving assembly line in Highland Park, which had been made possible, in part, by Taylor's, Fayol's, Gantt's, and Gilbreth's contributions to "scientific management." [14] By separating "planning" from "doing," or theory from practice, skill from activity, and thought from action, Taylorization stripped the American working classes of their skills, which aided the administrative regime of state bureaucrats and corporate managers in legitimating themselves as being worthy of their managerial powers, because of their unique grasp on "the art of bringing ends and means together—the art of purposeful action." [15] And, finally, in prefiguring the administrative welfare state of the New Deal, Woodrow Wilson's presidential administrations witnessed the federal government's turning down the road toward the regulatory-interventionist state, with the passage of the Clayton Anti-Trust Act (1914), the Federal Reserve Act (1913), the Underwood Tariff Act (1913), the Federal Trade Commission Act (1914), the Federal Farm Loans Act (1916), and the Eighteenth Amendment (1920).[16]

All of these conscious intensifications of capitalist production slowly evolved, under the pressures of World War I and the economic expansion of the 1920s, into the New Deal, as their collective effect—despite the vigorous radicalism of the Progressives—failed to forestall the Great

Depression of the 1930s. At first, much like the European nations, the United States embarked upon this transition by resorting to socially repressive legislation in order to discipline rigorously its industrial working classes. Yet, unlike many European nations, the United States soon dropped the exclusive strategy of harsh political and social oppression as the Eighteenth Amendment and the Palmer raids proved too overtly repressive in the rationalization of corporate capital. Instead, corporate capital more selectively applied force as it created "consumption communities" [17] in which workers as consumers were conditioned to repress themselves harshly in order to gain personal access to Woolworth's, Model Ts, the movies, and the suburbs. Yet, in doing so, much of the ethnic specificity, cultural otherness, and political negativity tolerated under entrepreneurial capitalism disappeared, as ethnic homogenization, mass consumption, and government regulation further advanced and finally fixed the social conditions for the complete rationalization of capital—the "one-dimensional society." [18]

To illustrate the tremendous expansion of state control over social relations during the transition to full monopoly capitalism, one need only consider the revolutionary labor and social welfare legislation of the New Deal. During the 1930s, the political caution that characterized the Progressives' limited rearrangement of the entrepreneurial capitalist market disappeared in an aggressive assault upon traditional entrepreneurial society by the federal governmental authority, which was intent upon integrating America's economic diversity into its bureaucratic plans for national industrial recovery. Before 1933, the American working classes remained basically craft oriented in terms of their skills, shop-floor society, and labor organization. Although partly broken by the scientific management movement and the assembly-line system after 1910, the American working classes up to the 1930s were still politically restive, collectively unorganized, and craft centered in their individual skills and values. Only one in ten American workers belonged to a union—mainly craft unions—and individual workers, as participants in an unorganized, prerationalized culture, were subject to the repressive measures of prohibition, political harassment, and a cultural assimilation policy based upon WASP conformity. [19]

Beginning in 1933, however, these unintegrated spheres of social specificity and political negativity were smashed apart by the totalizing logic of national industrial mobilization as state-mandated collective bargaining legislation and federal emergency employment programs incorporated the American working classes into the administrative regime of the interventionist state. Passage of the Norris-LaGuardia Act, the National Industrial Recovery Act, the National Labor Relations Act (Wagner Act), the Public Contracts Act (Walsh-Healy Act), and the Fair Labor Standards Act (Wage and Hour Act) made possible the rational administration of labor's hours, wages, unionization, hiring, firing, compensation, personal welfare, and contract bargaining by the bureaucratic rules of the federal bureaucracy, the large corporations, and the national labor unions. Similarly, the Civil Works Administration, the Public Works Administration, the National Recovery Administration, the Works Progress Administration, and the Reconstruction Finance Corporation provided millions of jobs, regimenting the labors of many hitherto unorganized and nonuniform American workers. After obliterating the social otherness of American labor, the administrative regime reconstituted the individual and communal fragments in national unions, standardized collective bargaining, public works employment, and the federally managed national economy. As the working classes were made more dependent upon the state-corporate regime, this state-corporate alliance repealed the Eighteenth Amendment in 1933 and adopted the Social Security Act in 1935, halting the repressive control measures of prohibition and economic insecurity.[20]

These early measures were further rationalized and continued to unfold during World War II in the manpower mobilizations of the Selective Service Administration, the War Manpower Commission, and the National War Labor Board. Later, with the Employment Act of 1947 and the Labor Management Relations, or Taft-Hartley, Act of 1947, the administrative regime sought to continue its rational command over the national economy and society to maintain standard levels of guaranteed employment and to effect the rationalized control of labor conflict. By 1948, one in three workers belonged to a labor union in the United States, and, even in the 1970s, one in four workers remained affiliated with the corporate-modeled, administratively rational unions.[21] Corporate capital and the federal state, then, efficiently reorganized a full range of organic communities, from Black sharecroppers to Polish ironworkers to female textile workers to Montana copper miners, in a vast administrative apparatus based on federal labor law, labor boards, and collective bargaining mechanisms. This policy network, in turn, merged the inherent contradictions between employees and management, workers and owners, labor and capital into the one-dimensional programming of the administrative state.

Yet, in faithfully creating the administrative conditions for the advanced rationalization of corporate capital, the transitional logic of the

New Deal—and its latter-day continuations in the Fair Deal, the New
Frontier, and the Great Society—systematically stifled the social logic
inherent to full monopoly capital. Bureaucratic decisionism and instrumental organization lost their purposiveness and rationality when they
fully penetrated prerational cultural and social interaction. Once the
prerational has been penetrated and transformed into the rationalized, any
further "rerationalization" self-destructs the original rationalized con-
structions. It is the lingering opposition, the unabsorbed specificity, the
negativity of the Outsider, that keeps the purposive-rational on its historical tracks and within its political limits. However, once these prerational
spheres are smashed or consumed as the Outsider becomes an Insider, any
further rationalization becomes increasingly *irrational.* Thus the total
domination of the concept, or the hegemony of the instrumental organization, over social specificity constitutes the deepest subversion of that
same abstract instrumental reason.

Consequently, during the transition, the state-corporate health delivery
systems trained more doctors and built more hospitals, significantly
improving national health care and individual life expectancy. Yet these
organizations—once in place and on line—continue to expand to the point
that highly capital-intensive hospitals and expensively trained doctors
mainly are dealing with high-tech heart transplants, ingrown toenails,
common colds, and routine pelvic examinations, while life expectancies
and other health indicators decline or hold steady in spite of massive new
health expenditures, federal health care, and redesigned delivery organizations.[22] Likewise, during the transitional phase, federally encouraged
electrification programs doubled energy consumption in the United States
from 1940 to 1960 to improve measurably the basic standard of living.
But, in turn, these rational instruments further stimulated another dou-
bling in national energy consumption from 1960 to 1978, with no new
immediately evident "improvement" in the "standard of living" beyond
living with more electrical consumer goods.[23] Similarly, by the logic of
the transition, federally subsidized mass education made possible a tremendous expansion of the schooling system. A complex array of educational institutions kept the young in class longer to learn increasingly
more sophisticated skills so that they could better integrate their labor
power into the technological productive forces of corporate capital. However, forced mass enrollments of entire generations in these educational
institutions, at the same time, has led to rampant indiscipline and a loss
of skills among elementary schools students, has fostered functional
illiteracy among secondary school graduates, and has allowed for the

systematic overtraining and underemployment of thousands of university graduates.[24]

Thus the total organization of social interaction under the state-corporate regime endangers the rational capitalistic development that it originally sought to advance, which necessitates, in turn, the reversal of this totalizing instrumental logic. Just as entrepreneurial capitalism exhausted its internal dynamic at the turn of the century by extending into the last pockets of the precapitalist world, by the mid-1960s, the transitional phase of state-corporate capitalism trespassed over its own counterbalancing limits as it intensified the instrumental administration of the lingering prerational sphere. As several sections of the Washington bureaucracy tried to rationalize the caloric intake of peasants in Bolivia, Zaire, and Thailand to combat the spread of Soviet communism, and as the Pentagon sought to win the hearts and minds of the Indochinese peoples by mounting airborne search-and-destroy sweeps against those same peoples in order to increase an abstract body count that statistically indicated total victory was near, and as several other bureaucratic instruments attempted to regulate the width, thickness, and composition of federally funded cement sidewalks in Oakland, East St. Louis, and Newark in the name of urban renewal and the War on Poverty, the transitional logic of New Deal liberalism and Cold War internationalism exploded *from within*.

The Age of Artificial Negativity

To comprehend fully how and why artificial negativity has dislodged the political and social formulae of one-dimensionality, one must reconsider the meaning of recent events taking place in several crucial social spheres. These developments, which are as profound and far-reaching as the reforms of the New Deal period, currently are obscured by outmoded interpretations and well-worn conceptualizations on both the left and the right. A correct understanding of the artificial negativity thesis, however, enables one to interpret these events and movements effectively as a tentative reopening of the public sphere. In the short run, this development may result merely in a reconsolidation of instrumental domination; but in the long run, it might ultimately make possible new forms of human emancipation.

In the last analysis, one-dimensionality boils down to corporate capital's efforts to impose instrumental rationalization of each moment in the everyday life of advanced industrial society. Its successes were dizzying as long as the totalizing designs of formal rationality confronted and consumed the prerational traditions of entrepreneurial society. But, as the diverse dimensions of regional culture, craft labor, ethnic community, popular politics, and the traditional family were administratively processed to fit a uniform conformity, state-corporate capitalism overshot its practical boundaries. Any sort of social specificity, personal autonomy, or political opposition necessarily was leached away in the homogenizing wash of mass-marketed commodities, mass public education, and collective benefits of state social welfare programs. Tradition succumbed to technique. Yet, technique could evince such superiority only against and over tradition. Once the purposive-rational mode of action turns back upon itself, as occurred during the 1960s, it proved neither purposive nor rational, either within its own formal operations or in terms of its efficient delivery of services.

To recognize this dual loss of purpose and rationality, one can reevaluate the meaning of the American policy of containment from the Truman to the Nixon administrations. Here, the logic of the transition prompted American decision makers to reorganize instrumentally the political alignments of the nation-state system following World War II to contain the expansion of the Soviet Union.[25] By skillfully exploiting its military and economic superiority, the United States instrumentally forced "the American way of life"—formal democracy, two-party parliamentary regimes, mixed capitalist economies, and a life-style rooted in material consumption—upon many unwilling and unworkable societies in Europe, Latin America, Africa, and Asia.[26] In Western Europe, Greece, and Korea, the totalizing domination of American world power barely won its border wars against the Soviet Union, successfully containing Soviet expansion, while making Europe, the Near East, and South Korea "safe" for the more advanced rationalization of American, European, and Japanese monopoly capital. Yet in Vietnam this logic went awry. In foolishly underwriting the outmoded leftovers of French colonialism, the United States bungled its opportunity to nurture a friendly, independent strain of national communism—an Indochinese Yugoslavia—as it instead sunk deeper into the bankrupt strategies of military assistance, political manipulation, and economic subsidy for the obviously unpopular "democratic" South Vietnamese governments.

Under entrepreneurial capitalism, such gunboat diplomacy, or the landing of the Marines, constituted the most effective mode of foreign domination. Yet, as I will suggest in Chapter 8, with the consummation of the transition these cumbersome techniques of naval blockades and troop movements were replaced with the more covert tools of political and economic domination, such as CIA operations officers organizing public safety, political sociologists surveying the populace for a "civic culture," and AID program directors bearing Food for Peace bundles. These changes, moreover, accurately reflect the course of American involvement in Vietnam after the defeat of the French in 1954. However, as I maintain in Chapter 9, these state-corporate instruments for international control were being proven obsolete even as they were deployed, inasmuch as transnational corporate enterprise devised an even more efficient mode of political control, namely, the material goods and cultural services of the transnational corporation, generating the "civic culture" of consumerist democracies among modern sector workers and consumers.

The administrative state's covert means of political control—undercover intelligence operations, international development agencies, or cultural shock troops such as the Peace Corps and the USIA—necessarily assumed the existence of a Cold War superpower struggle. When they failed, as in Vietnam, the administrative state could only resort to massive military intervention, which had already been proven by the French experience to be a policy of failure. Even more ironically, this massive expansion in American military involvement comes at exactly that moment in which the Soviet Union ceases to be a qualitatively different alternative to the American way of life. In fact, as Kennedy and Johnson committed more and more American troops to Vietnam, Khrushchev and the Soviet Politburo increasingly redefined socialism as more television sets, more washing machines, and more private autos—a development that finally has blossomed openly in Gorbachev's *perestroika*.

Under the transnational mode of control, however, the notions of Cold War and zero-sum superpower struggle become anachronistic, as the transnational corporation seeks to serve *any* potential customer seeking its goods and services. Thus recalcitrant peoples and maverick nation-states no longer need to be forced into submission at the end of a Marine's bayonet, nor do they need to be controlled covertly under an agricultural scheme set up by AID planners. Instead, they can submit willingly to their own self-control with each new commodity purchase and each new corporate-defined need as transnational corporations provide them with the material goods and cultural services of the "modern," or American, way of life. And, by the same token, political and economic control unfolds merely through the unequal exchange of transnational commerce.

Hence the Indochinese wars as they were waged by the United States are the turning point between the old and the new imperialism. From the vantage of the new corporate imperialism, Vietnam was a fiasco from start to finish inasmuch as the old state-based colonialism of France, and later of American Cold War imperialism, could only wage a bloody war that was doomed to failure. By the rules of the "old imperialism," before they produced counterproductive side effects such as the antiwar and student movements, control over Vietnam might have been attained with a few more hundred thousand troops, a full-scale invasion of the North, or, perhaps, a few strategically placed nuclear strikes. Instead, the "new imperialism" won by winning the phased withdrawal of American troops, the institution of "Vietnamization," and, then, the inevitable collapse of the southern regime.[27] In turn, the united communist Vietnam now seeks aid from the United States and Japan for oil technology, industrial capital, and renewed foreign trade in an effort to modernize her war-torn economy, which perfectly conforms to the inner logic of the transnational corporate enterprise and its new imperialism.[28]

The utter collapse of the New Left in the 1970s followed, in part, from its failure to understand these transformations in the international and national arenas. Still, in the 1960s, the New Left, along with the various counterculture movements of feminism, Black consciousness, and student activism, was part and parcel of the constitution process of artificial negativity. Here, then, the New Left served a function comparable to that of the Old Left prior to the New Deal. At that time, the various radical populist, socialist, and progressive movements in the cities and country-sides provided a telling critique, an innovative vanguard, or the essential otherness that challenged capital and the state to provide more political freedoms and economic benefits for the population at large.[29] Indeed, populism inspired many of first principles of Progressivism, and prairie socialism originally advocated many of the New Deal's welfare and labor policies.

Yet, once into the transition, these popular movements became highly suspect in the totalizing logic of one-dimensionality and were vigilantly repressed. Hence a series of government-sponsored red scares, witch-hunts, counterintelligence activities, and McCarthyism developing during the New Deal and Fair Deal years. The administrative regime, instead of recycling the opposition's political programs as sound political horse sense, diligently proscribed membership in such groups and forbade the propagation of their ideas to effect total control of the popular political process. But, inasmuch as it succeeded in the 1950s—the much-vaunted age of "the end of ideology"—the system seriously threatened its own continued development as it effaced the otherness that had hitherto kept it on its developmental tracks.

Consequently, the stimulation of the New Left—the free speech movements, the Black power groups, militant feminism, the drug culture, the antiwar organization, and the peace movement—prevented the complete derailment of advanced capitalist growth. These internally generated sources of negativity once again challenged the state-corporate social formation to reopen the public spheres and to reconsider the basic logic of many social and political policies. Unlike the Old Left under the logic of the transition, the New Left did not fall victim to the repressive countermeasures of the administrative regime. At many turns in its history, the movement was spied upon, infiltrated, and subverted by the FBI and CIA as these bureaus ineptly followed the repressive rules of the transition. But its members were not completely proscribed or vigorously repressed in a general antileftist hysteria. After all, in the 1950s, the Rosenburgs went to the chair marked as foreign agents; in the 1970s, Jane Fonda and company went to Hanoi lionized as culture heroes. Indeed, while she occasionally was boycotted in the 1970s and 1980s, Fonda nonetheless has prospered as the architect of new psychic self-management systems.

Thus, in a political situation in which it either had to overthrow the system entirely or strengthen it with its innovative notions, the New Left succumbed to the latter as the instrumental purposes of progressive corporate capital worked through the antiwar movement.[30] This unlikely alliance, in turn, ended the unpopular Vietnam War and weakened the popular commitment to fight any enemy at any time in any place to protect "the cause of freedom." But, unlike the old populist and socialist movements, which were grounded in organic communities, the New Left came from within the system's own universities, bureaucracies, and corporations—the growing elite of middle-class university students and the professional intelligentsia who had a large stake in the existing reward structure of the state-corporate system—to check the excesses and failures of the one-dimensional administrative regime.[31] Still, after having made these tremendous breakthroughs, the New Left failed to consolidate its gains and instead lapsed back into many of the divisive contradictions of the Old Left as many new splinter groups moved into ecological concerns, violent terrorism, electoral politics, or public interest lobbying.

The initial advances made during the 1960s by the New Left and other countercultural forces, however, gained greater force and full institutionalization in a second wave of counterbureaucratic movements. The administrative regime has tolerated, if not stimulated, these antagonistic forces in order to regulate more closely the old bureaucratic apparatus of the transitional period.[32] Clearly, the most important of these counterbureaucratic movements has been the transnationalization of corporate capital during the late 1960s, which has reopened the contradictions between state and corporation within advanced capitalist society. This "globalization process" has made the American economy and state "dependent upon economic activity outside the United States to an unprecedented degree."[33]

Between 1960 and 1970, fixed overseas investment of American transnationals rose from 21% to 41% of their fixed domestic investment.[34] In 1966, foreign corporate income was only 24% of domestic income, but by 1970 it was 44% of domestic income; in 1966, foreign sales of American transnationals were 30% of domestic sales, but by 1970 these overseas sales were nearly 40% of domestic transactions.[35] In fact, by 1970, more than 20% of all American transnational corporate profits came from overseas, and more than 25% of transnational corporate work forces were employed in foreign countries.[36] Until 1966, American exports had a higher labor component than American imports, but by 1970, American exports had lost their labor intensiveness as the United States had become "a service economy and a producer of plans, programs, and ideas for others to execute."[37]

For the most part, this managerial transformation occurred during the mid-1960s, as the transnational corporate managers reacted to the abject failure of the New Deal state in dealing successfully with either its domestic challenges or its international obligations. Recognizing the inability of their traditional home countries—given the massive decolonization and ill-fated colonial wars of the 1950s and 1960s—to protect their world markets, to ensure their international security, and to expand their economic operations, transnational corporations began to disguise their national origins. In adopting anational names such as Asarco, Amax, Exxon, Arco, Textron, Uniroyal, or United Technologies, transnational corporations also recruited management and labor worldwide, and established their own corporate-directed foreign, economic, employment, and investment policies. In the age of full monopoly capital, then, transnational corporate interests are *not* necessarily those of their former home or their present host countries.[38]

To appreciate this fact fully, one need only reconsider the post-1965 relations between the major oil corporations, the large nuclear technology

firms, the computer technology combines, and the arms builders and the
Arab states, the aggressive regional powers like Iran, Brazil, Pakistan
and India, the Eastern European states, and the world conflict zones—the
Mideast, the Indian subcontinent, and South Africa. American interests
usually *are not served* by such corporate deals with these nation-states.
National foreign policy, then, no longer instrumentalizes corporate interests to advance its national objectives. Rather, corporate policy needs
such as selling warplanes to aggressive regional powers or nuclear reac-
tors to hitherto nonnuclear nations, become the substance of national
foreign policy as the state serves the interests of corporate capital. Still
these contradictions have reintroduced an element of organizational otherness, political negativity, and unrationalized specificity into the conduct
of political bargaining and social policy that has been lacking for nearly
four decades.[39] At the same time, the knowledge-intensive, technology-
exporting industries that form the commanding heights of full monopoly
capital have exploited these contradictions in their efforts to organize the
entire world instrumentally—including the former great powers and the
superpowers of the nation-states era—in accord with their corporate
managerial designs.[40]

These developments perhaps also are witnessed in the attempts of
corporate capital to reverse the limited social advances of the welfare
state. Private corporate and foundation studies in favor of dismantling the
social security system and having its welfare functions "better served" by
private pension and benefit schemes, as well as corporate offensives to
forestall comprehensive national health care in favor of private health
delivery systems, are indicative of the corporate leadership's disenchantment with inefficient state bureaucracies. Similarly, the mounting militancy of corporate management in demanding "giveback" provisos in
labor contracts—that is, corporations are taking back many of the state
and corporate welfare benefits that they had conceded to organized labor
during the transition—also illustrates the opening of a counteroffensive
against the state-supported labor unions.

In addition to this counterbureaucratic movement by corporate capital
against the advanced industrial nation-state, the administrative regime of
the increasingly outmoded transitional state purposely has opened a
limited free space. Within its own structures, weak, negative forces are
nurtured as an adaptive control mechanism for the larger bureaucratized
social formation. The emergence and survival of professional public
interest lobbyists, such as Ralph Nader's task forces, Barry Commoner's
environmental studies, John Gardner's Common Cause organization, or

Howard J. Phillips's Conservative Caucus,[41] continue the critique of state-corporate capitalism by mobilizing interests "bureaucratically" against the *bureaucratic* decision making of large corporations or federal agencies. Instead of being systematically repressed, these weak oppositional forces are systematically subsidized and strongly encouraged to prod the bureaucratic apparatus to perform more efficiently or more humanely.[42] Such counterbureaucratic influences, however, are not allowed to become powerful enough to disrupt or dismantle completely the apparatus as it currently functions. Nader's failure to get a meaningful consumer protection agency established, Commoner's inability to effect passage of a real energy conservation bill, and Gardner's frustrations in constructing a systematic electoral reform program all suggest how weak these negative forces are. Undoubtedly, these reforms will be achieved, but only once they have been watered down to an appropriately symbolic level.

Along with these professional counterbureaucratic lobbyists, similar agencies also have been institutionalized within the government itself. Beginning with Nixon's slow sabotage of the various Great Society programs, a new form of federalism has been developing that seeks to halt the continued rationalization of state and local government by central decision makers. Instead of a single welfare state system operating from Washington, the instruments of revenue sharing, block grants, and community action programs are giving state and local decision makers back some of the discretion and authority appropriated by the federal bureaucracy since the New Deal. Therefore, the welfare state notion has been injected into cities, counties, and states, as they too set up social welfare divisions, community development agencies, and economic intervention bureaus that take the administrative load off the federal government's shoulders while extending its organizational clout. But, in doing so, these multiple centers of power and decision making are also checking and countervailing the organizational dictates of the federal administrative regime.

Similarly, Congress, the Justice Department, and the national media have counterattacked against the presidency to contain its imperial authority. Most important, the Senate Watergate investigations and the House impeachment committees finally resisted the overwhelming power of the president, ending an executive regime that sought to undermine the very democratic structures that made its rule possible. The War Powers Act of 1973, the Budget Act of 1974, and the extensive expansion of the congressional staff after 1974 all were significant efforts to impose new constraints on the president's ability to make war, to dispose arbitrarily of legally appropriated monies, and to manipulate information selectively by virtue of the executive's data-gathering and analysis monopoly. These important legal developments, in turn, are not simply fortuitous reactions to the Watergate affair. Rather, they amount to a systematic attempt to revitalize the constitutional contradictions and political conflicts between the executive and legislative branches to keep the federal government more manageable, responsive, and controlled. As a result, these artificially engendered negative forces have kept two presidents—Ford and Carter—well within the weakened scope of the postimperial presidency.[43]

Of course, it is no accident that the CIA, as well as the other federal intelligence services, underwent the most thoroughgoing transformation of its 30-year history during the 1970s. Beginning with Ford's initial reforms in 1976, which hobbled the operations directorate by outlawing political assassinations and domestic spying, and continuing through Carter's executive changes, the CIA fell subject to a number of important counterbureaucratic reforms. Armed with this new charter, which limits covert action in favor of using national technical means to gather information, the CIA also has been saddled with new congressional oversight committees and very tight budget restrictions. Although the basic capabilities of the CIA remain essentially the same, this executive agency has had to accept a series of real checks on its once entirely unchecked freedom of action. These reforms forced those who would follow the old formulae of power, like Colonel North, Admiral Poindexter, and Director Casey, to resort to illegalities to fund their secret wars in Central America and cloak-and-dagger operations in the Middle East.

In addition to these more formal expressions of artificial negativity, the system has fostered a variety of other internal reforms to correct for the totalizing excesses of the transition. Bureaucratic insurgency tactics, ranging from whistle-blowing to public employee unionization to information leaks, as well as new antibureaucratic legislation, such as sunshine laws, sunset provisions, and zero-based budgeting policies, are making bureaucratic decision making more accountable, as the aura of total power and knowledge is stripped away from bureaucratic practices. Similarly, the system accommodates artificial negativity by organizing increased citizen participation as part of its standard operating procedure. The administrative state now favors local action over federal action, neighborhood action over local action, and personal decision over state decision. Thus the revitalization of personal decision making, as a powerful source of negativity in the organizational society, is built into the posttransitional bureaucracy in the form of citizen committees, community liaison offices, and public hearings to improve the bureaucratic delivery system.

By the same token, mass culture has witnessed the partial reversal of mass media, which assume the passivity of the subject, in favor of media that entail the active participation of the subject. Consequently, instead of a culture industry rooted in the totalizing logic of central broadcasting, reified reproducible aesthetic experiences, and the passive acceptance of media-borne values and needs, the age of artificial negativity has witnessed the revival of individualized craft production, interactive electronic media with software—video cartridges and audiotapes—that allows for personal creativity and participation, and decentralized media broadcasting and production, with the competitive proliferation of software and hardware producers. In other words, with the relative reopening of a free space, the culture industry's totalizing logic of mass production and mass consumption of cultural experiences comes into question with the advent of interactive electronic technologies (CB radio, videotape systems, video games, small film and recording companies) and alternative media systems (personal presses, chapbook production, low-circulation journals, and multiple media publics) that could explode the totalizing culture industry from within. Yet these partial advances also undoubtedly could fail due to the lack of a sustaining social individuality.

What is more, the alternative cultural movements of the late 1960s and 1970s, such as the Black consciousness movement, feminism, the new ethnicity, environmentalism, and the new regionalism, represent popular cultural subversion of the homogenizing demands of the transition. In constituting abstract, reified, fungible labor units, the instruments of the transition did not allow for much unique personal or social specificity. Hence Blacks, Hispanics, women, Poles, and southerners also were all reduced in the transition to merely their labor power in labor law, union rollbacks, and federal job campaigns, much like the already-absorbed WASP male. Whereas this homogenization process took the destructive guise of anti-Semitism in Europe, in the United States the standardizing logic of the transition assumed the form of consumerism in the marketplace and the civil rights movement in politics, beginning with the women's suffrage movement in the 1920s and extending up through the Black civil rights movement of the early 1960s. The sudden burst in Black, Hispanic, and feminist consciousness in the mid-1960s defied the transition's totalizing logic of domination, as many Blacks, Hispanics, and women all sought to revive artificially the personal specificity and group-based otherness that the standardizing dictates of consumerism, civil rights, and labor legislation had been suppressing for four decades. In fact, the search for unintegrated otherness became so desperate that even highly integrated White ethnic communities began digging up their cultural roots. In ethnic festivals, traditional religions, and genealogy crazes, White ethnics celebrated an ethnic identity and community that had died with their grandparents or great-grandparents as the totalizing demands of WASP conformity smashed apart the working-class Eastern and Southern European ghetto in the large American industrial cities.[44]

At the same time, regional cultural identities within the mainstream of American society and politics—which had been contained effectively during the populist revolts of the 1890s—underwent a considerable resurgence as the artificial specificity of the Sunbelt, or the New South and the New West, wrestled with the Frostbelt of the Old North and the Old East for cultural and political preeminence.[45] Yet the common thread uniting all of these cultural crusades remains their *artificial negativity*, which denies the purposive-rational uniformity of the transition in favor of their self-defined specificity and collective otherness, which emanates from within monopoly capital but is directed against the state-corporate regime.

From Artificial to Organic Negativity?

Once all of the *prerational* aspects of American society submitted to the *rational* imperatives of purposive-rational management, the instruments of social administration lost their original purpose. The technical organization of the prerational as instrumentally rational activity, then, succumbed to its own mode of destructive totalizing "rationalization." Here, the state-corporate administration necessarily began to lose instrumental control over the economic and social processes of capitalist expansion as it "rerationalized" aspects of its interventionist apparatus. Yet, only the continued maintenance of this technical control over economic production, social consumption, and political administration guarantees the "rationality" of full monopoly capital in efficient ends-means terms. Once this technical control loosens, a crisis in the state-corporate system's "rationality" ensues.[46]

Furthermore, this slippage in the instrumental command over capital expansion and utilization further aggravated the ongoing economic crisis. As the state-corporate social formation emerged from the economic disorders and social conflicts of liberal-entrepreneurial capitalism, the essential mechanism of legitimation was its administrative effectiveness in providing the general social "goods" of political stability, economic growth, and expanded mass consumption of consumer goods and services, as well as the social welfare system. But, as the regime's overrationalization disrupts the management of the economy, polity, and society, the administrative ability to deliver the system's own self-defined social "goals" efficiently is weakened substantially.[47]

As this process unfolded, however, the American working classes suffered major social costs—systematic popular depoliticization, the rise of a technocratic administrative state, the loss of personal economic, political, and social skills, and the adoption of false material needs through consumeristic consumption—as they gained certain state-corporate benefits—political stability, relative material affluence, economic security, and a social welfare system managed by the state. But, once this technocratic system of state-corporate management had been constituted and the forms of social activity rationalized, any additional "rationalization" necessarily had to turn upon the agency of rationalization itself. Yet, in either streamlining or discarding aspects of the very interventionist apparatus that made possible the rational administration of the economy and society, the rational order began to self-destruct. And further rationalization strikes at the roots of personal motivation and endangers the economic logic of accumulation that drives the advanced industrial economy.

The rationality and legitimacy crises of the administrative state and monopoly capital present unprecedented opportunities to combat the continuation of political domination by this technocratic administration. By criticizing the positivistic natural and social sciences, which have served both to rationalize and to legitimate the administrative regime of instrumental control, organic negativity might recover from its repressive technocratic management under this administrative regime. Developing organic negativity, however, means more than simply reconstituting the free social spaces that ground critical analysis and debate. Emancipation today necessarily demands the *repoliticization* of mass society and renewed *education* of each individual in the cultivation of his or her own personal autonomy, political skills, and individual discipline. Without a new autonomous and rational subject, these efforts at massive change will collapse. It is necessary to push beyond merely defining and criticizing the nature of mass depoliticization under the transition. One must indicate how it is possible for individuals to escape from the naturalized social behaviors of personal commodity consumption and political apathy or the passive acceptance of bureaucratic policies and mass culture.

American political thinking must project new political needs for a *social individuality*—rooted in the organic community of the neighborhood, the family, or the city—instead of a commodified consumerist personality; for *personal political autonomy*—based upon renewed popular interaction and displacement of bureaucratic organization by popular participatory activity—instead of passive political clientage; and for *individual social judgment*—grounded in the contextual/substantive reasoning of autonomous personalities in revitalized organic communities—instead of the technical policy sciences of state-corporate administration.[48] Such forms of repoliticization, to be sure, will demand the reconstruction of new free spaces in both the public and private spheres from their current fragmentation under the regime of the administrative state. Still, these political movements and spaces, currently opening through the functioning of artificial negativity, are the institutional bases for organizing individual subjects to act subsequently as their own guides, their own administrators, and their own emancipators.[49] These repoliticized social spaces, in the last analysis, might allow for the renewal of personally initiated and collectively conciliated communicative interaction that is essential to the survival of organic negativity, even though it runs counter to the prevailing logic of corporate accumulation and state administration.

Notes

1. See Paul Piccone, "The Changing Function of Critical Theory," *New German Critique* 12 (Fall 1977), 29-38; Paul Piccone, "The Crisis of One-Dimensionality," *Telos* 35 (Spring 1978), 43-54; Tim Luke and Paul Piccone, "Debrizzi's Un-Dimensionality," *Telos* 37 (Fall 1978), 148-152; Paul Piccone, "Narcissism After the Fall: What's on the Bottom of the Pool," *Telos* 44 (Summer 1980), 112-121; Timothy W. Luke, "Rationalization *Redux*: From the New Deal to the New Beginning," *New Political Science* 8 (Spring 1982), 63-72; Timothy W. Luke, "The Modern Service-State: Public Power in America from the New Deal to the New Beginning," *Race, Politics, and Culture: Critical Essays on the Radicalism of the 1960s,* ed. by Adolph Reed, Jr. (Westport, CT: Greenwood, 1986), 183-205; Paul Piccone, "The Crisis of American Conservatism," *Telos* 74 (Winter 1987-88), 3-29; Paul Piccone, "Reinterpreting 1968: Mythology on the Make," *Telos* 77 (Fall 1988), 7-43; and Timothy W. Luke, *Screens of Power: Ideology, Domination and Resistance in Informational Society* (Urbana: University of Illinois Press, 1989).

2. For a historical and organizational discussion of this general cultural transformation, see James Burnham, *The Managerial Revolution* (Bloomington: Indiana University Press, 1960); Robert Dahl and Charles Lindblom, *Politics, Economics, and Welfare: Planning and Politico-Economic Systems Resolved into Basic Social Processes* (Chicago: University of

Chicago Press, 1976); Peter Drucker, *The New Society: The Anatomy of Industrial Order* (Boston: Harper & Row, 1971); Gunnar Myrdal, *Beyond the Welfare State* (New Haven, CT: Yale University Press, 1960); and Robert Presthus, *The Organizational Society* (New York: St. Martin's, 1962).

3. Herbert Marcuse, *Counter-Revolution and Revolt* (Boston: Beacon, 1972), 11.

4. See Daniel J. Boorstin, *The Americans: The Democratic Experience* (New York: Vintage, 1973); Lawrence Goodwyn, *Democratic Promise: The Populist Movement in America* (New York: Oxford University Press, 1976); Herbert G. Gutman, *Work, Culture and Society in Industrializing America* (New York: Vintage, 1966); and Frances Fox Piven and Richard A. Cloward, *Regulating the Poor: The Functions of Public Welfare* (New York: Vintage, 1971).

5. See Paul Piccone, "General Introduction," *The Essential Frankfurt School Reader,* ed. by Andrew Arato and Eike Gebhardt (New York: Urizen, 1978), ix-xxi.

6. More concretely, the New Deal coalition and its interventionist state successfully integrated the working-class vote as well as working-class wage and labor demands into the Democratic party and the national collective bargaining structures. Yet it was this same bloc of urban, blue-collar, often ethnic voters whose potential unrest and political militancy in the 1920s and 1930s elicited the formation of the New Deal state and the organized labor bureaucracies in order to deliver increased social services and jobs in exchange for docile loyalty. But, once the state satisfied these publics with economic growth, jobs, and services, the coalition lost its platform while failing to adjust to the new challenges and needs of the 1960s. Clearly, the system failed to respond to its internal controls and its initial purposes in Vietnam and Watts or Detroit during the 1960s.

7. In other words, the diverse counterculture movements of the 1960s, such as the Black power movement, the antiwar and peace movement, the new feminist groups, the student movement, gay activism, and religious revivalism, all directly contradicted the standardized cultural homogeneity of the transition period.

8. See Richard J. Barnet and Ronald E. Muller, *Global Reach: The Power of the Multinational Corporations* (New York: Simon & Schuster, 1974); John M. Blair, *The Control of Oil* (New York: Pantheon, 1976); and Richard Eells, *Global Corporations* (New York: Free Press, 1972).

9. See Immanuel Wallerstein, *The Modern World System* (New York: Academic Press, 1974).

10. Of course, less progressive elites, especially in latecomer imperialist states such as Germany, Japan, and the United States, pressed for continued colonial and imperial expansion, and, when matched against semicapitalist states on the capitalist periphery, such as Spain, China, Ethiopia, or the Boer Republics, the United States, Japan, and the European powers continued their expansion after 1885. In fact, World War I resulted, in large part, from Germany's expansionistic designs on Eastern Europe, the Ukraine, and the Near East. However, the other European powers, who already had embarked upon the *intensive* logic of capitalist expansion, necessarily resisted this outmoded *extensive* model of capitalistic development.

11. Herbert Croly, *The Promise of American Life* (New York: Macmillan, 1909).

12. Woodrow Wilson, *The New Freedom* (Garden City, NY: Doubleday, 1913).

13. Ibid., 22.

14. For a well-argued historical treatment of the scientific management of labor and production, see Harry Braverman, *Labor and Monopoly Capital: The Degradation of Work in the Twentieth Century* (New York: Monthly Review Press, 1974); Siegfried Giedion, *Mechanization Takes Command* (New York: Norton, 1948); and David Noble, *America by Design: Science, Technology and the Rise of Corporate Capitalism* (New York: Knopf, 1977).

15. American Institute of Management, "What Is Management?" *Dimensions in Modern Management,* ed. by Patrick E. Connor (Boston: Houghton Mifflin, 1974), 23.

16. Each of these pieces of legislation vastly expanded the interventionist mechanisms of the federal government. The Federal Reserve Act and the Federal Trade Commission Act gave the federal executive the tools to manipulate economic activity effectively through the money supply and commercial rulings, while the tariff and farm loans legislation enabled the central government to open the hitherto restricted American market to crucial world production centers and to finance farm activity—all new functions for the protoadministrative Progressive state. Moreover, Wilson's "New Freedom" legislation, in testing the totalizing logic of one-dimensionality, instituted strong means for controlling individuals—the direct national income tax and the Eighteenth Amendment—by empowering large new federal bureaucracies with the task of policing the general population's private finances and lives.

17. Boorstin, *The Americans,* 89-166.

18. See Herbert Marcuse, *One-Dimensional Man: Studies in the Ideology of Advanced Industrial Society* (Boston: Beacon, 1964), 1-55.

19. Jules Blackman, "Emerging Trends," *Labor, Technology, and Productivity in the Seventies,* ed. by Jules Blackman (New York: New York University Press, 1974), 19-25.

20. In addition to the suspension of such harsh repressive tools as Prohibition and the refusal to provide social security, the transitional social formation also instituted a series of covert control devices with the expansion of the Veterans Administration and the formation of the Federal Housing Administration after World War II. By providing easy credit to the masses of consumers, individualized housing and suburbanization provided another means for the homogenization of working-class cultures along with the massive expansion in private automobile production and consumption that together constituted a major instrument for the control of individuals through the manipulation of their material needs and wants in new mass markets.

21. Blackman, "Emerging Trends," 20.

22. See Odin W. Anderson, *Health Care: Can There Be Equity? The United States, Sweden, and England* (New York: John Wiley, 1972); and Ivan Illich, *Medical Nemesis: The Expropriation of Health* (New York: Pantheon, 1976). The impact of artificial negativity on health care systems seems quite radical inasmuch as many health professionals are beginning to favor reversing a century-old practice, namely, taking the individual's health care skills and responsibilities away and giving them to a scientifically trained doctor. Thus, in order to make the system more effective, individual subjects are to be given back their personal skills, individual decision, and family medical knowledge, which never should have been taken away to begin with. Instead of further integrating individuals into a standardized system, which has overloaded the once efficient system to its cost-effectiveness breaking point, health professionals are giving individuals back their autonomy and judgment in self-help health maintenance and sick care training.

23. Similarly, U.S. energy consumption per capita in 1972 was over twice that of West Germany and the Netherlands, but it is doubtful that this greater technical potential means a superior standard of living in the United States, despite its greater instrumental rationalization of energy consumption. See Amory B. Lovins, *Soft Energy Paths* (Cambridge, MA: Ballinger, 1977).

24. See Samuel Bowles and Herbert Gintis, *Schooling in Capitalist America: Educational Reforms and the Contradictions of Economic Life* (New York: Harper & Row, 1976); Ivan Illich, *De-schooling Society* (New York: Harper & Row, 1971); and Leo J. Ryan, "Our Public Schools Need to Be Reordered," *Los Angeles Times* (March 16, 1978).

25. See Raymond Aron, *The Imperial Republic: The United States and the World, 1945-1973* (Englewood Cliffs, NJ: Prentice-Hall, 1974); Ronald Steel, *Pax Americana* (New York: Viking, 1967); and Daniel Yergin, *Shattered Peace: The Origins of the Cold War and the National Security State* (Boston: Houghton Mifflin, 1977).

26. See Robert A. Packenham, *Liberal America and the Third World: Political Development Ideas in Foreign Aid and Social Science* (Princeton, NJ: Princeton University Press, 1973).

27. This reversal of the old imperialist domination, however, did not come soon enough to save Cambodia from near total destruction of the relatively peaceful and stable traditional political order. Indeed, the Cambodian incursion, perhaps better than any other recent imperial adventure, illustrates the bankruptcy of the old imperialism as the coercive logic of instrumental domination toppled the established government, smashed the rich particularity of Cambodian culture, and, in the space of five years, reduced its people to the dark barbarities of the Khmer Rouge—all in the name of "pacification."

28. And as the United States and Japan contend for the control of Indochina via the logic of monopoly capital's new imperialism, the Soviet Union and the People's Republic of China are embroiled in a proxy war in the tradition of the East-West Cold War, as Communist Vietnam and Communist Cambodia act out the old imperialist designs of the transition for the Soviets and the Chinese.

29. See John Gaventa, *Power and Powerlessness: Quiescence and Rebellion in an Appalachian Valley* (Urbana: University of Illinois Press, 1980), 220-251, for a discussion, for example, of how grass-roots political groups have used home video technology to document the environmental problems they were seeking to resist in Appalachia. Also see James Miller, *"Democracy Is in the Streets": From Port Huron to the Siege of Chicago* (New York: Simon & Schuster, 1987); Alison M. Jagger and Paula S. Rothenberg, *Feminist Frameworks: Alternative Theoretical Accounts of the Relations Between Women and Men* (2nd ed.) (New York: McGraw-Hill, 1984); Hazel Henderson, *Creating Alternative Futures: The End of Economics* (New York: Berkeley Windhover, 1978); and Murray Bookchin, *Toward an Ecological Society* (Montreal: Black Rose, 1980).

30. For an excellent discussion of this process, see Todd Gitlin, *The Whole World Is Watching: Mass Media in the Making and Unmaking of the New Left* (Berkeley: University of California Press, 1980). See also Adolph Reed, Jr., "The 'Black Revolution" and the Reconstitution of Domination," *Race, Politics, and Culture,* 61-95; and David Gross, "Culture, Politics and Lifestyle in the 1960s," *Race, Politics, and Culture,* 99-117.

31. The basis for these movements, perhaps, is best captured by the example of Daniel Ellsberg. A Harvard graduate, ex-Marine infantry officer, one-time RAND Corporation strategic analyst, Ellsberg turned from within the system against the system using the Pentagon's own strategic studies—and its own Xerox machines—against the bureaucratic administration of an impossible war made possible by the transitional organization of the state-corporate regime.

32. Although he did not say it in this context, President Nixon anticipated the intent and form of these counterbureaucratic movements throughout his first administration with his Federal Executive Service and the New Federalism doctrines, which were meant to reconstruct the New Deal state entirely. Indeed, he proclaimed, "This will be known as an Administration which advocated . . . more significant reforms than any Administration since Franklin Roosevelt in 1932." *New York Times* (November 10, 1972).

33. Barnet and Muller, *Global Reach,* 258.

34. Ibid.

35. Ibid.

36. Ibid., 259.

37. Ibid., 260.

38. Ibid., 216.

39. Obviously, this current division holds the possibility of transnational corporations, at some point in the future, totally obliterating the social specificity and political otherness of the nation-state system itself. And, although that point in the development of monopoly

capital is some time off, it has nevertheless begun. See Barnet and Muller, *Global Reach,* 213-362, on the "Latin Americanization" of the advanced capitalist nation-states by transnational corporate capital.

40. Ibid., 363-388.

41. See John Guinther, *Moralists and Managers: Public Interest Movements in America* (Garden City, NY: Anchor, 1976); and William J. Lanouette, "New Right Seeks Conservative Consensus," *National Journal: The Weekly on Politics and Government* 10, no. 3 (January 21, 1978), 88-92.

42. Indeed, these oppositional forces have even begun to form entire alternative policy practices in addition to providing systematic policy critiques as such institutions as the Brookings Institution, the American Enterprise Institute, the Institute for Policy Studies, and World Watch rationalize the interests and values of artificial negativity in their research and publications. See William J. Lanouette, "The 'Shadow Cabinets': Changing Themselves as They Try to Change Policy," *National Journal: The Weekly on Politics and Government* 10, no. 8 (February 25, 1978), 296-303.

43. These tendencies, of course, seem to have slowed under President Reagan and President Bush. Both seem committed to decreasing the size of the federal bureaucracy, but the secret wars of Ollie North as well as Grenada and Panama put both of their administrations back into an older model of American interventionism.

44. See Mark R. Levy and Michael S. Kramer, *The Ethnic Factor: How America's Minorities Decide Elections* (New York: Simon & Schuster, 1973).

45. See Kirkpatrick Sale, *Power Shift: The Rise of the Southern Rim and Its Challenge to the Eastern Establishment* (New York: Vintage, 1975); and Carl Oglesby, *The Yankee and Cowboy Wars: Conspiracies from Dallas to Watergate* (Mission, KS: Sheed Andrews & McMeel, 1976).

46. See Jürgen Habermas, *Legitimation Crisis* (Boston: Beacon, 1975), 50-68, 75-92.

47. See Alvin Gouldner, *The Dialectic of Ideology and Technology* (New York: Seabury, 1976), 195-273; James O'Connor, *The Fiscal Crisis of the State* (New York: St. Martin's, 1973); and Claus Offe, "Political Authority and Class Structure: An Analysis of Late Capitalist Societies," *International Journal of Sociology* (Spring 1972).

48. This critical debate already has begun; see Bruce Brown, *Marx, Freud and the Critique of Everyday Life* (New York: Monthly Review Press, 1973); Stuart Ewen, *Captains of Consciousness: Advertising and the Social Roots of the Consumer Culture* (New York: McGraw-Hill, 1976); Russell Jacoby, *Social Amnesia: A Critique of Contemporary Psychology from Adler to Laing* (Boston: Beacon, 1975); Henri Lefebvre, *Everyday Life in the Modern World* (New York: Harper & Row, 1971); William Leiss, *The Limits to Satisfaction: An Essay on the Problem of Needs and Commodities* (Toronto: University of Toronto Press, 1976); Claus Mueller, *The Politics of Communication: A Study in the Political Sociology of Language, Socialization, and Legitimation* (London: Oxford University Press, 1973); and Richard Sennett and Jonathan Cobb, *The Hidden Injuries of Class* (New York: Knopf, 1972).

49. See Luke, *Screens of Power,* 3-16, 207-239.

PART IV

Power, Discourse, and Culture in the Developing World

7

Cabral's Marxism:
An African Strategy
for Socialist Development

Despite being recognized as one of the most important new bodies of "ideological writings of any real vitality" [1] in modern Africa, Amilcar Cabral's theoretical project has received comparatively little critical attention or intellectual recognition.[2] In part, this lack of notoriety can be attributed to the relatively low visibility of both Guinea-Bissau and of the *Partido Africano da Independência da Guiné e Cabo Verde* (PAIGC) movement, which led the national liberation struggle of the indigenous peoples against the now collapsed Portuguese empire. Another part of this neglect follows from Cabral's own commitment to constant political activism rather than to sustained intellectual work. As a central organizer of the PAIGC in 1956 and as its preeminent national leader after 1959, Cabral devoted relatively little of his time and energy to producing a systematic body of political and social theory. Nonetheless, as this chapter shows, Cabral's carefully constructed Marxist theory is an effective strategy for attaining national liberation in a colonial situation. Ultimately, it outlines a uniquely African path of autonomous socialist development, especially as it addresses the special African problem of building politically a mass-based cultural renaissance, or a "return to the source."

Amilcar Cabral was born in 1925 in Guinea-Bissau. Highly atypical of Guineans, Cabral received a full education and eventually studied in Lisbon at the *Casa dos Estudantes do Imperio*. While in Lisbon, he began joint political discussions with Agostinho Neto and Mario de Andrade that soon convinced them of the need for revolutionary change throughout Africa, particularly in Portugal's African empire.[3] Cabral returned to

Guinea-Bissau and served in the colonial administration as an agronomist. Encouraged to leave Guinea because of his subversive attitudes, he returned first to Lisbon and then to Angola to work on a private sugar estate. He joined Neto as the founding member of the MPLA in 1956, and he later led in forming the PAIGC clandestinely in Guinea-Bissau during a visit there in 1956. After exhausting its legal options and political alternatives, the PAIGC took to organizing dockworkers in the coastal towns in the late 1950s—a strategy that led to the August 3, 1959, Pidgiguiti massacre of many African workers by the Portuguese authorities. In September 1959, Cabral left Angola and went underground with the PAIGC leadership to struggle against the Portuguese, politically and militarily. Working both within the colony and from Guinea-Conakry, Cabral launched the national liberation struggle in 1962 with a series of military attacks that soon enabled the PAIGC to take and hold large expanses of territory within the colony. The movement established itself as the functioning regime within the interior by 1966, and was able to declare the territory independent in September 1973. Cabral, however, was assassinated by Portuguese-backed agents in January 1973.

For politically aware Africans, who generally have been "conscious of a lack of a consistent, cohesive and powerful ideological dimension in the politics of their countries," [4] Cabral's theoretical work assumes a special importance. Even today, African societies face the difficult tasks of economy, nation, and state building with few compelling or convincing ideological options. Cabral's Marxism might provide the ideological tools for changing traditional ways of thinking as the members of African societies confront the challenges of building their economies, nations, and states both during and after their struggles for national liberation. As Cabral himself suggests, "The ideological deficiency, not to say the total lack of ideology . . . constitutes one of the greatest weaknesses of our struggle . . . if not the greatest weakness." [5] Thus, in contrast to almost every other alternative, as Chaliand notes, Cabral's Marxism remains one of Black Africa's most potent "modernizing and revolutionary ideolog[ies], one which, while exalting the sense of national identity, can also prune the socially and culturally conservative elements out of the national tradition and free the energies of the greatest number of people." [6]

In fact, Cabral's special contribution follows from his unique awareness of the ethnic and national dimension in revolutionary struggle, which expresses itself in his concern for cultural revitalization, in the struggle over the productive forces and state power in colonial and neocolonial situations. This contribution also is more than simply theoretical. Cabral's own leadership role in Guinea-Bissau's national liberation struggle allowed him to share many of the same experiences encountered by revolutionary militants in Angola and Mozambique. Cabral's special focus in Black Africa on the importance of culture in socialist development strongly parallels Antonio Gramsci's concern with similar issues in southern Europe. Indeed, as one traces out the crucial themes in Cabral's thought, many striking ties can be made between Cabral's "return to the source" and Gramsci's "philosophy of praxis." [7]

Moreover, as illustrated in Chapter 3, Gramsci's specifically European-oriented thought provided a theoretical critique and practical alternative for European political movements to the mechanically dogmatic vanguard party that forces industrialization down the bureaucratic collectivist path of the Soviet Union. Cabral's theoretical designs for a democratic party, a pedagogical movement, and a popularly rooted cultural renaissance as the basis of his socialist project establishes the most viable *African* alternative to the Soviet model of socialist development.[8] Like Gramsci, as I argued in Chapter 3, Cabral is very attuned to the problem of reorganizing economic production and state power as part of a larger cultural transformation. The continuing inspiration that his work has given to the militants in Angola, Guinea-Bissau, Mozambique, Namibia, and Zimbabwe, in spite of the considerable difficulties faced by all of these countries during and after the revolutionary national liberation struggle, attests to his significant theoretical influence.

Amilcar Cabral proves himself, like Antonio Gramsci, to be both a master dialectician and a sophisticated analyst of class contradictions. His theoretical output, which is greatly enriched by his practical experience as a political activist and natural scientist,[9] touches upon many themes, ranging from African history, colonial administration, cultural education, and international diplomacy to party organization, colonial economies, social psychology, and guerrilla warfare.[10] However, only a handful of Cabral's more salient theoretical concerns can be discussed here, namely, his theories of colonialism, of class, and of the party in the national liberation struggle as a form of socialist development.

On Colonialism

By almost every conventional measure, Guinea-Bissau is a small country. About the size of Switzerland, with an indigenous African population of fewer than a million,[11] its economy is almost exclusively agricultural and largely export oriented.[12] Still, as Davidson observes, Guinea-Bissau is more than interesting in itself because it is "a paradigm of the African situation," which makes it "a place not only worth observing for itself but also worth learning from." [13] In certain respects, Guinea-Bissau as well as Angola and Mozambique represented unusual colonial situations in that they were colonies of Portugal, which was itself a poor, semi-industrialized country. Portugal's colonies, then, tended to be considerably less developed than other nations' colonies, and their inhabitants were much poorer. Guinea-Bissau, nonetheless, prior to the opening of the national liberation struggle in 1959, was in other respects a textbook case in colonialism. Originally penetrated at the close of the fifteenth century as a slaving station, the Portuguese failed to define its boundaries until 1936.[14] Very few White settlers established residence in the colony. Instead, the entire colony was run along classic imperial lines by "the monopolist trading company, the *União Fabril*—which supplied Portugal with cheap colonial imports in return for Portuguese exports, the terms of trade fixed in order to turn the balance of payments as favorably to Portugal as possible." [15] Most of the rural population was compelled by administrative decree and tax legislation to cultivate cash crops for export, which "cut severely into the domestic food supply, and deepened the poverty and malnutrition of the peasants." [16] Hardly any significant industrial development occurred during the five centuries of Portugal's "civilizing mission." Instead, the health, education, and welfare of the native population were conspicuously ignored. At the onset of the national liberation struggle, the entire colony had only eighteen doctors, two hospitals, one secondary school, and eleven African graduates with higher education. Most of these social services were reserved for use by the tiny White Portuguese minority. Barely 1% of the African population could claim basic literacy, and only .3% of the Africans had attained "assimilated" legal status.[17]

This purposeful deformation of Guinea-Bissau's indigenous African societies, which was aimed at integrating the productive forces of their agrarian economies into the larger world economy through Portugal's trade networks, underlies, in the last analysis, Cabral's views on colonialism. While remaining thoroughly Marxist in his analysis, Cabral enriches this method with his uniquely developed emphasis on culture. "Colonialism can be considered," Cabral suggests, "as the paralysis or deviation or even the halting of the history of one people in favour of the acceleration of the historical development of other peoples." [18] Consequently, colonial relations amount to robbing the Africans not only of their agricultural produce, but, just as important, of their *history* and *culture*, which are immediately connected with the mode of production.

In taking this position, however, Cabral maintains that popular control of the productive forces is both the fundamental goal of the revolution and essential for the cultural liberation of the oppressed indigenous population. Colonialism, as "the negation of the *historical process* of the dominated people by means of violently usurping the free operation of the process of development of the *productive forces*," [19] Cabral sees as necessarily disrupting or destroying the African culture's "capacity (or the responsibility) for forming and fertilizing the seedling which will assure the continuity of history, at the same time assuring the prospects for evolution and the progress in the society in question." [20] For Cabral, then, colonial domination denies the organic economic and historical development of the indigenous culture from within in order to facilitate its more "rational" economic development from without, which requires "cultural oppression and the attempt at direct or indirect liquidation of the essential elements of the culture of the dominated people." [21]

Cabral's theory of colonialism immediately reveals itself to be highly sophisticated. It transcends the more common economic interpretation of colonialism in order to identify colonial relations as a complex mode of enforcing *cultural hegemony*, [22] which aims "to harmonize economic and political domination of these people with their cultural personality." [23] Indeed, colonialism "can be maintained," in Cabral's mind, "only by the permanent, organized repression of the cultural life of the people concerned." [24] Because culture is "the more or less conscious result of the economic and political activities of that society, the more or less dynamic expression of the kinds of relationships which prevail in that society, on the one hand between man (considered individually or collectively) and nature, and, on the other hand, among individuals, groups of individuals, social strata or classes," [25] the colonizer purposely altered the indigenous culture to synchronize it more completely with the needs of the world economy. And, in making this move, the colonialist's repression of culture seeks to destroy the African's historical forms of subjectivity, stigmatizing them as "primitive," "barbaric," or "backward," and to replace these organic forms of action with the more narrow, objectified forms of economic, social, and political domination that are largely grounded not in *African* but in *European* history and culture. By replacing the African institutions for dealing with nature, society, and the productive forces that mediate them, the European colonizers paralyzed the Africans' creation of an indigenous culture and history in order to rationalize further their Western capitalist productive forces and historical development.

For Cabral, this historical process proves to have important dialectical dimensions inasmuch as the European influence always turns out to be partial, temporary, and politically unsuccessful despite the economic and technical superiority of European culture. Ultimately, he maintains, "it is not possible to harmonize the economic and political domination of a people, whatever may be the degree of their social development, with the preservation of their cultural personality," [26] in Africa, because of the tremendous "differences between the culture of the dominated people and the culture of the oppressor." [27] More important, however, Cabral admits that this partial suspension of the African's history and culture "was not just a negative reality." [28] On the contrary, by partially *paralyzing* the ongoing organic development of the African culture, the colonizer actually begins to ensure eventual progress for the indigenous peoples as colonial economic and social institutions begin transferring more universal forms of historical subjectivity—embodied in modern technology, formal education, empirical science, bureaucratic organization, the world economy and market, or international law—to the colonized population in their everyday life.[29]

Colonialism, then, reveals itself as the mediation of modernity to be both constructive and destructive, progressive and regressive, developmental and deconstructive. Cabral recognizes that "it gave new nations to the world, the dimensions of which it reduced and that it revealed new stages of development in human societies and in spite of or because of the prejudices, the discrimination and the crimes which it occasioned, it contributed to a deeper knowledge of humanity as a moving whole, as a unity in the complex diversity of the characteristics of development." [30] Thus, as colonialism politically mediates the gradual universalization of particular European cultures in modern science, the world market, and advanced technology, at the same time it facilitates the particularization of this universal culture as part of the partially and temporarily repressed African histories and cultures.

Obviously, in most colonies, the European colonizers successfully took control within their colonial domains of the indigenous African societies' productive forces, reorganizing these forces by administrative decree, tax legislation, large engineering works, and forced labor arrangements to strengthen their own metropolitan economies. Quite often, Cabral recognizes that the African peoples' initial resistance was "crushed by the technical superiority of the imperialist conqueror, with the complicity of or betrayal by some indigenous ruling classes. Those elites who were loyal to the history and to the culture of the people were destroyed." [31] Yet, even as the political and intellectual elites who served as the guardians of the African history and culture were destroyed or compromised by colonialism, Cabral maintains that "the cultural resistance of the African people was not destroyed. Repressed, persecuted, betrayed by some social groups who were in league with the colonialists, African culture survived all of the storms, taking refuge in the villages, in the forests and in the spirit of the generations who were victims of colonialism." [32] For Cabral, then, the pretheoretical cultural understanding of the African peoples, who also are the major productive forces of the colony, contains the emancipatory forms of collective subjectivity, or history-making and culture-building potential, that can overcome colonialism. Because the popular masses have always resisted the colonizer's domination, Cabral believes that a movement working for its liberation from colonialism "must, on the cultural level just as on the political level, base its action in popular culture" [33] in the struggle "both for the preservation and the survival of the cultural values within a national framework." [34] Furthermore, as the productive agents of the export-oriented agricultural economy, these peoples in reclaiming their culture might also begin to regain power over their economic resources.

In other words, to combat the political domination, economic exploitation, and cultural hegemony of the Portuguese colonizers, Cabral advocates the politically organized and scientifically rationalized *reconstitution* of the traditional African peoples' history-making and culture-building capacities in a nationwide movement to oppose the colonizer's cultural hegemony with the colonized's counterhegemonic culture. Indeed, his own careful survey of the political strength, economic importance, and cultural potential of Guinea-Bissau's native peoples in the mid-1950s illustrates the salience that he gave to cultural preparation in the national liberation war. Like Leopold Senghor, whose writings profoundly influenced him early in life, Cabral firmly advocated "the re-Africanization of minds" as the method of this cultural struggle. But, in having experienced colonial rule, the revitalized African cultures must be conscious of their place "in the framework of universal civilization" [35] as "a conquest of a small piece of humanity for the common heritage of humanity." [36] However, the particular social strata and bloc of class forces that could, on the one hand, resist this anticolonial movement and, on the other hand, organize and lead this re-creation of the African peoples' history and culture for Cabral requires a more detailed examination of his analysis of the class antagonisms present in colonialism.

Class Contradictions Under Colonialism

To attack the European colonizers' cultural domination and economic exploitation, Cabral successfully sketches out a comprehensive class analysis of Guinea's native social forces and colonial state. At times, Cabral's analysis verges on a conventional materialist interpretation as he strives systematically—even if unsuccessfully—to relate every group to the mode of production. Still, as a political analyst of class contradictions and political opportunities, he skillfully employs Marxism not as a dogma but as a *method*.[37] Consequently, Cabral's class analysis, in Guinea-Bissau, again much like Gramsci's considerations of Italian history and politics, can be described as "the product of scientific study of empirical material, in the classic sense in which this was practiced by the founders of historical materialism." [38]

In Guinea-Bissau, Cabral spent at least two periods of several years each familiarizing himself with the diverse peoples and social institutions of the colony. From 1952 to 1954, in discharging his duties as a colonial agronomist, Cabral "tramped the length and breadth of his country acquiring detailed local knowledge, growing into an intimacy with village life," [39] and later, from 1959 to 1961, in carefully selecting cadres for the PAIGC underground, he also undertook a comprehensive review of social conditions. In doing so, Cabral carefully considered several concrete contradictions among classes (the peasantry, the urban petty bourgeoisie, the Portuguese settlers, the small working class, the urban lumpen elements, and the intellectual groups), ethnonational groups (the Fula, the Balanta, the Mandinga, and the Pepel), religious blocs (Christians, Moslems, and animists), status groups (women, the traditional chiefs, students, and traditional religious leaders), regions (urban, rural, coastal, and interior), and institutions (tribal differences, family structure, kinship groups, age groups, religion, and political structures).[40] Here, Cabral's method suggests that "the position of each group must be defined—to what extent and in what way does each group depend on the colonial regime? Next we have to see what position they adopt toward the national liberation struggle. Then we have to study their *nationalist capacity* and, lastly, envisaging the post-independence period, their *revolutionary capacity*." [41]

In asking these questions of the groups he identifies, Cabral recognized that in Guinea-Bissau those social forces that were most dependent upon the colonial regime—such as the Moslem Fula chiefs, the White working class, the urban traders, many obedient Fula peasants, some African petty bourgeois officials, and some of the African lumpen elements—lacked any nationalist or revolutionary capacity. Similarly, those social forces that "have maintained intact their tradition of resistance to colonial penetration" [42] had the greatest nationalist capacity—for example, most of the animist peasants, the Balantes, the small African class of farm owners, many of the underemployed mestizo and African petty bourgeoisie, many politicized lumpen elements, some of the White petty bourgeoisie, the few African "intellectuals," and some discontented Fula peasants. Because of the complexities of the colonial situation, Cabral implements Marxism, not as an unyielding application of foreign categories grounded in the European bourgeois and proletarian class struggle to a recalcitrant African reality, but rather as a method for creating categories and concepts suitable to the African context. Cabral constantly maintains that "national liberation and social revolution are not exportable commodities; they are, and increasingly so every day, the outcome of local and national factors . . . essentially determined and formed by the historical reality of such people, and carried to success by the overcoming or correct solution of the internal contradictions between the various categories characterizing this reality." [43]

By taking Marxism as a *method* for political analysis, Cabral frees himself from the doctrinal necessity of finding a revolutionary proletariat, by the orthodox Marxist-Leninist canon, or a revolutionary peasantry, by the classic Maoist formula, in a concrete situation where the forms of colonialism prevented the development of such radicalized classes. In Guinea-Bissau, Cabral notes that the tiny proletariat was not "easy to mobilize" and he knew "from experience what trouble we had convincing the peasantry to fight." [44] Consequently, Cabral does not seek to construct his ultimate collective subject from a nonexistent class consciousness. On the contrary, he concentrates instead on the potential *nation* and not the actual *classes* as a form of revolutionary collective subjectivity. By cultivating the *nationalist capacity* of various subnational, parochial social forces, Cabral advocates that the colony of Guinea-Bissau be recognized as a "nation-in-itself." Under African conditions, Cabral holds that only such a liberated "nation-for-itself" can reclaim the "inalienable right of every people to have their own history" based on its right to control "the process of development of national productive forces." [45]

From one perspective, anyone might question the need to identify this program of building a "national" socialism as having a Marxist pedigree. In passing over the proletariat and the peasantry as the primary revolutionary agents, Cabral would seem to have little in common, for example, with Lenin, Mao, or Ho. While this is true, from another perspective it becomes a major strength of Cabral's project. Instead of being uncritically wedded to an orthodox perspective, and having to endure the experience of a "July days" in Petrograd, a 1927 Shanghai debacle, or a Nghe An collapse, Cabral and the PAIGC adapted their strategies to the nationalist plane from the start. Cabral saw himself and his theory as Marxist; yet, for the most part, he did not let the historical traditions of Marxism overburden his analysis of colonial Africa's unique revolutionary situation.

Nevertheless, the decisive agency behind this national mobilization and social revolution comes from a more or less distinct class, or the "indigenous lower middle class," which remains the group most directly affected by the "influence of the colonial power's culture and most capable of creating the new revolutionary nation." [46] This African petty bourgeoisie, for Cabral, fuses together in itself all of the contradictions and conflicts of colonialism. It is composed purely of indigenous peoples, yet it is the most "Europeanized" native group. It largely shares in the everyday administration of the colony with the Europeans, but it is never fully trusted or rewarded. It also is purely a creation of colonialism, and thus it cannot fully identify with either the European colonizer or the African colonized masses. Cabral observes:

> This drama is the more shattering to the extent to which the petite bourgeoisie in fulfilling its role is made to live alongside both the foreign dominating class and the masses. On the one side the petite bourgeoisie is the victim of frequent if not daily humiliation by the foreigner, and on the other side it is aware of the injustice to which the masses are subjected and of their resistance and spirit of rebellion. Hence, arises the apparent paradox of colonial domination; it is from within the indigenous *petite bourgeoisie*, a social class which grows from colonialism itself, that arise the first

important steps towards mobilizing and organizing the masses for the struggle against the colonial power.[47]

Of course, Cabral does not see this gradual radicalization of the indigenous petty bourgeoisie as either an automatic or a necessary development. On the contrary, the petty bourgeoisie's marginal privileges under colonialism, its distressing tendency to seek personal rewards over genuine public service, and its often mestizo racial makeup all contributed to the difficulty of mobilizing this class. Thus, by questioning their marginal status, and building radical consciousness, Cabral saw that the petty bourgeoisie instead must "return to the source," [48] or to the rich but suppressed history and culture of the popular masses, by denying "the pretended supremacy of the culture of the dominant power that of the dominated people with which it must identify itself." [49]

Although Cabral is not always explicit on this point, the "return to the source" assumes special importance inasmuch as many of the petty bourgeois activists in Portugal's African colonies were mestizo, often of Cape Verdean extraction, like Cabral himself. Hence their genuine reunion with the cultural traditions of the African workers and rural producers was critical in allaying some of the racial suspicions and ethnic prejudices that came between the class and racial groups. Furthermore, Cabral maintains:

It is a slow process, broken up and uneven, whose development depends on the degree of acculturation of each individual, of the material circumstances of his life, on the forming of his ideas and on his experiences as a social being. This unevenness is the basis of the split of the indigenous petite bourgeoisie into three groups when confronted with the liberation movement: a) a minority, which, even if it wants to see an end of foreign domination, clings to the dominant colonialist class and openly opposes the movement to protect its social position; b) a majority of people who are hesitant and indecisive; c) another minority of the people who share in the building and leadership of the liberation movement.[50]

After surveying both historical precedents set in other nations and social alternatives within Guinea-Bissau, Cabral correctly realized that the African struggle for national liberation must rely on the indigenous petty bourgeoisie because European colonialism in Africa did not create a substantial proletariat, a radicalized peasantry, or a revolutionary intelligentsia. As a result, entirely new and unorthodox political strategies, such as Cabral's, must necessarily be created to match the unusual class structures and contradictions of colonial society.[51]

In recruiting leadership for the national liberation struggle, Cabral did not place any special emphasis on the traditional avant garde or the literary intellectuals common in European and even Asian revolutions. As he observes, "There were none, because the Portuguese did not educate people." [52] Still, in the petty bourgeoisie, with its diverse skills and talents, Cabral found his revolutionary vanguard, which "knew the general situation very well, who had some knowledge, not profound theoretical knowledge, but concrete knowledge of the country itself and of its life, as well as of our enemy," that, at the same time, "was still closely connected to the rural areas and contained people who spoke almost all the languages that are used in Guinea. They knew all the customs of the rural areas while at the same time possessing a solid knowledge of the European urban centers. They also had a certain degree of self-confidence, they knew how to read and write (which makes a person an intellectual in our country) and so we concentrated our work on these people and immediately started giving them some preparatory training." [53]

In the last analysis, these few mestizo and African petty bourgeois activists, who "return to the source" by engaging in political activity among the peasant masses, are Cabral's "organic intellectuals" for the African national liberation struggle. As Gramsci suggests, "Every social group, coming into existence on the original terrain of an essential function in the world of economic production, creates together with itself, organically, one or more strata of intellectuals which give it homogeneity and an awareness of its own function not only in the economic but also in the social and political fields." [54] And, while these "organic intellectuals" are not all drawn directly from the peasantry, they have intimate ties with the indigenous masses whose awareness, identity, and interests basically are served by the emergence of the mobilized petty bourgeoisie as the leading group in the national liberation movement.

In Guinea-Bissau's political situation, then, Cabral placed his theoretical bet on the petty bourgeoisie as the class with the greatest nationalist and revolutionary capacity. With the intellectual and practical skills learned from the European colonizer, the petty bourgeois activist could organize and rationalize the "culture of the rural and urban working masses" [55] in his own cultural reconversion as the political leader of

Africans making their own history and culture. Still, this cultural re-awakening also demanded an effective political organization. Indeed, this fusion of petty bourgeois activists, urban wage earners, and the rural producers into a coherent political bloc capable of reclaiming and recreating their *national* autonomy and identity required, for Cabral, the construction of a powerful national liberation movement, or political party.

The National Liberation Movement as a Party

Cabral records that as a "group of petty bourgeois who were driven by the reality of life in Guinea . . . to try and do something," [56] he and the PAIGC leadership set about building a political party that could successfully organize a liberation movement within a nation lacking a revolutionary working class, peasantry, or intelligentsia. Following his largely cultural conception of colonialism, Cabral describes national liberation as the total rejection of the historical stasis imposed by colonial rule "in which a given socio-economic whole rejects the negation of its historical process. In other words, the national liberation of a people is the regaining of the historical personality of the people, its return to history through the destruction of the imperialist domination to which it was subjected." [57] So armed with "a greater revolutionary consciousness, and the capacity for faithfully interpreting the aspirations of the masses in each phase of the struggle and for identifying themselves more and more with the masses," [58] he maintains that only the petty bourgeoisie can return the people and the nation to their history by creating a party capable of organizing and leading an armed struggle. Even though Cabral tried again and again to work out a negotiated peace with Portugal, he still saw the necessity of waging an armed struggle to keep pressuring Lisbon.

Yet, as it constructs the national liberation movement, the party must not become a tightly disciplined and rigidly centralized Leninist party of the new type. On the contrary, Cabral saw that the relatively undeveloped cultural and social conditions of Guinea-Bissau and other colonized countries necessitate the construction of a party whose essential tasks are pedagogical. That is, in a situation in which colonial exploitation and oppression are manifested in cultural destruction, the revolutionary political party had to concentrate on cultural re-creation and renewal. The most important task of this pedagogical party, which was to be performed hand in hand with the national struggle, is *education*. It should aim at "creating in the countryside and in the towns not only a new life but also—and even more important—a New Man, fully conscious of his national, continental and international rights and duties." [59]

Moreover, Cabral did not see the party as an omniscient intellectual vanguard charged with the historical task of enlightening the dimly aware masses with its omnicompetent scientific doctrine. Instead, for Cabral, the party, as the "representative and defender of the culture of the people, must be conscious of the fact that, whatever may be the material conditions of the society it represents, the society is the bearer and creator of culture. The liberation movements must furthermore embody the mass character, the popular character of the culture—which is not and never could be the privilege of one or of some sectors of society." [60] Thus the PAIGC's institutions were organized to provide new, unprecedented opportunities to the population to participate in new cultural, economic, political, and social environments—schools, clinics, village assemblies, people's militias, popular stores, agrarian collectives, party committees, or army units—that the colonizer had denied to them. Ultimately, "national liberation is necessarily an act of *culture*," [61] and the party that guides this popular re-creation of culture, in Cabral's eyes, is nothing but "the organized political expression of the culture of the people who are undertaking the struggle." [62]

Cabral's idea of the party as a national liberation movement engaged in cultural re-creation closely parallels Gramsci's idea of the party as "the Modern Prince," discussed in Chapter 3. Both are what Gramsci would consider the national and organizational "germs of a collective will tending to become universal and total." [63] Clearly, Cabral would agree with Gramsci that the party pedagogically must awaken and develop "a national-popular collective will" [64] by imparting the insights of its organic intellectuals to the mobilizing classes from which these intellectuals are drawn. Cabral, like Gramsci, realizes also that "any formation of a national-popular collective will is impossible, unless the great mass of peasant farmers burst simultaneously into political life." [65] Still, the constitution of this revolutionary will and consciousness remains a pedagogical process in which the party, under the conditions of colonialism, in Gramsci's words, "must be and cannot but be the proclaimer and organizer of an intellectual and moral reform, which also means creating the terrain for a subsequent development of the national-popular collective will towards the realization of a superior, total form of modern civilization." [66] That is, as Cabral contends, "a reconversion of minds—of mental sets—is thus indispensable to the true integration of people into the liberation movement." [67]

Nevertheless, this moral reconversion of popular consciousness cannot occur without, as Gramsci states, "a programme of economic reform—indeed the programme of economic reform is precisely the concrete form in which every intellectual and moral reform presents itself." [68] Since the colonial administration expropriated the colonized people's productive forces, the national liberation movement also must undertake a systematic program of economic reform (or the repossessing of the nation's economic development from outside control) that underpins its equally wide-ranging program of intellectual (or the rebuilding of a new consciousness and new social individuality) and moral (or the re-creation of popular national history and self-rule) reform by staging the national liberation struggle. Given the situation of anticolonial struggle, the party serves as the liberated nation-state *in nuce* and, again as Gramsci suggests, "must be conceived of as an 'educator,' inasmuch as it tends precisely to create a new type or level of civilization." [69]

Cabral sees the party as it leads the national liberation struggle as the most effective mediation of the national movement's history-making role. As Gramsci maintains with regard to the practice of party building, "an historical act can only be performed by 'collective man,' and this presupposes the attainment of a 'cultural-social' unity through which a multiplicity of dispersed wills, with heterogeneous aims, are welded together with a single aim, on the basis of an equal and common conception of the world, both general and particular, operating in transitory bursts (in emotional ways) or permanently (where the intellectual base is so well rooted, assimilated and experienced that it becomes passion)." [70] For the masses of the people, who are for Cabral "the only social sector who can preserve and build it up and make *history*," [71] the party provides new social structures, political institutions, and cultural education. As Gramsci suggests, it is within the popular party that "a new way of conceiving the world and man is born and this conception is no longer reserved to the great intellectuals, to professional philosophers, but tends rather to become a popular, mass phenomenon, with a concretely world-wide character, capable of modifying (even if the result includes hybrid combinations) popular thought and mummified popular culture." [72]

To educate the party leadership, Cabral emphasizes the need for training "people with a mentality which could transcend the context of the national liberation struggle," [73] and preparing these cadres with the skills for continuing the pedagogical and democratic functions of the party after the national liberation struggle. Even once political liberation has been attained, Cabral affirms the principle that the population's ongoing cultural, economic, and social "liberation should be the work of the people themselves, who should rely primarily on their own resources to attain this goal." [74] In Guinea-Bissau, as Davidson remarks, these educationally oriented party leaders were the PAIGC's backbone in the national liberation struggle, even though "they have no political power, no physical security, no reassurance in numbers. . . . Always they can act only by personal courage and persuasion." [75] Still, the party's impact comes from the persuasiveness of its pedagogical leaders, who, in "having to live day by day with various peasant groups in the heart of the rural populations, come to know the people better. They discover at the grass roots the richness of their cultural values (philosophic, political, artistic, social and moral), acquire a clearer understanding of the economic realities of the country, of the problems, sufferings, and hopes of popular masses." [76] With this equal, open, democratic exchange between the party cadres and the villages, or "this tireless work of listening and talking, explaining, watching, correcting, suggesting, guiding and generally *representing* the Party to the peasant and the peasants to the party," [77] Cabral asserts that his experience showed

> the leaders realize, not without a certain astonishment, the richness of spirit, the capacity for reasoned discussion and clear exposition of ideas, the facility for understanding and assimilating concepts on the part of populations, groups who yesterday were forgotten, if not despised, and who were considered incompetent by the colonizer and even by some nationals. The leaders thus enrich their cultures—develop personally their capacity to serve the movement in the service of the people. [78]

Because of its essentially pedagogical role, Cabral did not see the party developing into an organizational weapon to be wielded exclusively by militant intellectuals who are above and beyond the masses of the people. Instead, the pedagogical party provides "the weapon of theory" [79] that both the people and the party leaders must learn to use collectively for their mutual self- and group development as more autonomous history-creating and culture-constituting subjects. Although the party leaders are relatively more literate, more conscious, and more educated than the rank and file, the mass membership under their guidance soon must prove their own potential for becoming literate, conscious, and educated with the reforms brought by the national liberation movement.

Ultimately, the party succeeds through confronting and understanding the concrete conditions of African colonialism, which reduce the essential struggle to *"the struggle against our own weaknesses."* [80] Specifically, the party struggles against illiteracy, superstition, passivity, and disorganization as a means of attacking the colonizer. By recognizing that "culture is simultaneously the fruit of a people's history and a determinant of history, by the positive or negative influences which it exerts on the evolution of relationships," [81] Cabral seeks to turn the indigenous culture, which had been suppressed under colonialism to dominate and weaken the indigenous masses, into a positive force that makes strengths out of weaknesses, turns diversity into unity, ignorance into enlightenment, and paralysis into progress.

To Cabral, the pedagogical party "must be capable of distinguishing the essential from the secondary, the positive from the negative, the progressive from the reactionary in order to characterize the master line which defines progressively a *national culture*." [82] As both a product and a determinant of culture, the pedagogical party and its weapon of theory works to create a new moral milieu in which a new form of social individuality can emerge without the deformations imposed by colonialism, which sought to reduce the indigenous peoples into completely passive, dominated, and weak objects. In contrast, the new social individuality seeks to reclaim the indigenous peoples' history and culture by encouraging them to learn the new skills and universal values appropriate for active, autonomous, and strong political subjects no longer hobbled by the ignorance, poverty, and dependence caused by colonial relations.

Consequently, Cabral's idea of the party, which assumes the form of a national liberation movement and uses the techniques of armed struggle, can be seen as a powerful agent for furthering political development in colonized countries. The party attains its educational goals to the extent that it instructs its cadres and followers in the practical responsibilities of *political subjectivity*. Instead of remaining passive political objects, treated like children by colonial tax collectors, labor bosses, and police, the Africans can regain and elaborate their own political subjectivity by fighting with guerrilla militias, working in party stores and clinics, learning at party-established schools, and participating in party political committees and bureaus. The defensive passivity of the rural producers, rooted in their political powerlessness, begins to break down as the mobilized peasant villagers—men, women, young, and old—increasingly learn the personal and communal skills for acting as conscious, responsible, and free political subjects engaged in collective political action.

Also, as it organizes a new political consensus, or Gramsci's "national-popular collective will," along formal lines, the party projects a new form of modern *social individuality*. The social organizations of the national liberation movement embody formal institutions and personal opportunities for the once colonized individual to "mentally decolonize" him- or herself, redefining his or her personal identity and roles in new age, sex, family, communal, economic, political, and technical relations. Thus the political party, with its popular army, village schools, popular clinics and stores, village assemblies, and political committees and bureaus, teaches both party activists and followers new forms of personal and communal interaction largely unknown to them under colonialism. And these new forms of human interaction and individual models are mediations of socialist development that can begin to break down the oppressive social customs involving young-old, male-female, intrafamily-extrafamily, or intervillage-extravillage relations in colonial society.[83]

Finally, for Cabral, the party must attempt to open a sphere of *cultural universality* as it creates the opportunities for relatively parochial rural peoples collectively to construct their own specifically national culture, society, and state. As he states:

> In the framework of the conquest of national independence and in the perspective of developing the economic and social progress of the people, the objectives must be at least the following: *development of a popular culture* and of all positive indigenous cultural values; *development of a national culture* based upon the history and the achievements of the struggle itself; constant promotion of the *political and moral awareness* of the people (of all social groups) as well as *patriotism*, of the spirit of sacrifice and devotion to the cause of independence, of justice, and of progress; development of a technical, technological, and scientific culture, compatible with the requirements for progress; development, on the basis of a critical assimilation of man's achievements in the domains of art, science, literature, etc., of a *universal culture* for perfect integration into the contemporary world, in the perspectives of its evolution; constant and generalized promotion of feelings of humanism, of solidarity, of respect and disinterested devotion to human beings.[84]

Thus, as the party generates a national political symbolism, a secular political mythology, and a national political language, which did not exist under colonialism, this nascent national culture also can gain access to more universal cultural forms. By partially eroding the narrow ethnic, linguistic, racial, and regional parochialism of the diverse peasant cultures, Cabral saw the party, at least, providing chances that may or may not be exercised for its followers to participate in systems of sophisticated cultural action, ranging from modern science, world culture, scientific medicine, advanced military technology, and modern communications to formal ideology, the political party, and the nation-state.

The party's program for initiating socialist development, then, starts a modernizing process in colonial societies that hitherto and otherwise would not have experienced much of the emancipatory secularization, social differentiation, and personal autonomy implicit in modern social forms, but not present under European colonialism. In turn, Cabral saw this experiment in citizenship and partisanship as laying, potentially, the complete foundations for full socialist development and a more participatory democratic society after the winning of the national revolution.

Conclusions:
Cabral and Socialist Development

For Cabral, socialist development in western and southern Africa implied more than merely declaring the collective state ownership and party control of the means of production in economic and social development, which was the practical outcome of orthodox Marxism-Leninism from East Germany to North Korea. In part, of course, socialism implies this technical moment, or the *rationalization* of ownership and control in the productive forces by altering existing *technical-administrative relations* to serve the immediate producers more rationally. However, socialism also implies the concomitant development of equality, emancipation, and liberation. That is, socialism entails, in addition to rationalization, an economic moment, or the *equalization* of access to, and use of, productive forces in order to serve more equitably the individual and group needs of the immediate producers by changing existing *property relations*; a political moment, or the *emancipation* of the immediate producers from irrational, unequal, and oppressive social and political institutions by restructuring existing *authority relations*; and a social psychological moment, or the *liberation* of the immediate producers from outmoded, limiting, and inhumane personal and social practices and beliefs by reconstructing existing *cultural relations*. In the last analysis, full socialist development assumes the complete creation of each of these transformations, along with their rational integration into a new social formation under the collective control of the immediate producers.

Cabral's preeminence as a theorist of socialist development lies in the equal emphasis that he places on each of these integral aspects of socialism.[85] He correctly refuses to settle for simple political independence in the national liberation struggle or for the mere nationalization of the means of production as the strongest step toward socialism.[86] Political independence must not be a mystifying outcome of neocolonial relations of domination; it must embody the political emancipation and social psychological liberation implicit in the "inalienable right of every people to have its own history." [87] Cabral demands that local forces retain command of the economy, or that "economic activity will be governed by the principles of democratic socialism," [88] which also must reclaim the nation's right to control "the process of development of the national productive forces." [89] Yet, in the process, the nation's control of its own productive forces must not be franchised out to domestic or foreign special interests. Rather, it must embody domestic control of the economy through new local forms of technical-administrative rationalization and economic equalization that the previous colonial regime repressed.

This entire process of slowly developing a socialist society in all of its aspects is, at the same time, to be achieved by the democratic means of collective control. For Cabral, socialist development begins to emerge and can be attained only by means of *popular collective control* by

> a group of persons constituted as a group, and not by a single person or some persons of that group. Collectively to control, in a given group, means to study problems together so as to find the best solutions; means to take decisions together; means to profit from the experience and intelligence of each member, and thus of all members, so as better to direct, to instruct, to command.[90]

Of course, one must note that, in actual practice, the fortunes of Guinea-Bissau have not been particularly auspicious since Cabral's assassination and the declaration of independence by the PAIGC on September 24, 1973. Although the formal structures of the PAIGC village committee system functioned relatively well, the economic weaknesses of Guinea-Bissau's meager productive forces dogged the PAIGC leadership after the Portuguese withdrawal in 1974. The small size of the nation's population, productive land, and natural resources, coupled with poor weather, insufficient foreign aid, and the destruction of experienced cadres during the war, have kept Guinea-Bissau in a deep economic slump not unlike that in Angola and Mozambique.

At the same time, even though Cabral's institution-building acumen allayed many tensions for quite some time, two new threats, also being experienced in Angola and Mozambique, have surfaced in Guinea-Bissau's public life. First, the serious racial tensions between Cape Verde and the mainland, between Cape Verdean mestizos and African cadres in the PAIGC and between the largely mestizo-staffed state organs and the African population that Cabral was very concerned about have broken out into violent conflict.[91] These contradictions, which have been manifest in the ongoing debates over totally unifying the Cape Verde islands with the mainland of Guinea-Bissau, finally exploded on November 16, 1980, as anti-Cape Verdean elements in the PAIGC successfully staged a coup against President Luis de Almeida Cabral and his Cape Verdean supporters.[92] Dissatisfaction over the adoption of a new constitution earlier in the month sparked these moves among the military and Africans in the PAIGC, who were unhappy with the new constitutional definition of Guinean nationality, government powers, and presidential authority.

This unfortunate development, in turn, tied into the second threat that Cabral himself recognized as intrinsic to the revolutionary role of the alienated petty bourgeoisie. That is, once these elements successfully pulled off the revolution, as the revolutionary vanguard possessing considerable moral authority and political power, they must choose between "betrayal or suicide as a class."[93] Like Fanon, Cabral saw that the petty bourgeoisie did have a propensity to betray its best interests in favor of power, privilege, and position; hence he constantly stressed the "struggle against our weaknesses." In betraying the revolution, they would, Cabral felt, set themselves up as a new privileged ruling caste, exploiting the indigenous population for the benefit of outside interests. In committing "class suicide," Cabral hoped, the petty bourgeoisie would work themselves out of a job by educating the populace to be their own rulers. Yet, the events of November 16, 1980, suggest that instead the revolutionary petty bourgeoisie had used the party to commit another kind of "class suicide" and, as Chaliand notes, only "to be reborn as a bureaucracy."[94] Thus, instead of furthering the project of popular collective control, the tendency toward bureaucratization in the PAIGC party, military, and state has slowed even more the painfully slow progress of Guinea-Bissau's agrarian economy. The stagnation in the nation's political and economic life during the 1980s only reemphasized the dismal prospects of Guinea-Bissau after these counterrevolutionary events.

Still, Cabral's theoretical vision of socialist development, with its equal attention to cultural liberation, political emancipation, and economic equalization as well as technical-administrative rationalization, provides an alternative to African elites intent upon an indigenous socialist mode of development. Like Machel and Mondlane in Mozambique,[95] Cabral addresses himself cogently to the problems of reclaiming the nation's suppressed history and culture from both colonialism and neocolonialism; building a popular, democratic, and collectively controlled party; quickly educating people who have been denied the possibilities of fully learning their own indigenous culture, world culture, and modern science; correctly identifying the social class forces and political blocs of colonial society; and developing a humane socialist order fully conscious of the political, cultural, and social dimensions of the socialist tradition.

Amilcar Cabral's Marxism represents in Africa, like Antonio Gramsci's thought in Europe, one of the most comprehensive and serious efforts to constitute an organically rooted, historically grounded, and nonstatist form of Marxism yet conceived in that region. Rather than formally recapitulating some of the successes and many of the failures of Soviet Marxism in new historical situations, both Cabral and Gramsci approach Marxism as a flexible method, a philosophy of praxis. Thus both the PAIGC and the Italian Communist Party (PCI) developed into radically different institutions, far more suited to their own immediate milieux, as well as to widespread imitation, than the Communist party of the Soviet Union. Perry Anderson has argued that only Antonio Gramsci, of all the major theoreticians among the diverse enrollment of the Western Marxist schools, has successfully "embodied in his person a revolutionary unity of theory and practice of the type that had defined the classical heritage."[96] If Anderson, however, had increased his theoretical scope to include that region of the "West" usually denied by the West—Africa—he would have realized that Cabral, like Gramsci, also continues in his own way "the classical traditions of historical materialism" with his considerations of the "motion of capitalism as a mode of production, analysis of the political machinery of the bourgeois state, [and] strategy of the class struggle necessary to overthrow it"[97] under African conditions of colonial domination. The extent of Cabral's theoretical achievements is even more impressive, as Chapters 8 and 9 will reveal, in view of the prevailing discourses of modernization and development or the conceptual understanding of political culture in developing countries typically used outside of the Third and Fourth Worlds to interpret change in these regions.

Notes

1. Paul A. Beckett, "Frantz Fanon and Sub-Saharan Africa: Notes on the Contemporary Significance of His Thought," *Africa Today* 19, no. 2 (Spring 1972), 60.

2. For recent discussions, see Patrick Chabal, *Amilcar Cabral: Revolutionary Leadership and People's War* (Cambridge: Cambridge University Press, 1983); and Ronald Chilcote, *Amilcar Cabral's Theory and Practice: A Critical Guide* (Boulder, CO: Lynne Reinner, 1990). Also see David A. Andelman, "Profile: Amilcar Cabral," *African Report* 15, no. 5 (May 1970), 18-19; Robert Blackey, "Fanon and Cabral: A Contrast in Theories of Revolution for Africa," *Journal of Modern African Studies* 12, no. 2 (June 1974), 191-210; Gerard Chaliand, *Armed Struggle in Africa: With the Guerrillas in "Portuguese Guinea"* (New York: Monthly Review Press, 1969); Gerard Chaliand, *Revolution in the Third World* (New York: Viking, 1977); Ronald Chilcote, "The Political Thought of Amilcar Cabral," *Journal of Modern African Studies* 6, no. 3 (October 1968); Basil Davidson, *The Liberation of Guiné: Aspects of an African Revolution* (Harmondsworth: Penguin, 1969); Bernard Mugbane, "Amilcar Cabral: Evolution of Revolutionary Thought," *Ufahamu* 2, no. 2 (Fall 1971), 71-87; Charles McCollester, "The Political Thought of Amilcar Cabral," *Monthly Review* 24, no. 10 (March 1973); Michael S. Morgado, "Amilcar Cabral's Theory of Cultural Revolution," *Black Images* 3, no. 2 (1974), 3-16; and Stephanie Urdang, "Towards a Successful Revolution: The Struggle in Guinea-Bissau," *Objective: Justice* 6 (January-March 1975). For compilations of Cabral's writings in English, see Amilcar Cabral, *Unity and Struggle: Speeches and Writings* (New York: Monthly Review Press, 1979); and Amilcar Cabral, *Return to the Source: Selected Speeches of Amilcar Cabral* (New York: Monthly Review Press, 1973), 59.

3. Davidson, *Liberation of Guiné*, 29-30.

4. Beckett, "Frantz Fanon and Sub-Saharan Africa," 60.

5. Amilcar Cabral, *Revolution in Guinea: Selected Texts* (New York: Monthly Review Press, 1969), 92-93.

6. Chaliand, *Revolution in the Third World*, 70.

7. See, for example, Antonio Gramsci, *Selections from the Prison Notebooks,* ed. and trans. by Quintin Hoare and Geoffrey Nowell Smith (New York: International, 1971), 381-419.

8. For further discussion, see Carl Boggs, *Gramsci's Marxism* (London: Pluto, 1976); Joseph LaPalombara, "The Italian Communist Party and Changing Italian Society," *Eurocommunism: The Italian Case,* ed. by Austin Ranney and Giovanni Satori (Washington, DC: American Enterprise Institute, 1978); and Paul Piccone, "Gramsci's Marxism: Beyond Lenin and Togliatti," *Theory and Society* 1, no. 3 (1976), 485-512.

9. Cabral's job as an agronomist allowed him tremendous opportunities to do what few, if any, African intellectuals have ever done, namely, gain firsthand experience of his country's people, geography, economy, agriculture, and society in a systematic survey of Guinea-Bissau's rural sectors. See, for example, his "Agricultural Census of Guiné," *Unity and Struggle,* 4-16.

10. For an excellent bibliographical and biographical overview of Cabral's work, see Ronald H. Chilcote, "Amilcar Cabral: A Bio-Bibliography of His Life and Thought," *African Library Journal* 5 (Winter 1963), 289-307.

11. In addition to the indigenous African population, 3,000 to 4,000 Portuguese settlers and nearly 30,000 Portuguese military personnel resided in or were stationed in Guinea-Bissau. See Richard Gibson, *African Liberation Movements: Contemporary Struggles Against White Minority Rule* (London: Oxford University Press, 1972), 247.

12. See David M. Abshire and Michael A. Samuels, *Portuguese Africa: A Handbook* (New York: Praeger, 1969).

13. Davidson, *Liberation of Guiné,* 21.

14. Ibid., 22.

15. Ibid., 26.

16. Ibid., 27.

17. Ibid., 28.

18. Cabral, *Revolution in Guinea,* 76.

19. Cabral, *Return to the Source,* 41-42.

20. Ibid., 42.

21. Ibid., 43.

22. Gramsci, *Prison Notebooks,* 261-264. For further discussion, see Boggs, *Gramsci's Marxism,* 36-54.

23. Cabral, *Return to the Source,* 40.

24. Ibid., 39.

25. Ibid., 41.

26. Ibid., 40.

27. Ibid., 48.

28. Ibid., 57.

29. Cabral perpetually attempted to justify the PAIGC's activities in terms of international law and before the public forums of international organizations. See *Revolution in Guinea,* 24-49; and *Return to the Source,* 15-38.

30. Cabral, *Return to the Source,* 58.

31. Ibid., 49.

32. Ibid. Cabral continues by observing the effectiveness of the colonizer's hegemony-building policies: "Recognizing this reality, the colonizer who represses or inhibits significant cultural activity on the part of the masses at the base of the social pyramid, strengthens and protects the prestige and the cultural influence of the ruling class at the summit. The colonizer installs chiefs who support him and who are to some degree accepted by the masses; he gives these chiefs material privileges such as education for their eldest children, creates chiefdoms where they did not exist before, develops cordial relations with religious leaders, builds mosques, organizes journeys to Mecca, etc. And above all, by means of the repressive organs of colonial administration, he guarantees economic and social privileges to the ruling class in their relations with the masses." Ibid., 46.

33. Ibid., 47.

34. Ibid., 52.

35. Ibid.

36. Ibid., 51.

37. Georg Lukács, *History and Class Consciousness* (Cambridge: MIT Press, 1971), 1.

38. Perry Anderson, *Considerations on Western Marxism* (London: New Left, 1976), 80.

39. Davidson, *Liberation of Guiné,* 30.

40. Cabral, *Revolution in Guinea,* 56-75.

41. Ibid., 59.

42. Ibid., 61.

43. Ibid., 92.

44. Ibid., 62, 61.

45. Cabral, *Return to the Source,* 43.

46. Ibid., 60.

47. Ibid., 69.

48. Cabral, *Revolution in Guinea,* 62-63.

49. Cabral, *Return to the Source,* 63.

50. Ibid., 64-65.

51. Cabral, *Revolution in Guinea,* 105. Here Cabral remarks that "the generally embryonic character of the working classes and the economic, social and cultural situation of the physical force of the most importance in the national liberation struggle—the peasantry—do not allow these two main forces to distinguish true national independence from fictitious political independence."

52. Ibid., 66.

53. Ibid., 66-67.

54. Gramsci, *Prison Notebooks,* 5.

55. Cabral, *Return to the Source,* 47.

56. Cabral, *Revolution in Guinea,* 66.

57. Ibid., 102.

58. Ibid., 109.

59. Ibid., 90.

60. Cabral, *Return to the Source,* 43-44.

61. Ibid., 43.

62. Ibid., 43-44.

63. Gramsci, *Prison Notebooks,* 129.

64. Ibid., 130.

65. Ibid., 132.

66. Ibid., 133.

67. Cabral, *Return to the Source,* 44.

68. Gramsci, *Prison Notebooks,* 133.

69. Ibid., 247.

70. Ibid., 349.

71. Cabral, *Return to the Source,* 61.

72. Gramsci, *Prison Notebooks,* 417.

73. Cabral, *Revolution in Guinea,* 67.

74. Ibid., 42.

75. Davidson, *Liberation of Guiné,* 83.

76. Cabral, *Return to the Source,* 54.

77. Davidson, *Liberation of Guiné,* 83.

78. Cabral, *Return to the Source,* 54.

79. Cabral, *Revolution in Guinea,* 90.

80. Ibid., 91.

81. Cabral, *Return to the Source,* 54.

82. Ibid., 47-48.

83. See Stephanie Urdang, *Fighting Two Colonialisms: Women in Guinea-Bissau* (New York: Monthly Review Press, 1979), 167-186, 238-259.

84. Cabral, *Return to the Source,* 55.

85. For a statement of his theory as policy, see "PAIGC Program," *Guinea-Bissau: Toward Final Victory* (Richmond, BC: Liberation Support Movement Press, 1974), 10-14.

86. For a detailed discussion of this problem in the socialist transition, see Wlodzimierz Brus, *The Economics and Politics of Socialism* (London: Routledge & Kegan Paul, 1973); and Wlodzimierz Brus, *Socialist Ownership and Political Systems* (London: Routledge & Kegan Paul, 1975).

87. Cabral, *Revolution in Guinea,* 102.

88. Ibid., 171.

89. Ibid., 102.

90. Davidson, *The Liberation of Guiné,* 128.

91. See Amilcar Cabral, *P.A.I.G.C. Unidade e Luta* (Lisbon: Nova Aurora, 1974), 69-132.

92. *New York Times* (November 16, 1980).

93. Chaliand, *Revolution in the Third World*, 188.

94. Ibid., 189.

95. See Samora M. Machel, *O Processo a revolucao democratica popular em Mozambique* (Lisbon: Garcia & Carvalho, 1975); and Eduardo Mondlane, *The Struggle for Mozambique* (Baltimore: Penguin, 1970).

96. Anderson, *Considerations on Western Marxism*, 45.

97. Ibid., 44-45.

8

Discourses of Modernization
and Development:
Theory and Doctrine After 1945

There are many voices speaking in the discourses of development. They are all multilayered, complex, and multidimensional. In addition to the discourse of national liberation articulated by such thinkers as Cabral and Fanon, there are entire disciplines of analysis constructed around the notions of modernization and development. Because of this diversity, the discourse on developmental change often has proven conflicted, contradictory, and confusing. Indeed, the "conventional wisdom" in development studies dismisses the entire gamut of traditional modernization and development theory from the 1950s, 1960s, and 1970s as totally irrelevant today. This attitude is gravely mistaken. When reexamined for its ironies and unintended consequences, the discursive grid of modernization and development thinking actually can reveal much about the nature of power and change in the contemporary world-system. This insight, in turn, will be affirmed in the next chapter, with its reexamination of how political culture and individual subjectivity have been defined in many social scientific analyses of the developing countries.

For more than three decades, American and European social scientists as well as their students in the Third and Fourth Worlds have sought to formalize a scientific theory of modernization and development by using a particular type of language within a peculiar political discourse. This discourse, for example, suggests the following:

Modernization . . . depends upon, "the systematic," sustained and purposeful application of human energies to the "rational" control of man's physical
and social environment for various human purposes.[1]

Modernization involves the diffusion of what one expert calls the "world
culture"—"based on advanced technology and the spirit of science, on a
rational view of life, a secular approach to social relations, a feeling for
justice in public affairs and, above all else, on the acceptance in the political
realm of belief that the prime unit of the polity should be the nation-state." [2]

"Modernization" may be defined as the process by which historically
evolved institutions are adapted to the rapidly changing functions that reflect
the unprecedented increase in man's knowledge, permitting control over his
revolution. This process of adaptation had its origins and initial influence in
the societies of Western Europe, but in the nineteenth and twentieth centuries
these changes have been extended to all other societies and have resulted in
a worldwide transformation affecting all human relationships.[3]

Modernity, restated in the terms of this discursive framework, means
gaining rational control of the physical and social environment, building
a liberal democratic state, participating in world culture, and joining the
scientific revolution. The meaning assigned to the complex processes of
modernization and *development* by this discourse similarly boils down to
finding practical ways to engage certain states and societies in these
macrosocial processes. Yet, in posing their discourses this way, and
perhaps even contrary to their conscious intentions, these general *social
scientific theories* actually have served as *ideological legitimations* for
the "modernized"—North America and Europe—to dominate the "modernizing"—the so-called Third World of Asia, Africa, and Latin America—as the former developed "underdevelopment" among the latter.
Cabral's project of national liberation, cultural revolution, and political
transformation, on the other hand, was aimed directly at discrediting these
ideological pretensions in Western political discourses about modernity
and development.

Conventional discourses of social scientific explanation often portray
the development process, *in theory*, as a largely voluntary and fully
progressive inner transformation of a society's native potential to accommodate greater social complexity, which follows from economic, political, and social policies adopted by its more than willing leadership and/or
actions by its more than willing populace. This scientific discourse's
neutral chronicle of events, however, clearly disguises the interests of
those social forces—such as multilateral aid institutions, transnational

corporations, and the industrial nations—that actually are behind the modernization process. Ultimately, *in practice*, this process involves the mainly involuntary and basically destructive transfer of new foreign institutions and their values to a less than willing populace by means of political domination, military coercion, and economic manipulation. Hence, in appearing as a general theory for scientifically explaining macrosocial change, modernization and development discourses, in actuality, serve as a vitally important ideology mystifying the real processes whereby the individuals and societies of *modernizing* countries "adapt" themselves to the passage through modernization's "stages" or "phases." Behind these stages and beyond these phases, the social forces of *modernized* countries sophisticate their "rational control," extend the "world culture," and expand the "scientific revolution," especially over the modernizing countries.

Since the end of World War II, a diverse range of American and European social scientists have devoted their energies to constructing elaborate and sophisticated theories of modernization and development. At the same time, a significant number of government programs, beginning in the United States with the bilateral aid packages built into the Truman Doctrine and the multilateral development assistance schemes of the European Recovery Program and continuing to the present operations of the World Bank and International Monetary Fund, have been put on line by the NATO and OECD nations to facilitate the modernization and development of their organizations' members as well as that of their major Third and Fourth World trading partners. In many respects, the central premises of these social scientists' *theories* did not significantly inform or influence the basic precepts of the policymakers' *doctrines*. Still, Packenham argues that "the doctrines and the theories were similar in important ways, and that both were profoundly affected by some largely inarticulated premises of American political ideology." [4] Indeed, the hegemonic American political ideology of classical liberalism has often misdirected both the theory and the doctrine of development since 1945.[5] Here, however, I want to indicate how another set of inarticulate assumptions, premises, and values present in the discursive grids of American social science theory and government doctrine also decisively have misdirected development policies under the post-1945 era of *Pax Americana*.

On the whole, the entire conceptual program of modernization and development doctrines since 1945 has embodied the cultural assumptions, political premises, and economic values of the United States as it fought the Cold War from within the bulwarks of the NATO and OECD bloc. In fact, the first and most important policy experiences acquired by American development agencies came in administering the European Recovery Program, the Economic Cooperation Administration, and the Technical Cooperation Administration in Europe. These experiences in an already developed European context, in turn, were misapplied to less developed Asian, African, and Latin American contexts in the 1950s and 1960s by means of Title IV of the Economic Cooperation Administration, the Act for International Development, the Development Loan Fund, and the Foreign Assistance Act.

In taking these American government and corporate policies to the Third and Fourth Worlds, however, the doctrines of development there largely have meant the acceleration of "underdevelopment," as the development theories created to deal with "metropolitan" Europe have destructively misdirected the actual developmental needs of Asian, African, and Latin American nations.[6] Hence what has been labeled "development" in the Third and Fourth Worlds since 1945 has meant the "corification" or the "metropolitanization" of certain classes, industries, and institutions there in order to integrate certain key sectors of their economies into the larger transnational economic system constructed by major transnational banks and corporations and the OECD states, under American leadership, since 1945. The initial motivation behind these efforts was, of course, anticommunism, as the United States sought to contain the USSR as a threatening alternative to transnational capitalism. As the USSR has declined as a credible threat, the maintenance of the same modern global economy and transnational civil society made possible by resisting Soviet aggression has become the dynamic force sustaining the discursive disciplines of development.

Consequently, the discourses of development as well as the social scientific theories constructed to explain the modernization and development processes mistakenly are rooted in the cultural, technological, historical, and political premises of North American and Western European society rather than in the actual needs and real experiences of the Third and Fourth World countries—articulated autonomously in local terms by the indigenous peoples—that are working on their development. Like Western Europe after 1945, the developing world has been remade in the discursive design of American containment thinking. Now, new development theories and doctrines need to be constructed that address the actual needs, real limits, and concrete potential of Third and Fourth World countries in terms of their own histories, their own means of making choices, and their own structures of decision constraints and benefit allocations. I cannot even pretend to undertake that task within the confines of this chapter. Still, I can identify some of the flaws and failings of prevailing theories and doctrines that have prevented such tasks from being undertaken.

The Social Origins of the Theory

World War II represented a major crisis for the internal regulation of the advanced industrial metropolitan economy. Having lost out on the heyday of European imperialism because of their relative latecoming to great power status, the Axis bloc of Germany, Italy, and Japan had attempted to "imperialize the imperium" by seeking colonial possessions in North Africa, the Balkans, the Near East, the Soviet Union, China, and Indochina, which threatened the great European powers of Great Britain and France as well as the commercial and industrial networks of the United States. Yet, in the process of defeating the Axis, the entire pre-1939 metropolitan order was virtually destroyed. The great European powers were eclipsed by the new American and Soviet superpowers. The already weakened European colonial system began to unravel completely before the demands for decolonization and the rising costs of empire. Finally, the economic relations between the industrialized Northern Hemisphere and preindustrial Southern Hemisphere were knocked off their Eurocentric axis as the powerful American economy expanded its business dealings abroad.

The entire experience of the World War I and World War II generation totally contradicted the nearly three-centuries-old European ideology of enlightenment, which discursively had cast the European (and later the North American) White man with the burden of bringing the fruits of European science, technology, industry, and statecraft to the non-Western world in the form of material progress, rational enlightenment, and advanced civilization. As Cabral argued, these self-serving discourses of European cultural superiority served to mystify how the European empires in Asia, Africa, and Latin America were built upon the foundations of racism, genocide, and forced labor.

By 1945, the dynamics of this European "enlightenment," which had promised civilizing progress as the by-product of technologically guided instrumental reason, finally was recognized even in Europe as having created brutalizing chaos as part and parcel of the Western civilization. Instead of continually expanding civilization, the finest minds, the fullest energies, and the widest array of resources in the European metropole had spent years to create Auschwitz, Hiroshima, and the Gulag. The political discourses grounded in the transcendent logos of European civilization, enlightenment, and progress, then, by 1945 had been shattered in the political transformations unfolding across Europe since 1914. As a result, both intellectual and power vacuums were created that the former European empires and colonizers could not begin to fill. The weak reed of "Westernization," which conjured up images of the wartime struggle by the democratic, capitalist Western nations resisting, first, German and Japanese fascism, and then Stalinist totalitarianism, was partly salvaged by social scientific theory and government doctrine in the United States, as such programs as the Marshall Plan, the Point Four Doctrine, and the Agency for International Development had to be legitimated and explained. However, with their desire to overcome the European idioms of imperialism—such as the "White man's burden," the "civilizing mission," and "civilization"—American social scientists and policymakers soon adopted the more neutral notions of "modernity" and "development" to account for and explain the process of social transformation after 1945.

As a result, in government bureaus, multilateral development agencies, and the social science departments of universities throughout the United States, urban anthropologists, rural sociologists, development economists, public administrators, and area specialists all accepted, to some extent, the modernization and development discourses to interpret and, then, to manipulate the processes of "modernization." Rather than seeing the emerging nations starting down the *European* road to "civilization," "enlightenment," or "progress," these new theorists recast these macrosocial changes in a somewhat new and different *American* ideology, which stressed the traditional American myths of economic growth, national self-determination, democratization, and technological innovation. The most obvious and widely accepted example of this transformation is, of course, W. W. Rostow's *The Stages of Economic Growth: A Non-Communist Manifesto*. Explicitly anticommunist and allegedly non-ideological, Rostow sought to build a positive scientific model of modernizing economic and social development, which he ironically pegged discursively to metaphors of aerial flight. Seeing "uniformities in the sequence of modernization but also—and equally—the uniqueness of each nation's experience," he identified five stages of growth—the traditional society, the preconditions for takeoff, the takeoff, the drive to maturity, and the age of mass consumption—that all societies must traverse to become modern.[7] By rejecting the allegedly "ideological" language of European colonialism, or Marxism-Leninism, these American theorists believed they were creating new and more rigorously defined social concepts, such as aggregate economic growth, the takeoff, growing democratization, and extensive industrialization, which could be measured through statistical indicators. By monitoring and measuring variations in these objective indicators, it was believed, social theorists might more "scientifically" explain how and why the emergent nations could be steered into the unavoidable transition to modernity and development in a new *Pax Americana*.

These new thinkers, whom one might describe as *modernizationists*, have worked to realize a very modern discursive ideal, namely, the formalization of a methodologically rigorous and value-neutral conceptual language that could nomologically explain and technologically manage macrosocial change. At best, however, the modernizationists only replaced the discursive and conceptual idioms of European colonialism with ones rooted in America's economic and technological domination of the world economy. The preeminence that the modernizationists' new theory plainly places upon the rational control of the environment, the technological view of life, and the secular approach to social relations engendered by the scientific revolution reveals a substrata of assumptions, beliefs, and intentions deeply rooted in everyday American life. Likewise, the theoretical emphasis put upon liberal capitalist goals—such as rapid economic growth, the autonomy of the nation-state, democratic political processes, and national industrialization—contradicts the alleged scientific neutrality of the modernizationists' new discursive development.

Given the economic and political shifts occurring in the international relations of the industrial metropole after World War II, this conceptual reengineering undertaken by the modernizationists becomes more understandable. By ever-increasing degrees, the modernizationists and their theories gained a "more practical provenance in the expanding commitments of the United States government to the 'development' of many so-called underdeveloped areas." [8] International financial institutions, multinational corporate operations, and international aid agencies, all largely dominated by the United States, preoccupied themselves after 1947 with generating new economic development in Europe and in the Third World. At the same time, these social forces cultivated new discourses, aimed at fostering the development of liberal-democratic regimes and mixed capitalist economies in the emergent colonial countries.

European industrial society, which had organized the nations of the world-system's periphery with formal political empires that mixed statist-entrepreneurial capitalism with an ideology of the enlightened White Christian's civilizing mission, was supplanted by North American technological society. This new industrial state managed the world economy through an informal economic empire based upon the rational-bureaucratic cooperation of an interventionist democratic state and large multinational corporations, which integrated key sectors of the emerging colonial periphery in an economic and political "partnership in beneficence." [9] Hence the conceptual and theoretical innovations begun 30 years ago in the comparative studies of economics, politics, and society are not a fortuitously evolved new phase in the elaboration of a scientific paradigm. On the contrary, modernization and development theories discursively express the social scientific community's response to changes in the political practices of the larger society. They also can be reconsidered ironically as a distorted ideological narrative revealing the actual meaning of these new forms of political domination. Under European hegemony, the advanced industrial metropole wrapped its actions in the ideology of the White man's burden and the Christian civilizing mission. Under American hegemony, the advanced industrial metropole mobilized the ideology of the corporate-managed scientific revolution and its philosophies of "getting science down to business."

The advanced industrial metropole's political values—administered political stability, centralized technical control, cultural secularization, and incremental evolutionary reform—are reflected in the modernizationists' social theories. In fact, "when we strip away the terminology of the behavioral sciences," as Chomsky observes, one witnesses among the modernizationists "the mentality of the colonial civil servant, persuaded of the benevolence of the mother country and the correctness of its vision of world order, and convinced that he understands the true interests of the backward peoples whose welfare he is to administer." [10] Instead of the "White man's burden" in bringing civilization to the periphery, the modernizationists filled their discourses with the "modern man's burden" of bringing the scientific-technological revolution to the periphery. Rather than being merely ethnocentric by virtue of some Eurocentric assumptions, as the old colonialists' myths were, the discourse of the modernizationists suffers from a definite *metrocentricity* inasmuch as many of their allegedly neutral assumptions, premises, and values in fact directly derive from the more culturally homogeneous forms of life being simultaneously imposed by the same material forces in the advanced industrial cores of North America and Western Europe.

Myriad social scientific theories are available to explain modernization—explanations based on structural-functionalism, comparative history, political culture, political psychology, critical historical junctures, collective choice theory, and Marxist political economy, as well as orthodox political sociology.[11] Admittedly, some currents in these discourses seem more powerful than others, some approaches might appear more plausible than others, and a valuable debate might emerge from criticizing and amending the various flaws or strengths of each perspective. I believe, however, that the ideological content and conceptual crisis of modernization and development theory lies deep within each and every one of these particular approaches. The deeper axiological structure that unites these frameworks, then, is more crucial here than the superficial terminological or conceptual particulars that divide them.

While many of these theories differ in their political values or economic assumptions, they largely share a discursive perspective that assumes the desirability of adopting core forms of life. Most of these formulas cast modernity, in some form or another, as the telos of development; they differ merely over "the conditions of change and stability of different types of society, the descriptions of the characteristics and internal dynamics of such different types, the process of the transition from one type to another, and the extent to which such transition evinces an evolutionary tendency to be organized in relatively universal stages." [12] Therefore, the deeper underlying continuities in the diverse concepts and methods of modernization and development theory as well as how these continuities contain a powerful ideological message favoring "metropolitanization" will be the subject of the following critical observations on the language, the explanatory forms, and the concepts used in the modernizationists' discourse.

The Lexicon of Modernization

Throughout history, intellectuals have created a number of different kinds of categories and scales for classifying societies. Social systems have been categorized in technological terms, for instance, as hunting and gathering, agrarian, manufacturing, industrial, or cybernetic systems. They have also been categorized along racial, cultural, geographical, religious, political, economic, or evolutionary scales of comparison. Yet it was only after 1945 that the *chronological* classifications of the modernizationists gained wide acceptance. Using this metaphorical language, based on time, societies are seen as postmodern, modern, modernized, modernizing, premodern, or nonmodern. From this perspective, the metaphor of modernity apparently provides the most general and least value-laden classification system available to explain macrosocial change. It collapses technological, economic, and political measures into a single indicator without raising the problems of race, region, religion, or culture, as did the "Westernization" model. Hence Japan, Israel, China, and the Soviet Union could be labeled "modern" when many balked at regarding them as "Western." Likewise, modernity solved the geographical problem inherent in "Westernization" by allowing the analyst to ignore Greece, Ireland, Mexico, and Portugal when looking at the "modernized" nations of Western Europe, Asia, and North America.

Yet, in staking its claim as a set of extremely objective categories, the modernity metaphor also can be seen as a complex mystification expressed in a time term. Modernity mystifies the actual complex relations of race, culture, geography, religion, politics, economics, and technology by reducing them to a solitary abstract time expression. Modern societies are those systems that already have modernized. To be modern in this discourse is to participate in or to share in one kind of sociocultural totality, namely, an advanced technological, state or corporate capitalist, secularized society such as has mainly developed in the Northern Hemisphere. To be premodern in this discourse is to participate in another less complex social totality. By setting them in this discursive grid as "premodern," moreover, such peoples are automatically defined as wanting modernization or as willing to be forced into modernity as it evolved in the "modernized" regions.

In eighteenth-century Europe, the term *modern* was used to distance and to distinguish the culture and society of that time from those of the "ancients." In the twentieth century, *modernity* is used to distance and to distinguish the culture and society of certain regions from that of "backward" and "emerging" regions. Deep within the discursive structure of modernization and development theory rests the assumption that the "moderns" of today became so by changing in certain inescapable ways from their "backward" condition just as the "moderns" of the eighteenth century underwent endless changes in changing from being among the "ancients." The discourse of modernity, then, not only categorizes different societies; it also characterizes their present position and future tasks in terms of participating in certain types of social change. Thus "backward" developing nations of today, as the contemporary correlates of the "ancients," must follow the same fateful path that the modernized did in order to attain modernity.

When used as this discursive construct, "modernity" substantially addles the actual processes of social change inasmuch as it abstractly constructs an explanatory scale for the modernizing out of the concrete historical experience of the modernized. The metaphors of modernity abstractly express the historical, social, and cultural development of the modernized in a dehistoricized, desocialized, and deculturized social theory that guides and justifies the modernization of premodern. These metaphorical grids suggest that the diverse chronicles of Third World societies' history conceal the same unilinear program for modernization as that which formed during the modernized's transition to modernity. Hence the modernity metaphor holds that history is not the unique unfolding of each people's particular potential, but rather that all of these diverse changes conform to a universal historical program.

The ideological import of this discursive construction of history seems quite manifest. The modernizing regions are not even entitled to build autonomous narratives of their own history and culture. Instead, the "latecomer" modernizing nations are simply following the same paths blazed by the "early-comer" modernized nations. Hence the latecomers are discursively defined as having a great deal to learn and borrow from the early-comers. The class terms of modernity cast the modernized region's history—or past progress into its present situation—as the modernizing regions' future; therefore, the modernizationists discursively reorganize the emerging nations' understanding of their economic, political, and social present in order to anticipate the creation of their foreordained future—the *historiography* of the *modernized* becomes the *futurology* of the *modernizing*.

The term *development*, as it is and has been used by the modernizationists, also implies that nations or peoples come to participate in the structural elaboration of an existing form or state of being. A developed nation is seen as having attained a certain perfection of improvement in its social structures and cultural processes, whereas a developing nation, in the modernizationist discourse, displays a positive commitment for applying its potentials in adopting the existing "developed" forms and states of being. Nevertheless, the existing forms and states of being are those of the modernized regions. The entire thrust of the language usage of "development" is to show the modernized how better to "bring about changes in the underdeveloped societies, how to 'develop' them" [13] along the lines of the modernized. Likewise, even the term *underdevelopment* becomes the modernizationists' expression of a new kind of "developmental" or "modern" existence. An underdeveloped nation becomes, in the modernizationist language, by definition a "developmental" form or state of being that is not yet realized or that is, in some way, retarded. Still, by stipulating that nations are "underdeveloped," the modernizationists can imply discursively that these nations' leaders and populations nurture powerful desires to become part of the developed forms of social being and that they will submit to the "bringing about" or the "development" of massive changes.

Of course, the notion of "modernization" represents the latest sophistication in the modernizationists' secularization of old imperialistic language meanings to suit new political relations with the developing countries. Whereas European intellectuals openly saw their nations' political dominion in the Third World as the pretext for that region's "Anglicization," "Franconization," "Latinization," "Europeanization," "Christianization," or, in its later forms, "Westernization," American intellectuals transcended the political and social connotations of *place* by resorting to *time* terms. Under the older terms, the "West" was explicitly defined as the cultural center of the world, from which all other regions borrowed or learned in order to evolve or progress. At the same time, the borrowing or learning process always followed a unilineal path from the advanced center to the nonadvanced peripheries as "primitive" and "backward" peoples "Westernized" themselves. In fact, the advanced metropolitan core was violently forcing its own ways and values upon the periphery; and, in doing so, it aroused a great deal of anger and anguish by forcing the manners of foreign peoples and places upon largely unwilling societies and peoples.

By resorting to *time* terms, however, many of these relations are mystified and obscured by the null referents of "modernization" and "modernity." Elements of modernization and modernity can be readily detected in any nation, and they do not need to be associated with any single cultural or political region in order to have meaning; hence they are more difficult to rebel against or to reject as "foreign." By the same token, the modernizationists can appear to be far more progressive and respectful of cultural traditions by advocating the *modernization* rather than the *Westernization* of the developing world. A definite geographic region and a specific sociocultural totality underwrites modernization language by being the most modern; however, it is no longer as much the

"West" as it is the "core" or the "North," that is, North America, Europe, and Japan. If the terms of the modernization were to be given a geographic expression, then one would have to call the current development of the Third World "Northernization."

A great deal of added legitimacy also accrues to the North by not labeling its development of the periphery or the South as "corification" or "Northernization" even though the process is largely one of transferring modern "core" or "Northern" practices and values to the premodern peripheral "Southern" regions. For the postimperial peripheries, it is much easier to justify change as the neutral and almost natural effects of *modernization* than it would be to explain it as the culturally biased and socially rooted outcome of embracing the "North's" social totality, while mainly forsaking native traditions. Even though some in the peripheries see through this ideological ploy, the modernizationist discourse continues to use these linguistic terms to legitimate the expansion of "world culture" and to mystify the social interests that ultimately are served by this ideological worldview. The alleged but implicit cultural superiority of the North and the social backwardness of the South remain key premises in the modernizationists' language, just as the superiority of Europe and the inferiority of its colonial peoples were crucial to imperialist language.

In addition to concealing the original *sources* of modernity, the modernizationists also have employed a number of terms that confuse the nature of the modernization *process*. Although the theory of modernization and development paints the process entirely as one of voluntary adoption or willing imitation, the process also often in practice involves many instances of the old imperial strategy of involuntary conversion. In the discursive theorizing of the modernizationists, the possessors of "modernity" closely parallel the community of "Christianity." Modernity, like Christianity, is seen by the modernizationists as an expanding world-historic force, the final fulfillment of which is taken to be the collective charge of the modernized.

The modernized partake in a community of well-being whose boundaries must be expanded. Consequently, the modernized, by virtue of their superior well-being, assigned to them in this discourse, are under an obligation to convert or to modernize the nonmodern. The general advantages of the scientific revolution and its world culture are seen as reason enough to convert, induct, or transform the premodern into joining the modernizing state of being. And, in so doing, the modernizationists' eschatological ideology of modernity (with its stages of modernization discursively drawn as they unfolded for the liberal capitalist economies of the metropolitan countries) becomes, in turn, an ideological eschatology for modernizers in the peripheral countries.

The extent to which the process of modernization is a forced conversion, an induction under duress, and a compulsory transformation into modernity surfaces in the conceptual language chosen by the modernizationists in their theoretical discourses. In the final analysis, the language of the modernizationists is an ironically accurate description of the actual practice of modernization inasmuch as almost all of the theoretical concepts are derived by creating verb constructs using the suffix *ize*. A nation or a people is modern*ized* as it becomes increasingly bureaucrat*ized*, industrial*ized*, rational*ized*, urban*ized*, and so forth. In ordinary language use, the dictionary records that the suffix *ize* has three closely parallel meanings of importance for creating the modernizationists' theoretical constructs: (a) *to subject to* action, process, or treatments, as in to catechize, cauterize, or satirize; (b) *to render, make into, put into conformity with* or *to make like*, as in to galvanize, Christianize, or sterilize; and (c) *to act in the way of*, or *practice*, or *carry on*, as in to apostatize, botanize, or philosophize.[14] The ideological content of this sort of language is overpowering.

The same coercive conceptualizations run through the notion of "developing." Again, in ordinary language use, the meaning of *developing* reveals these dynamics of normalization as it implies such activities as (a) changing the form of a surface, mass, or process; (b) making clear by or as if unfolding some enclosing, enfolding, or obscuring cover; (c) making visible or manifest the invisible or latent; (d) opening up, causing, or revealing hidden qualities or unexpected potentialities; (e) elaborating or expressing in an expanded form; and (f) laying out or evolving into a clear, full, and explicit presentation. The developing nation is set into the dividing practices of this conception of social truth to change the form of its existing processes and structures. In turn, the agendas of economic growth lay out or evolve into a clear, full, and explicit representation of where, when, why, and how its structures and processes must change. As with all other growing societies, "developing" then opens up, causes, or reveals the hidden qualities (domestic economic efficiency, an orderly internal house, or aggressive export-led trading policies) that release the unexpected potentialities (attaining economic success, joining the world economy, participating in global growth) of the nation. Within the discourse of modernity, the invisible and latent power of self-interest, economic rationality, and market forces are made visible and manifest as these unleashed social forces are elaborated and expressed in an expanded form—wholly in keeping with the disciplinary expectations of the liberal development regime that simply clears away the enclosing and obscuring cover of tradition. As elements of the discursive grid of development, which are able to articulate the meaning of modernity and to explain the process of becoming modern, the discourse of modernity unconsciously expresses with its language what it has meant "to develop" under the post-1945 era of *Pax Americana*. Yet, the modernizationists are almost totally insensitive to these deeper meanings in their own theoretical language, because they are, for the most part, North Americans, Westerners, Northerners, or "modernized." As persons from the core modernized regions, anxious to articulate the meaning of modernity and to explain the process of becoming modern, the modernizationists unconsciously express, as beneficiaries of modernity and of their positions in the metropole's policymaking structures, what it means to modernize by their language. They are insensitive to these meanings because they *do not* see them, in fact, as *problematic*. And, in the last analysis, these theoretical meanings fully capture the ultimate, if unintended, meaning of modernization's practical process.

The meanings that the modernizationists express in their discourse reflect and reproduce violent dynamics of the modernization process. The modernized metropolitan countries and their social forces *subject* the premodern and the modernizing nations to political actions and social processes in order to quicken their transition to modernity. Such core social forces, and local modernizers in the periphery, laboriously work *to make* the peripheral societies *into* "modern" social complexes, *to make* these peoples *like* "modern" men, *to put* the Third and Fourth Worlds *into conformity* with the metropolitan world, and *to render* the premodern culture *into* a "modern" state of existence. And, of course, the modernizationists continually advocate that the peoples of the developing periphery *must carry on like*, or *act in the way of*, or *practice as* the peoples of the core economies. Such relations, whether they come from within or without under the aegis of native or foreign modernizing forces, are largely relations of coercion, domination, and manipulation. These events do not represent the "diffusion" of a "world culture." On the contrary, they reveal how the dominant regions of the world and their political forces enforce the transfer of their own culture, economy, and society into subjugated dependent regions of the world. The developing periphery is *made into*, is *put into conformity with*, and is *made like* the metropolitan core. The rationalization, the standardization, and the uniformization are *acted* out *in the way of* the developed core's rationality, standards, and uniformity. For the most part, and in spite of some significant national variations, the developing countries' bureaucratization, industrialization, mobilization, rationalization, and urbanization largely are *induced by* and mainly are *managed for the benefit of* core social forces in accordance with metropolitan values and practices.

The Mystification of Forces:
Metrocentricity

In the genetic explanation of modernization, the discourses of modernization present the periphery's unfamiliar culture and society by reducing them to more familiar metropolitan patterns of action. That is, the modernizing can be made to be modernized only by inducing a rejection of their familiar forms of existence in favor of unfamiliar states of being. Both of these assumptions reveal the wholly metrocentric nature of modernization and development theory. On the one hand, "modernity" and "modernization" tend to be associated closely with all the positive qualities and virtues of the modern world. Yet, on the other hand, these associations mystify and obscure the negative qualities and vices of the modern world, especially those incumbent upon the developed core societies' modernization of the periphery. As Huntington has observed, "All good things are modern and modernity consequently becomes a melange of incompatible virtues. In particular, there is a failure to distinguish between what is modern and what is Western." [15] This failure can be best witnessed in the discursive underpinnings of modernizationist theory.

Modernization and development theory and its constituent concepts are regarded as objective, fully formulated, and scientific in nature. They are viewed as simple reality recorders, neutral idea expressers, and value-free logic communicators. With the failure to distinguish between what is "modern" and what is "Western" (or, more accurately, "core" and "metropolitan"), the concepts of modernization and development theory serve as the vessels of metrocentricity: They become complex reality creators, biased idea makers, and value-laden logic benders that express the practice and the theory of a certain sociopolitical context—metropolitan domination and peripheral dependence.

In a somewhat similar frame of mind, Huntington notes:

> The one thing which modernization theory has not produced is a model of Western society—meaning late twentieth century Western European and North American society—which could be compared with, or even contrasted with, the model of modern society. Implicitly, the two are assumed to be virtually identical. Modern society has been Western society writ abstractly and polysyllabically. But to a non-modern, non-Western society, the processes of modernization and Westernization may appear to be very different indeed.[16]

However, the processes of modernization, or "corification" and "metropolitanization," *do* indeed *appear* differently in the periphery. Moreover, these "differences" can be discerned, at least in part, by reconsidering how the modernizationists virtually identify the "modernity" of the core with "modernization" seen as metropolitanization.

The "metrocentrism" of the modernizationists prejudges and pre-evaluates actions, institutions, and thoughts as being valuable, or useful, or valid only if they are part of the modern social totality. Those cultures that exist outside and independent of the modern social totality are not valuable, useful, or valid because they are premodern, modernizing, or underdeveloped. "Metrocentricity," however, involves more than an ethnocentric prejudice—that is, it subsumes an ethnocentric meaning by valuing only metropolitan culture and society. Ethnocentrism alone does not convey its full implications. Metrocentrism also involves good measures of what might be termed "chronocentrism" and "technocentrism." In addition to having assimilated metropolitan culture and societal institutions, the developing countries are expected to take part in "modern times" or to be "of their time." Likewise, the ultimate symbol of modernization remains working toward the total mechanization and technologization of everyday life. Hence the theory of modernization and development also has fallen down in its ability to distinguish a model of metropolitan society, metropolitan time, and metropolitan technology that can be contrasted with that of a modern society. The reasons this differentiation has not taken place are clear: Modern society, modern time, and modern technology *are* the sociocultural, temporal, and technological expressions of the developed core countries.

The modernizationists, through their various discourses of change, perpetuate and sophisticate the use of this wholly metrocentric perspective, casting an ideological shade over modernization and development theory. To become "modern," a nation must become "metropolitan" by adapting to and adopting from the ways of the core or metropole, which are implicitly identical to "modern society," "modern times," and "modern technology." Such patterns of thought are more than a "conceptual ambiguity," as Huntington suggests. Such thinking mystifies the corporate and political forces behind the modernizing of the periphery, as its "unfamiliar ways" are reduced to fit the needs and to serve the interests of the modern social totality. The identity of the most corelike core country, at any one time, is equally ambiguous. Is it Great Britain, the United States, Sweden, Japan, West Germany? Or is it networks of metropolitan regions linking urban capitalist centers in all of the above *plus* key cities in the developing countries? Modernization and development theory intellectually embodies the core's culture in practice and its practice in culture. What Huntington labels as a *scientific failure* to distinguish between the "modern" and the "Western" is, in fact, an *ideological success* because in political and economic practice they become indistinguishable in the elaboration of the present transnational order.

Ethnocentricity

For the modernizationists, modernization involves the diffusion of the "world culture." Still, like the diffusion of any culture, it requires those who are being "enculturated" to accept certain new values, institutions, and practices in favor of their current ones. In other words, what the modernizationists describe as the "diffusion" of culture also requires a "deculturization" to accept the new "enculturation" of modernity. This remains within the reproduction of "world culture"—based on advanced technology or the spirit of science, on a rational view of life, a secular approach to social relations, a feeling of justice in public affairs, and the political belief that the prime unit of the polity should be the nation-state. The "world culture" plainly is not a true world culture; rather, it is narrow representations of the culture of the hegemonic world power, the actual political metropole. Its hegemonic cultural forms and economic functions are those of metropolitan life. The criteria of advancedness, of technology, of spirit, of science, of rationality, of life, of secularism, of social relations, of feeling, of justice, of public affairs, of political realm, of belief, of prime unit, of polity, and of nation-state are all derivations of the modern social totality that has presented itself as home base of the "world culture." It becomes the "world culture" because of its worldwide domination and manipulation of the other global cultures that are slowly being caught up in its "diffusion." The peripheral states' own values, institutions, and actions are then "underdeveloped" or "developed" to complement the core.

Nevertheless, this new "enculturation" also involves processes that the modernizationists often mystify and the modernizers usually ignore: the deculturalization of the periphery as it forsakes or modifies its familiar ways to adopt unfamiliar states of everyday existence. As the periphery bureaucratizes, industrializes, mechanizes, mobilizes, rationalizes, secularizes, and urbanizes, it also disorganizes, deagriculturalizes, dehumanizes, desolidarizes, deanimates, desacralizes, and deruralizes. The modernizationists, however, both accept and advocate their losses as necessary dues of entering "modernity." As Rostow suggests, this simply is part of the normal "takeoff." Old roles, as Chapter 9 discusses in closer detail, are dropped in favor of acting like "modern" subjects—the actions of traditional life are modified to imitate the metropolitan citizen, city dweller, consumer, industrialist, merchant, student, urbanite, and worker. Old institutions are entrapped in the diffusion of the metropolitan city, corporation, factory, laboratory, market, party, plan, school, and state. These events, nonetheless, are not inevitable, nor are they natural. Rather, such changes represent the increasing domination and growing dependence of the periphery as its individual residents confront this colonization of their everyday lifeworld. Concepts such as "world culture," "the scientific revolution," "a rational view of life," "a secular approach," and the "spirit of science" purport to explicate modernization in nonideological, unbiased, and neutral terms. Still, such concepts also articulate and legitimate the discourse of metropolitan domination.

Chronocentricity

During 1831, in reflecting on the cultural impact of European imperialism, John Stuart Mill expressed the main sense of "chronocentricity" in these terms:

> Before men begin to think much and long on the peculiarities of their own times, they must have begun to think that those times are, or are destined to be, distinguished in a very remarkable manner from the times which preceded them. Mankind are then divided, into those who are still what they

were, and those who have changed: into men of the present age, and men of the past. To the former, the spirit of the age is a subject of exultation; to the latter, of terror; to both, of eager and anxious interest.[17]

With the advent of domination by the core, nations divide into those "of the present age" and those "of the past age." In doing so, the time or the time sense of the core, or Mill's "men of the present age," becomes the norm for the entire world's time.

The time sense expressed by the concept of *modernity*, for instance, is no longer measured by the passing of the months, years, or decades. Instead, "modernity," or being in and "of the present age," comes to be measured in particular discursive grids tied to cultural sophistication, economic growth, political organization, and technological strength. Literally speaking, persons "of the present age" and persons "of the past" both exist in the temporal present, whether it is 1831, 1945, or 1990. Still, at the same time, to be in "1990" in most areas of what is labeled as Afghanistan, Chad, or Paraguay in these terms means something entirely different from being in "1990" in many areas of Japan, Sweden, or the United States. Because they are poor peripheral societies, the former nations are in, but not "of their time," while, in comparison to these nations "of the past," the latter nations are *both in and of their time* because they are core parts of the modern social totality that defines being "of the present age." "Modernity" must not be understood as a literal time concept; it is a discursive sociopolitical frame whose scales and indicators are attuned culturally to the "chronos" of the developed core regions.

Modernity has meaning only when connected to the concrete *contemporary* practices of the core. The spirit, the style, and the content of the core's contemporaneous moments constitute modernity. Therefore, modernity and modernization are constantly redefined and reconstituted with changes in the spirit, style, and content of the metropolitan social totality. To be "of the present," a nation or a people must cultivate and adopt the spirit, style, and content of the core zones, with all of the rapidity and mutability associated with life in the core. As the modern "ethos" increasingly becomes convergent with the other modern nations' "ethos" because of the cultural sophistication and social differentiation attending modernization, the collective convergent spirit, style, and content of modern life, or "chronos," serves as the ethos of the core. Change becomes a way of life in a very real sense as it creates new sociocultural values. Modernity is not a simple time concept that marks off the passing of clock time or calendar time; it is instead in these discourses a concept that marks off sociological, technological, economic, and political demands as the metropolitan core defines them.

Modernity, as a time concept, homogenizes the entirety of world history into a single sociologically stipulated continuum whose endpoints are continually redefined. Black contends that "modernization must be thought of not as a simple transition from tradition to modernity but as part of an infinite continuum from the earliest times to the indefinite future." [18] If modernity actually could be described by a finite continuum with distinct endpoints and midpoints, then modernization and development theory would not be quite as chronocentric. One could discover what it should look like once it reached the point of modernity. If modernity is seen as an infinite continuum, however, the chronocentric quality emerges strongly. For example, in the nineteenth century, as England attained its industrial "takeoff," it was the nation "of its age" and all others were of the past. Yet, as England and the other metropolitan powers all slowly passed through Rostow's metaphorical stages of "takeoff," "maturity," and "mass consumption," the definitions of being "of the present" and "of the past" changed. What was an innovative modernization for the core as it modernized, becomes, by virtue of a chronocentric assessment, a near traditional commonplace for the periphery as it modernizes. For the core, the attainment of industrial maturity denoted the achievement of "modernity." Still, today, given the core's subsequent development, the periphery's attainment of industrial maturity marks off only a small additional step in its modernizing status. For a peripheral nation to achieve in 1986 what a metropolitan nation accomplished in 1896 does not necessarily make the peripheral nation "modern," even though its achievement might have made the metropolitan nation "modern" 80 years ago.

Indeed, the core's more rapidly advancing and more fully differentiating collective culture, or "chronos," has led to the unceasing devaluation in these discourses of the modernizing's accomplishments along with a continuing inflation in the value of the modernized region's contemporaneous spirit, style, and cultural values. The core remains the trendsetter, yet it continually resets and redefines the trends. Hence the periphery has a difficult time deciding upon what must be done to attain modernity. What Japan's modernizing elites did in the 1880s-1890s, what Argentina's business leadership did in the 1900s-1920s, what China's Maoist economic program did in the 1950s-1960s, and what Brazil's and India's leaderships are doing today to become part of the metropolitan state of being vary significantly because of how and why the core kept changing

during these periods. The spirit, the style, and the culture of the metropolitan region varied widely and thereby set a differing sense of what
being "of the present age" meant to these peripheral nations—some of
which succeeded at becoming part of the modern social totality while
others are still trying.

"Chronocentrism" confronts the modernizers in the periphery as they
seek to modernize their peoples and nations. As Indira Gandhi observed
about India, "India lives in many layers. Many centuries exist in our land.
Parts of India are as advanced as you will find elsewhere in the world.
The rest are bound in tradition." [19] In truth, such a situation confronts
modernizers everywhere, for the differing spirit, style, and content of
many "centuries" denotes the degree to which the periphery fails to
participate in the one important "century," namely, the core's "present
age." The "modernity" of "men of the past," or "tradition," must be
eradicated by the modernizers in order to extend the hegemony of the
advanced layers down into the entire society. The ways of the "many
centuries" in the periphery must be forgone for a society to adapt to the
ways of the "present century," which are, by definition, more advanced
and more beneficial.

Unfortunately, for most peripheral nations, by the time their cultural
sophistication and social differentiation develop to the point of being in
the "layer" of what was the nineteenth century, the core has already
pushed into what will be the twenty-first century, leaving much of the
periphery behind in spite of all its modernizing efforts. Some parts of it
may make the transition, but most do not. By painting modernity as an
infinite continuum, the hegemonic core system can maintain its "chronocentric" superiority. As the infinite continuum of modernity stretches
into the indefinite future, the metropolitan pace of cultural sophistication
and economic growth sets the scale for the modernizationists' and the
modernizers' theory and practice. Yet, such theoretical and practical
actions are faulty inasmuch as the advancements of the periphery are
prejudged and preevaluated from the discursive perspective of one "advanced layer" of time, or the core's "chronos," in order to serve the needs
and the interests of the metropolitan social forces in the modernizing of
these "men of the past." Those who exist in a state of being resting upon
tradition's "many centuries" are dominated by and are made dependent
upon those who make and manage the "one century" of metropolitan
time. Indeed, the concepts of "tradition" and "modernity" in the modernizationist discourse both record contemporary and modern states
of being. The only difference is that "tradition" represents an inferior

contemporaneousness that is shared by "men of the past," whereas "modernity" represents the superior contemporaneousness that is collectively advanced by "men of the present" who are truly "of their time," not merely "in their time," like the "men of the past."

Technocentricity

The most basic component of metrocentrism, however, follows from the modernizationist discourse's nearly absolute faith in technology. The most fundamental flaw of modernization and development theory arises in the "technocentricity" of its concepts and frameworks. The technological factor allegedly creates the common cultural, economic, political, and social functions and structures underlying the cultural and temporal convergence of the metropolitan and peripheral nations. The "historically evolved institutions" of both metropolitan and peripheral society are adapted to the "unprecedented increase" in human knowledge and control of the environment through the "scientific revolution." [20] The modernizationist discourse is quite open about this point of conceptual order. In fact, "it does draw attention to the principal cause of everything connected with modernization—transformation of the world by technology." [21] Rather than just any sort of human or social change, technical control over nature and, consequently, over people through the control of natural processes and resources repeatedly appears as the essence of modernization. In these discourses of change, Huntington declares, "the essential distinction between modern and traditional society, most theorists of modernization contend, lies in the greater control which modern man has over his natural and social environment." [22] Moreover, he suggests, "this control, in turn, is based on the expansion of scientific and technological knowledge." [23]

In vindication of the ideological and economic needs of the core, the final proof and ultimate symbol of modernization remains the total mechanization and technologization of everyday life. In the conceptualizations of the modernizationists, modernization equals the more efficient manipulation and exploitation of nature, which leads, in turn, to the more efficient manipulation and exploitation of people, especially the people of the periphery. To reinforce this point, one need only survey a sampling of the modernizationists on their conception of modernization:

It [modern society] is characterized by its far reaching ability to control or influence the physical and social circumstances of its environment and by a value system which is fundamentally optimistic about the desirability and consequences of this ability.[24]

[Modernization] involves a "rapidly widening control over nature through closer co-operation among men." [25]

[A society is] more or less modernized to the extent that its members use inanimate sources of power and/or tools to multiply the effects of their efforts.[26]

"Modernization" may be defined as the process by which historically evolved institutions are adapted to rapidly changing functions that reflect the unprecedented increase in man's knowledge, permitting control over his environment, that accompanied scientific revolution.[27]

Modernization depends upon the "systematic, sustained, and purposeful application of human energies to the 'rational' control of man's physical and social environment for various human purposes." [28]

Without technological development and economic growth, modernization is inconceivable.[29]

They [modern societies] are characterized by . . . a culture that emphasizes the values of science, knowledge and achievement.[30]

[Modernization of] the "world culture" [is] based on advanced technology and the spirit of science, on a rational view of life, a secular approach to social relations.[31]

Modernization, then, consists of the growth and diffusion of a set of institutions rooted in the transformation of the economy by means of technology.[32]

Here modernization is used primarily with regard to the spread and use of industrial-type roles in non-industrial settings.[33]

Industrialization is that aspect of modernization so powerful in its consequences that it alters dysfunctional social institutions and customs by creating new roles and social institutions on the use of the machine.[34]

By *industrialization* I refer to *economic* changes brought about by a technology based on inanimate sources of power as well as on the continuous development of applied scientific research. Modernization . . . refers to all those social and political changes that accompanied industrialization in many countries of Western civilization.[35]

All of the core's cherished social myths—the belief in social advancement through science, a faith in collective improvement through expanding knowledge, the desire to master nature to improve human life, and the accomplishment of better living through technology—are articulated in these passages. However, few of the benefits of these myths accrue for the periphery. The "technocratic" quality of modernization and development theory mystifies the intrusion of the world capitalist economy and the machine process into the underdeveloped world with technological rationality "spreading and diffusing" into "nonindustrial settings." The core, having already undergone the reconstitution of its social fabric by the capitalist machine process, now rationally manages the periphery's reorganization by capitalist industry to serve its own interests and needs. Still, the metropolitan modernizationist discourse persists in describing the process as a natural economic transformation voluntarily agreed to and accepted.

The core, in modernization and development theory, allegedly is *not* forcing the metropolitanization of the periphery. On the contrary, "technology" is transforming the peripheral economy, causing the growth and diffusion of a new set of institutions that are more functional and responsive. Modernization results from industrialization, or applied scientific research, or a widening control of nature, or a culture of science, or the use of inanimate sources of energy, or the spread of industrial roles, or the rational view of life, but not from the forced subjugation of peripheral economy to benefit core social forces. Such discursive formulas seek to totally mask and utterly obscure the state agencies, multinational banks, transnational corporations, and trade networks that prosper behind these screens of "technological change." It is these core corporations, banks, development agencies, and their locally based native affiliates who are "systematically and purposefully" applying their human energies in a sustained fashion to *rationally* control their physical and their human environments. The advanced technology is metropolitan, the spirit of science is metropolitan, the secular approach is metropolitan, and the values of science are metropolitan; hence the "rapidly widening control over nature" is affected by a core-organized and core-serving "closer cooperation among men." The periphery remains a "nonindustrial setting" that is to be spread into, used, altered, and rationally controlled for the advantage of metropolitan social forces.

All of these political and social implications, however, are concealed by the naturalistic, universalistic, and mechanistic certainties of a discourse seeing "technology" transforming allegedly dysfunctional social institutions and customs. "Technology," "industrialization," and "rationality" serve as mystifications that obscure a political struggle by typing it as a predetermined process, that turns a violent social process into an automatic natural behavior, and that renders a self-serving economic activity into a historical certainty. Technology is *not* transforming the periphery; industrialization is *not* altering dysfunctional social institutions; and the scientific revolution is *not* adapting historically evolved institutions. Instead, metropolitan and metropolitanized persons are making these changes. Moreover, they are doing so to serve their own sociocultural, economic, and political interests in the metropolitan social totality. The best approach to such discursive opacity can be had by paraphrasing Marx: *Modernity* does *nothing*; it does *not* possess immense riches, it does *not* fight battles. *It is men*, real living men, who do possess things and fight battles. It is not "modernity" that uses men as a means of achieving—as if it were an individual person—*its* own ends. Modernity is nothing but the activity of men in pursuit of their ends.[36]

The "technocentric" nature of modernization and development discourse prompts the modernizationists to conceive of the periphery and its state of existence largely in technological terms. For the modernizing, modernization becomes incomprehensible without adoption of metropolitan technology and technical thought. For the modernizers in the periphery, "Western society has little meaning apart from its technology for these countries, and its institutions are inextricably linked together—politics and science, inventions and parliaments." [37] As the imports of core technology grow, the machine process of core country life increasingly reproduces the alienation and exploitation of everyday life in a technological society throughout the periphery's modernizing societies. In addition to the modernizers' urgings of the modernizing into modernity, modern technology prompts these premodern peoples and nations to adapt modern behaviors into their lives simply to operate and implement their imported techniques. The technocentric view of modernization and development sees the periphery's modernizers thinking of their modernization, almost exclusively, in terms of mechanization and technics. As the agents of their own "metropolitanization," then, "they have regarded their steel mills, dams and fertilizer factories as the tangible manifestation of such development. Aswan, Volta or Bhakra-Nangal *are* development." [38] Beyond these traditional industrial goals, the informationalization of the core economy now demands that computerization and automation can also be expected from peripheral economies, pushing their prospects for modernization even further away from realization.[39]

The technocratic thrust of modernization and development discourses forces the modernizing to become persons "of the present age" by learning the rational control, calculability, and systematic purposiveness of technology. To be persons "of their age," in the last analysis, means to be persons working the modern machines and serving the metropolitan technology "of the present age" in the world capitalist economy. In other words, modernization becomes "normalization," as I will illustrate in greater detail in Chapter 9. Modernity is a condition in which the modernizing will be like the modernized as they extend the use of inanimate energy and tools, as they broaden the more rational control of scientific reason, and as they deepen the greater control of the environment. In doing so, however, the modernizing arguably are not merely liberating themselves through the use of technology; rather, they also are engaging in their own self-domination by adopting an alien form of technical existence from the core. As the periphery modernizes, social choices, political options, technical alternatives, and cultural diversity are sacrificed in order to gain rapid entry into the metropole-dominated modern economy. Knowledge and values other than those of science, technology, and the "secular approach to social relations" are largely precluded from the peripheral frame of action by the preexisting structure of the metropolitan world-system. Choices are already made, options are foreclosed, alternatives are discounted, and diversity is not encouraged as the modernizers mobilize their nations and peoples for their transformation through systems of coercive normalization.

The discourses of the modernizationists, then, are riddled with metrocentrism, and their conceptual appraisals suffer from definite inadequacies because of their discursive ethnocentricity, chronocentricity, and technocentricity. For a nonmodern, nonmetropolitan society, the processes of "modernization" appear very different from those that have unfolded in the core. Indeed, in the process of these changes, modernization has led to the subjugation of local culture, local time, and local technologies by the core in favor of imported visions of metropolitan culture, time, and technology. As I will argue in Chapter 9 with regard to political culture, familiar states of being are supplanted by unfamiliar alien ways of being, both in theory and in practice. Acting under the discursive directives of a metrocentric theory and the exigencies of the world economy, the modernizers of the periphery often must act not as creative but as imitative elites, who prevent their peoples from becoming what they might have been or from remaining what they are by persuading them to become what they are not by adopting practices and values from the discourses of the modernizationists.

Notes

1. Robert E. Ward, "Political Modernization and Political Culture in Japan," *World Politics* 15, no. 4 (July 1963), 570. Cited in Claude E. Welch, *Political Modernization: A Reader in Comparative Political Change* (Belmont, CA: Wadsworth, 1971), 4.

2. Lucian W. Pye, *Aspects of Political Development* (Boston: Little, Brown, 1965), 8. Cited in Welch, *Political Modernization,* 4.

3. C. E. Black, *The Dynamics of Modernization: A Study in Comparative History* (New York: Harper & Row, 1967), 7.

4. Robert A. Packenham, *Liberal America and the Third World: Political Development in Foreign Aid and Social Science* (Princeton, NJ: Princeton University Press, 1973), xv.

5. See, for example, Gar Alperovitz, *Cold War Essays* (Cambridge, MA: Schenkman, 1970); Raymond Aron, *The Imperial Republic* (Englewood Cliffs, NJ: Prentice-Hall, 1974); T. Bauer, *Dissent on Development* (Cambridge, MA: Harvard University Press, 1976); Irving Louis Horowitz, *Three Worlds of Development* (New York: Oxford University Press, 1972); Gabriel Kolko, *The Roots of American Foreign Policy* (Boston: Beacon, 1969); Arthur M. Schlesinger, Jr., *The Imperial Presidency* (Boston: Houghton Mifflin, 1973); Ronald Steel, *Pax Americana* (New York: Viking, 1967); William A. Williams, *The Tragedy of American Diplomacy* (New York: Dell, 1972). Also, for earlier critiques of ideology in modernization and development theory, see Suzanne J. Bodenheimer, *The Ideology of Developmentalism* (Beverly Hills, CA: Sage, 1971); Andre Gunder Frank, "The Development of Underdevelopment," *Monthly Review* (September 1966); John H. Kautsky, *The Political Consequences of Modernization* (New York: John Wiley, 1972); Charles Douglas Lummis, "Modernization Theory as Ideology," paper presented at the Western Political Science Association Convention (1974); James Peck, "The Roots of Rhetoric: The Professional Ideology of America's China Watchers," *Bulletin of Concerned Asian Scholars* 2, no. 1 (October 1969); Dean C. Tipps, "Modernization Theory and the Comparative Study of Societies: A Critical Perspective," *Comparative Studies in Society and History* 15, no. 2 (March 1973); and Howard Wiarda, "The Ethnocentrism of Social Science: Implications for Research and Policy," *Review of Politics* 43 (April 1981), 163-197.

6. See Samir Amin, *Accumulation on a World Scale* (New York: Monthly Review Press, 1974); Andre Gunder Frank, *On Capitalist Underdevelopment* (Bombay: Oxford University Press, 1975); and Raul Presbisch, *Towards a Dynamic Development Policy for Latin America* (United Nations, 680/Rev. 1, 1963).

7. See W. W. Rostow, *The Stages of Growth: A Non-Communist Manifesto* (Cambridge: Cambridge University Press, 1960), 1-3.

8. Roy C. Macridis and Bernard E. Brown, *Comparative Politics: Notes and Readings* (4th ed.) (Homewood, IL: Dorsey, 1972), 428.

9. Originally conceived by Secretary of State John Hay in 1898 to rationalize and to legitimate the American acquisition of its Pacific colonies and territories, "the partnership in beneficence" has proven to be the touchstone of the North American development of the world economy after World War II. Exploitation, when cast in this sense, no longer implies the looting of one region by another; rather, it suggests the mutual sharing of social costs and benefits—except that one partner's "mutual" share is far more beneficial and much less costly than the other partner's share of the exchange.

10. Noam Chomsky, *American Power and the New Mandarins* (New York: Vintage, 1969), 41.

11. The range of this literature is quite broad and diverse in both conceptualization and methodology, but a small sample of such modernizationist works, in addition to those already mentioned, might include Gabriel Almond and G. Bingham Powell, *Comparative Politics: A Developmental Approach* (Boston: Little, Brown, 1966); Gabriel Almond and James S. Coleman, *The Politics of Developing Areas* (Princeton, NJ: Princeton University Press, 1960); David E. Apter, *The Politics of Modernization* (Chicago: University of Chicago Press, 1967); Peter L. Berger et al., *The Homeless Mind: Modernization and Consciousness* (New York: Random House, 1973); Reinhard Bendix, *Nation-Building and Citizenship* (Garden City, NY: Anchor, 1964); Leon Binder, *Iran: Political Development in a Changing Society* (Berkeley: University of California Press, 1962); S. N. Eisenstadt, *Modernization: Protest and Change* (Englewood Cliffs, NJ: Prentice-Hall, 1966); S. N. Eisenstadt, *Tradition, Change, and Modernity* (New York: John Wiley, 1973); G. Lowell Field, *Comparative Political Development: The Precedent of the West* (Ithaca, NY: Cornell University Press, 1967); Robert L. Heilbroner, *The Future as History* (New York: Harper & Row, 1959); Robert L. Heilbroner, *The Great Ascent* (New York: Harper & Row, 1963); Irving Louis Horowitz, *Three Worlds of Development* (New York: Oxford University Press, 1972); Samuel Huntington, *Political Order in Changing Societies* (New Haven, CT: Yale University Press, 1967); Daniel Lerner, *The Passing of Traditional Society: Modernizing the Middle East* (Glencoe, IL: Free Press, 1958); Marion J. Levy, *Modernization and the Structure of Society* (Princeton, NJ: Princeton University Press, 1966); Marion J. Levy, *The Structure of Society* (Princeton, NJ: Princeton University Press, 1952); S. M. Lipset, *Party Systems and Voter Alignments* (New York: Free Press, 1967); S. M. Lipset, *Political Man* (Garden City, NY: Anchor, 1959); Lucian Pye, *Politics, Personality, and Nation Building* (New Haven, CT: Yale University Press, 1962); Dankwart A. Rustow, *A World of Nations* (Washington, DC: Brookings Institution, 1967); and I. Robert Sinai, *The Challenge of Modernization* (New York: Norton, 1964).

12. S. N. Eisenstadt, *Tradition, Change, and Modernity*, 12.

13. Ibid., 11.

14. *Webster's Ninth New Collegiate Dictionary*, 644, for example, provides this insight into the structural meaning of *ize* and its cognitive form *ization.*

15. Macridis and Brown, *Comparative Politics*, 414.

16. Ibid., 414-415.

17. John Stuart Mill, "The Spirit of the Age," *Essays on Politics and Culture*, ed. by Gertrude Himmelfarb (New York: Peter Smith, 1962), 3.

18. Black, *Dynamics of Modernization*, 54.

19. Norman D. Palmer, *The Indian Political System* (Boston: Little, Brown, 1971), 8.

20. Black, *Dynamics of Modernization*, 7.

21. Berger et al., *The Homeless Mind*, 8-9.

22. Macridis and Brown, *Comparative Politics*, 410.

23. Ibid.

24. Robert W. Ward and Roy C. Macridis, *Modern Political Systems: Asia* (Englewood Cliffs, NJ: Prentice-Hall, 1963), 445.

25. Rustow, *A World of Nations*, 3.

26. Marion Levy, *Modernization and the Structure of Societies* (Princeton, NJ: Princeton University Press, 1966), 11.

27. Black, *Dynamics of Modernization*, 7.

28. Benjamin Schwartz, cited in *Changing Japanese Attitudes Toward Modernization*, ed. by Marius B. Jansen (Princeton, NJ: Princeton University Press, 1965), 23-24.

29. Frank Tachau, *The Developing Nations: What Path to Modernization?* (New York: Dodd, Mead, 1972), 9.

30. Macridis and Brown, *Comparative Politics*, 388.

31. Lucian Pye, *Aspects of Political Development*, 8. Cited in Welch, *Political Modernization*, 4.

32. Berger et al., *The Homeless Mind*, 9.

33. David E. Apter, "Political Systems and Developmental Change," *Comparative Politics: A Reader*, ed. by Harry Eckstein and David E. Apter (Glencoe, IL: Free Press, 1963), 157.

34. Apter, *Politics of Modernization*, 68.

35. Bendix, *Nation-Building and Citizenship*, 6-7.

36. Karl Marx and Frederich Engels, *The Holy Family*, cited in T. B. Bottomore, ed., *Karl Marx: Selected Writings in Sociology and Social Philosophy* (New York: McGraw-Hill, 1956), 63.

37. Apter, *Politics of Modernization*, 45.

38. John Kenneth Galbraith, *Economic Development in Perspective* (Cambridge, MA: Harvard University Press, 1964), 51.

39. See Timothy W. Luke, *Screens of Power: Ideology, Domination and Resistance in Informational Society* (Urbana, IL: University of Illinois Press, 1989).

9

Foucault and the Discourses of Power: Developing a Genealogy of the Political Culture Concept

Michel Foucault is recognized widely for influencing many fields of inquiry, ranging from criminology to architecture to literary criticism. His impact on political science, however, has been fairly limited. On one level, Foucault's lack of acceptance is doubly strange given his interest in such themes as power, knowledge, and truth. Yet, on another level, his implication of the naturalistically grounded social sciences in the administrative domination of modern society undoubtedly encourages many political scientists to dismiss his work almost entirely. While Foucault's project obviously works at cross-purposes with much of Marxian/Marxist thinking, in this chapter I aim at possibly broadening his appeal by continuing the critique of modernization and development theory from Chapter 8. And, in contrast to Cabral's notions of political culture and revolutionary activity, I explore how the problematic concepts of "political culture" and "individual subjectivity," as they emerged in the techniques of American empirical political analysis after 1945, might be understood more critically in light of Foucault's style of interpretative analysis.

Foucault's Theoretical Project

In terms of his own categories, Michel Foucault can be seen as a "founder of discursivity" in the social sciences. That is, his work provides "a paradigmatic set of terms, images and concepts which organize thinking and experience about the past, present, and future of society." [1] His images and concepts can reveal much about the modern discourses of political culture and political socialization. Here, Foucault's work can be made more relevant to modern political science, and it also can show hidden tendencies in the conceptual workings of this "human science" as it has operated in the present generation. As products of "specific intellectuals," or empirically trained social and political scientists, discourses about political culture and individual subjectivity also must be contextualized against different criteria of truth and knowledge than those central to political theory as a discourse of "specific" and "universal" intellectuals.[2] To indicate how Foucault's works might improve our understanding of political culture, a brief overview of his terms, images, and concepts is needed. More concretely, his approach to the questions of the subject, power, truth, and knowledge as well as the arts of government are the most important here.

The Origins of the Subject

Foucault's work has been characterized in many ways.[3] In his earlier work, Foucault focused on the nature of knowledge and its production. However, in retrospect, and particularly after 1975, he increasingly saw himself undertaking a key project—developing genealogies of the modern subject. With this recognition, his entire project came to center upon "the procedures of power" that he labels "disciplines," or the myriad techniques of social control "by which the body is reduced as a 'political' force at the least cost and maximized as a useful force." [4] For Foucault, the acquisition of power over the individual's body and power over the mass population's bodies marks the advent of modernity. In modernizing Western society, "the disciplines of the body and the regulations of the population constituted the two poles around which the organization of power over life was deployed." [5] "My objective," he claims, "has been to create a history of the different modes by which, in our culture, human beings are made subjects." [6] This construction of the modern subject is bound up intimately with the disciplines of power tied to the discourses and procedures of "dividing practices" in expert cultures of the human sciences. Through the manipulative methods of human or social science, "the subject is objectified by a process of division either within himself or from others." [7]

These practices develop initially in the social management of disease, madness, criminality, and sexuality. Foucault's analyses in *Madness and Civilization, The Birth of the Clinic, Discipline and Punish,* and *The History of Sexuality* all concentrate upon how humans are assigned identity, roles, social stigma, norms, and meaning as social scientists divide anonymous masses of population into carefully differentiated classes and categories. In defining madness, crime, illness, and deviance, the dividing practices both objectify and subjectify through expert discourse and disciplinary technologies. The mad, criminal, ill, and deviant are dominated in these groupings, but they also gain new, special identities rooted in the complex professional discourses that define and police their behavior. In these discourses, then, the body and mind of individuals are reduced through scientific classification and objectification to *things,* enabling their powers to be spatialized, temporalized, and mobilized more rationally. These "atypical" groups, however, are not atypical. Rather, they are dealt with in the same disciplinary fashion as the normal populations; the "normal" populations simply are not as aware of these rituals of power extending control over their abnormal and normal behavior.

The powers of the human sciences and the state become interdependent on the ability of both forces to specify, measure, and manipulate information about individuals and groups. Discovering and controlling anomalies in the individual and social body preoccupy the discourses of expert cultures and the practices of the state as they engage in "the measurement of overall phenomena, the description of groups, the calculation of the gaps between individuals, their distribution in a given 'population.' "[8] One set of operations detects the anomalies. Another related set of therapeutic, corrective, or remedial interventions eliminates the anomalous quality in the individual or social body.

Yet these elaborate means of objectifying, classifying, and subjectifying the subject cannot be disentangled from the increasingly interventionist power of the state. Not only is the state a kind of macrosocial force aimed at policing the "totality," it also is a microsocial power organized around the "individualization" of subjects. As Foucault observes, "the state's power (and that's one of the reasons for its strength) is both an individualizing and a totalizing form of power. Never, I think, in the history of human societies—even in the old Chinese society—has there been such a tricky combination in the same political structures of individualization techniques, and of totalization procedures."[9] The regime of power/knowledge highlights the two-sidedness of subjectivity, namely, as "subject to someone else by control and dependence, and tied to his own identity by a conscience or self-knowledge." [10] The subject comes to self-knowledge and develops a conscience in the modern era, therefore, only inasmuch as it becomes increasingly subject to or dependent upon the networks of power/knowledge elaborated by the state and human sciences.

Discipline, Biopower, and the State

In addition to documenting the formative processes of the subject on the plane of microsocial "individualization," Foucault also elaborates the genesis of the modern state on the plane of macrosocial "totalization." Here, then, the modes of biopower emerge in both their individual and social forms. As Foucault claims:

> One of these poles—the first to be formed, it seems—centered on the body as a machine: its disciplining, the optimization of its capabilities, the extortion of its forces, the parallel increase of its usefulness and its docility, its integration into systems of efficient and economic controls, all this was ensured by the procedures of power that characterized the *disciplines*: an *anatomo-politics* of the *human body.* The second, formed somewhat later, focused on the species body, the body imbued with the mechanics of life and serving as the basis of the biological processes: propagation, births and mortality, the level of health, life expectancy and longevity, with all the conditions that can cause these to vary. Their supervision was effected through an entire series of interventions and *regulatory controls: a biopolitics of the population.*[11]

The emergence of centralized autocratic states in Western Europe from the sixteenth through the eighteenth centuries is the event used by Foucault to explore these new links between the state and the individual. Specifically, Foucault focuses upon the policing powers of these new states, as discussed in professional treatises on the "art of government," which developed an instrumentally rational concern over "how to introduce economy, that is the correct manner of managing individuals, goods and wealth with the family . . . into the management of the state." [12]

Rather than discoursing about sovereignty and moral right, these new treatises stress economic or instrumental rationality in the state's organization of humans interrelating with things. Foucault cites Guillaume de la Perriere's *Miroir de la Politique* (1567) to support this shift: "Government is the right disposition of things arranged so as to lead to a convenient end." [13] Guided by these discursive insights, Foucault believes the state assumes administrative responsibility over every dimension of group and individual life.

> Consequently, the things which the government is to be concerned about are men, but men in their relations, their links, their imbrication with those other things which are wealth, resources, means of subsistence, the territory with its specific qualities, climate, irrigation, fertility, etc.; men in their relation to other kinds of things which are customs, habits, ways of doing and thinking, etc.; lastly, men in their relation to that other kind of things which are accidents and misfortunes such as famine, epidemics, death, etc. [14]

In turn, the arts of government promoted the development of empirical knowledge over the state's and its subjects' resources and behavior, measured and judged in statistical terms. The administrative concern with population, family, economic, and health statistics after the eighteenth century reflects this interest by the state in documenting the growth and health of individual subjects and the totality of subjects.

Yet Foucault also sees this new administrative regime as one of new powers, or "biopower," which designates "what brought life and its mechanisms into the realm of explicit calculations and made knowledge-power an agent of transformation of human life." [15] Biopower, at the individual level and the level of the social totality, concentrates upon creating the "docile body that may be subjected, used, transformed and improved." [16] The technologies of discipline and surveillance mobilized by the state to police its social activities work to objectify the body of individuals, as subjects in schools, prisons, hospitals, factories, barracks, or asylums, and the body of society, as totalities of "populations" in health, population, fertility, production, and mortality statistics. Two new entities, then, are created through the disciplinary technologies of bio-power—the society as state-administered totality and the individual subject as state-managed individuality—and its objectification of the body. The disciplinary technologies derive their power, as Foucault observes, from "the ensemble of minute technical inventions that made it possible to increase the useful size of multiplicities [i.e., a workshop, school, army, or nation] by decreasing the inconveniences of the power which, in order to make them useful, must control them." [17]

Similarly, Foucault sees these disciplinary technologies of bio-power, using "anonymous instruments of power . . . such as hierar-chical surveillance, continuing registration, perpetual assessment and classification," [18] as inextricably bound up with the emergence of capitalism. In fact, the logic of reification in the disciplines of biopower mirrors and parallels the commodification logic of exchange. With capitalism and the regime of biopower, "each makes the other possible and necessary; each provides a model for the other." [19] Foucault, then, maintains that

> if the economic take-off of the West began with the techniques that made possible the accumulation of capital, it might perhaps be said that the methods for administering the accumulation of men made possible a political take-off in relation to the traditional, ritual, costly, violent forms of power, which soon fell into disuse and were superseded by a subtle, calculated technology of subjection. In fact, the two processes—the accumulation of men and the accumulation of capital—cannot be separated; it would not have been possible to solve the problem of the accumulation of men without the growth of an apparatus of production capable of both sustaining them and using them; conversely, the techniques that made the cumulative multiplicity of men useful accelerated the accumulation of capital.[20]

This ultimate "subtle, calculated technology of subjection" generated during the modern era is epitomized by "panoptic" technology, typified by Bentham's design for a prison organized as a panopticon. Under the "eye of power," the occupants of modern panoptic social structure live in "small theatres, in which each actor is alone, perfectly individualized and constantly visible." [21] This pure technology of control forces its occupants and controllers by virtue of its structure to order their own behavior through its powers. As Foucault concludes, "Power is not totally entrusted to someone who would exercise it alone, over others, in an absolute fashion; rather, this machine is one in which everyone is caught, those who exercise this power as well as those who are subjected to it." [22]

The other consequence of developing biopower in the modern state is "the growing importance assumed by the action of the norm, at the expense of the judicial system of the law." [23] Biopower, unlike legal punitive mechanisms based on death, is a power "whose task is to take charge of life," using "continuous regulatory and corrective mechanisms." Therefore, normalization and enforcing normal behavior through disciplinary technologies now drive modern states' policing of individuals and society.

> It is no longer a matter of bringing death into play in the field of sovereignty, but of distributing the living in the domain of value and utility. Such a power

has to qualify, measure, appraise, and hierarchize, rather than display itself in its murderous splendor; it does not have to draw the line that separates the enemies of the sovereign from his obedient subjects; it effects distributions around the norm. I do not mean to say that the law fades into the background or that the institutions of justice tend to disappear, but rather that the law operates more and more as a norm, and that the judicial institution is increasingly incorporated into a continuum of apparatuses (medical, administrative, and so on) whose functions are for the most part regulatory. A normalizing society is the historical outcome of a technology of power centered on life.[24]

Likewise, normalization underlies the modern "rights," "to life, to one's body, to health, to happiness, to the satisfaction of needs." [25] The rights to these states of enjoyment largely are imperatives to distribute one's behaviors correctly around the norms of living, health, happiness, and bodily maintenance set under biopowered disciplines.

These developing schemes of normalization from the social sciences entail a definite regression in judicial power and sovereignty. Here, Foucault claims, "we should not be deceived by all the constitutions framed throughout the world since the French Revolution, the codes written and revised, a whole continual and clamorous legislative activity: these were the forms that made an essentially normalizing power acceptable." [26] Under this regime, individuals and societies suffer a new political "double bind," which is the simultaneous individualization and totalization of modern power structures that impose new forms of "individualization" on persons as well as new modes of "totalization" on societies.

Truth, Intellectuals, and Power

Foucault argues that truth in these normalizing regimes of biopower "is linked in a circular relation with systems of power which produce and sustain it, and to effects of power which it induces and which extend it." [27] The struggle "for truth" actually is a contest about how truth is defined, created, and administered in the economy and polity. Truths are not "discovered" to be so and accepted as such; on the contrary, they are "systems of rules" for defining and dividing the true from the false in attaching power to the true. Truth, in turn, "is to be understood as a system of ordered procedures for the production, regulation, distribution, circulation and operation of statements" within an elaborate "political, economic, institutional regime of the production of truth." [28]

In the case of the social sciences, these relations of truth production are interlocked completely with relations of power. They become, as discussed in Chapter 5 in light of Marcuse's critique of technology, a basis for "the research of total administration." Specifically, Foucault claims:

> "Truth" is centered on the form of scientific discourse and the institutions which produce it; it is subject to constant economic and political incitement (the demand for truth, as much for economic production as for political power); it is the object, under diverse forms, of immense diffusion and consumption (circulating through apparatuses of education and information whose extent is relatively broad in the social body, notwithstanding certain strict limitations); it is produced and transmitted under the control, dominant if not exclusive, of a few great political and economic apparatuses (university, army, writing, media); lastly, it is the issue of a whole political debate and social confrontation ("ideological" struggles).[29]

Within these networks, intellectuals also can occupy a "specific" rather than a "universal" position, a class position (serving capital or the proletariat), a professional position (the field of research, laboratory position, academic job, or work environment), and a social power/knowledge position (the relation to the larger social apparatus of truth creation and management).

The "political problems of intellectuals," however, must not be thought of "in terms of 'science' and 'ideology' but in terms of 'truth' and 'power.' "[30] Truth cannot be separated from power, but Foucault suggests that intellectuals can constitute "a new politics of truth" by "detaching the power of truth from the forms of hegemony, social, economic, and cultural, within which it operates at the present time."[31] Like the disciplinary technologies, the apparatus of truth materially assists the productivity of power in modern social regimes. Specific intellectuals build and operate the discourses of truth production, circulation, and consumption. The object of analysis, classes of truth, and policing of meanings coexist with "systems of power which produce and sustain it, and to effects of power which it induces and which it extends it."[32]

When one accepts Foucault's characterization of these modes of power and knowledge, the diverse scientific claims made by empirical political analysis in the present era perhaps assume a different quality. What powers are producing what kinds of truth in naturalistic, empirical political analysis today? How do specific intellectuals, such as empirical political scientists, fit into the apparatus of truth and disciplinary technologies of modern biopower? What concepts and categories are used in empirical political analysis as "interpretations" to classify, objectify, and manipulate bodies and groups? How do the individualization and totalization of biopower fit into social science discourse today? What is the disciplinary intent behind the arts of government in the present? A reinterpretation of the role played by the concept of political culture/political socialization in empirical political analysis might shed light on these questions. Admittedly, this account is only a partial interpretation. Yet, it does uncover several suggestive parallels to Foucault's analysis, forcing one to reevaluate, at least tentatively, the naturalistic dimensions of modern American political research, as I also advocated in Chapter 8.

Political Culture and Biopower

For the most part, Foucault's system of analysis relies on historical examples and cultural materials from the sixteenth through the nineteenth centuries. Having revealed the logic of biopower and the disciplinary technologies at the time of their initial inception, he largely leaves open the subsequent manner of their further development.[33] So, like Foucault, one must look for ruptures, discontinuities, or abrupt shifts in discourses to find shifts in theory and practice, because small turns in a formal tradition or apparently minor turns in professional discourse reveal much about power and knowledge. Here, the shift from the pre-World War II concern with "making citizens" to the post-1945 fascination with "political culture/political socialization" in development discourses can be closely analyzed to examine how new "disciplines" might be assisting the creation of "biopower" in the present.

In naturalistic schools of American political science, such disciplinary techniques seem to be mobilized continually to serve power today. From Foucault's standpoint, one only has to scan the labor market notices in American political science to witness the search for "specific intellectuals" by agencies of the state to operate particular "apparatuses of truth" with their disciplinary knowledge. For example, in the July 1984 *American Political Science Association Personnel Service Newsletter*, a notice from the U.S. Information Agency (USIA) advertised employment for a "Social Science Analyst—Latin American Branch," who "will design and analyze sample surveys of Latin American elite and general public opinion on ideas relevant to U.S. foreign policy or dealing with media habits and information sources of Latin American politics." [34] In the December 1985 *Newsletter*, the U.S. Central Intelligence Agency (CIA) sought to employ political scientists in analytical positions as "political methodologists" with "training in one or more of the following: elections, electoral behavior, public policy, mass attitudes or elite studies . . . preference will be given to those with research experience in the field of comparative politics." [35] The USIA also sought in the March 1986 *Newsletter* "a full-time Social Science Analyst to work on the People's Republic of China. . . . the work involves planning and executing . . . studies on audiences, mass media . . . public opinion, and images of U.S. society and policies relevant to agency interests in the PRC." [36] Similar searches for African, Asian, Middle Eastern, and European specialists by the USIA and CIA also appear frequently in the "Positions in Applied Settings" section of the APSA's *Personnel Service Newsletter.* Obviously, in noting these phenomena I am not claiming that the CIA and USIA run the modern world. However, these notices do illustrate what Foucault argues—the modern state does employ the talents of specific intellectuals, who manipulate specialized apparatuses of empirical truth construction, to rationalize its rule with special disciplinary knowledge.

As in Europe before the "social revolutions of the 18th century," the "citizen-at-large" in Africa, Asia and Latin America prior to the 1960s was nothing more than a "shadow figure on the political stage." [37] Social scientists, on the whole, did not "give much attention to what the man on the street thought or how he came to hold these thoughts" throughout the Third World.[38] For American decision makers, elite and mass public opinion in Latin America as well as Asia, Africa, or the Middle East was ignored or seen as nonexistent. These CIA and USIA searches for methodologically sophisticated analysts indicate that times have changed.

Still, what has changed? Why is public opinion abroad now a subject of professional truth generation? Has a mature public, a civic political culture, and a complex tradition of political opinion developed worldwide in less than 20 years? What do these searches for political analysts by the American state reveal about individual political subjectivity and our understanding of political culture in the Third World? How can the conceptions of political culture and individual subjectivity guiding these CIA and USIA "political methodologists" and "social science analysts" contribute to the decision-making circles of the American government? Arguably, the production of "scientific truths" by political methodologists goes hand in hand with the bipolar ideological struggles of the post-1945 era. The system of democracy, development, capitalism, and freedom produced by power in the West seeks normalizing control and disciplinary tools to maintain itself, to contain the Soviet bloc, and to expand abroad. Appraising the receptivity of new subjects and monitoring the acceptance of existing ones for the system of power drives these apparatuses of truth. Foucault sees the kinds of subjectivity that the CIA and USIA are monitoring as the product of power relations, working out of "systems of rules" or "interpretations."

Since interpretation is "the violent or surreptitious appropriation of a system of rules, which in itself has no essential meaning, in order to impose a direction, to bend it to a new will, to force its participation in a different game, and to subject it to secondary rules, then the development of humanity is a series of interpretations." [39] Accordingly, CIA and USIA mapping of public opinion, elite attitudes, and media debates abroad may represent the attempt of *Pax Americana* to "develop humanity" in terms of its "interpretations." Thus Foucault also would be adamant about how individuality and subjectivity would be defined by these analytical agencies: "The individual is no doubt the fictitious atom of an 'ideological' representation of society; but he is also a reality fabricated by this specific technology of power that I have called 'discipline.' " [40] On one plane, the search for social scientific analysts to survey and sample individual opinion in the Third World may suggest that these societies are becoming less stable; hence the social scientific focus on managing public opinion and mass attitudes in Third World nations with a new "system of rules." Yet, on another plane, the scientization of patterns in their political behavior also suggests that these populations are becoming implicated in the complicated normalizing processes of advanced industrial societies. Creating a discourse about public opinion, political culture, and individual socialization, on one level, is an attempt to do empirical research. On another level, however, it also may become an effort to reduce individuals to political forces and maximize their useful forces at the least cost. Such processes include, as Foucault claims, the social scientific manufacture of "artifacts," such as political culture, elite attitudes, political socialization, and public opinion, in the power/knowledge discourses of social science. It represents the modern impulse to reduce the bodies and minds of individuals through scientific classification and objectification to *things*, making it possible for the state to mobilize their energies more rationally. Ironically, in terms of Rousseau's project, as discussed in Chapter 4, these tendencies show how real Rousseau's worst fears about manipulating human perfection have become as well as how far away from his notions of "civic virtue" modern democracies have wandered.

Here it is useful to develop a genealogy of political culture, retracing the discourses of political socialization and cultural change that have evolved out of it. Genealogy, as Foucault outlines, "deals with series of effective formation of discourse: it attempts to grasp it in its power of affirmation, by which I do not mean a power opposed to that of negation, but the power of constituting a domain of objects, in relation to which one can affirm or deny true or false propositions." [41] These investigative rules, as Dreyfus and Rabinow admit, lead one to "the relations of power, knowledge and the body in modern society." Genealogical analysis, therefore, records the history of "interpretations" or "the history of morals, ideas, and metaphysical concepts. . . . they must be made to appear as events on the stage of historical process." [42] Yet, at the same time, such genealogical study "leads to a strange and complex attitude: one has to take the world of serious discourse seriously because it is the one we are in, and yet one can't take it seriously, first because we have arduously divorced ourselves from it, and second because it is not grounded." [43] These attitudes are quite useful for investigating how the discourse of political culture tries to constitute a new domain of objects, reflecting the statecraft of the contemporary world system.

Like Foucault, then, this discussion of the political culture concept involves a pragmatically oriented interpretation of historical events and practices. Most important, the workings of power and the construction of truth can be observed in the cultural practices that fuse the expression of power and knowledge in social science. Such practices underpin the contemporary understanding of "truths" about the individual subject, society, and the social sciences. As Dreyfus and Rabinow suggest, one must study "those doubtful sciences thoroughly enmeshed in cultural practices, which in spite of their orthodoxies show no sign of becoming normal sciences; study them with a method which reveals that truth itself is a central component of modern power." [44] No "doubtful science" among the human or social sciences reveals its integration of truth and practice with modern power as well as contemporary empirical political analysis. The discourse of political culture/political socialization, which may find its foundations in the modern state's need for stability through the civic cultural training and effective political socialization of "democratic subjects," might reveal a great deal about truth and power as they are understood in today's doubtful human sciences.

Simply because it is the first, the most comprehensive, and the best known example of such research on political culture/political socialization, this investigation will focus on Almond and Verba's *The Civic*

Culture.[45] This modern text seems to exemplify best the type of scientific discourse that Foucault treats in his critiques of the human sciences. The engagement of power/knowledge with political culture/political socialization in post-World War II works of American political science, like Almond and Verba's *The Civic Culture,* descends in part from Charles E. Merriam's earlier work on "the making of citizens." [46] Merriam's naturalistic research program identified the objective practices of social science as part of a larger, formal series of sciences immediately responsible for explaining and manipulating the interrelations of political groups and individuals. "If biology explains the lower forms of life," he argues, "psychology the subhuman groupings, and anthropology the primitive human developments, it remains for social science to account for the behavior of the social groupings on a higher level; and for politics to interpret the special governmental or patriotic cohesions." [47]

"Cohesions," or the mechanisms or techniques for generating the cohesiveness of the political self and political regime, guide Merriam's work. To a very real extent, Merriam's "cohesive influences," exerted through formal schooling, the state, patriotic organizations, the family, religious institutions, and the political press as "mechanisms of civic education," parallel Foucault's analysis of "disciplinary technologies" generating "biopower." Like Foucault, Merriam senses that the search for "cohesions" must not be confined "to political society alone, for the same query may be raised in any group, whether civil or ecclesiastical, or business or social. For in all these societies there appear similar patterns of obedience and conformity, so well developed as to become almost automatic in action and yet capable of disintegration and destruction. What are, we may ask, the essential elements in the texture of group cohesion?" [48]

These same patterns of "almost automatic obedience and authority" in the individual behavior of subjects in political groups, which, in turn, "produced" or "made" them as citizen objects, became the focus of political culture studies in the 1950s and 1960s. However, in the tense setting of superpower conflict, these studies celebrate the individual subject's global acceptance as an important new political actor. "In all the new nations of the world," Almond and Verba note, "the belief that the ordinary man is politically relevant—that he ought to be an involved participant in the political system—is widespread." [49] Likewise, "political elites are rare who do not profess commitment to this goal." [50] Implicitly, Almond and Verba concede that the emergence of individual subjectivity for "the ordinary man" unfolds hand in hand with statization of "the new nations of the world." This populist rupture with the classical autocratic traditions in most of the developing nations was made by colonialism, war, or corporate penetration. As a result, the idea of the subject and state, as critical social institutions, also was implanted with this spread of Western capitalism. Almond and Verba's empirical political analysis, by the same token, can be seen as the first scientific cross-national attempt of naturalistic analysis to define and classify the cohesions of biopower in this new world of nations. In *The Civic Culture Revisited*, nearly two decades later, which also was produced in a context of continuing superpower conflict, these theoretical intentions are reaffirmed.[51] As Verba claims, "*The Civic Culture* asked the right questions. It did not always ask them as precisely as they might have been asked, nor did it ask all the relevant questions about democratic stability. But it opened important areas of study."[52]

Building a Microapparatus
of Truth Generation

Learned treatises on "the arts of government" such as Almond and Verba's *The Civic Culture* and *The Civic Culture Revisited* are not simply an academic exercise existing *in vacuo*. Both works are grounded in the post-1945 East-West struggle over creating political stability and instability within a new *Pax Americana*. Similarly, both works assess the unity of employing "*survey techniques* to study citizen attitudes and values within a set of quite varied nations to deal with the macropolitical problem of *democratic stability*." [53] Thus psychic states or psychosocial dispositions also now become the objects of formal administration and disciplinary control. And, despite Almond's view that they continue an ancient tradition in political analysis, they represent a break from many earlier works on civic institutions and political education.[54] The scope of their work is much broader. Their research programs are linked to creating a microapparatus of truth relevant to the pressing practical problems of building nations, constructing states, and training citizens in the middle of the twentieth century as the colonial and fascist empires of Europe collapsed.

As Verba admits, "One feature of *The Civic Culture* was its focus on democratic stability. We were concerned with why some democracies survive while others collapse more than with the question of how well democracies perform." [55] From Foucault's standpoint, this text could manifest how biopower, as it is revealed by contemporary social scientific discourse, is developing on a global scale. "Men in relation to other kinds of things which are customs, habits, ways of doing and thinking" [56] are the targets of this empirical political analysis. Such works, set at the limits of their scientific discourses' powers, "have codified and interpreted our knowledge of one of the most central and abiding themes of political theory—how men are inducted into their politics." [57] In deploying their discursive strategies, these works disclose one dimension in the workings of biopower and reveal new rituals of power in the modern state.

In political culture/political socialization discourses, the "docile body," which is to be used, transformed, improved, and controlled, is the *citizen* and the *political culture*. The individualization strategies, as Merriam would claim, are those of "making citizens," while the totalization strategies, as Almond and Verba illustrate, are those of "developing a civic culture." Biopower brings to life both of these new entities, making the psychic state of the citizen, as revealed in attitudes and values, and the political culture, as typified by model distributions of attitudes and values, objects of explicit calculation, revealing, once more, how "modern man is an animal whose politics places his existence as a living being in question." [58]

To elaborate the power/knowledge of "the civic culture and open polity" [59] Almond and Verba recognize that

> if we are to come closer to understanding the problems of the diffusion of democratic culture, we have to specify the content of *what* has to be diffused, to develop appropriate measures for it, to discover its quantitative incidence and demographic distribution in countries with a wide range of experience with democracy. . . . with such knowledge we can speculate intelligently about "how much of what" must be present in a country before democratic institutions take root in congruent attitudes and expectations.[60]

But instead of *speculating* about democratic institutions, they define their content by examining attitudes in a number of operating democratic systems through the normalizing techniques or "the test of empirical-quantitative analysis." This examination of individuals and nations in terms of disciplined methods trains their attention and activity on the norms of "operating democratic systems." [61] The "working democracies" constitute a norm, which is a controlled distribution of qualities and traits, restructuring the image of "how much of what" must be present to make a nation fit into the grid of normalized expectations. These specified contents, then, seem to be the "truths" that identify anomalies and set standards for their neutralization or correction once the qualities of democratic culture and citizenship are produced.

Unlike traditional political theory, or the moral-juridical studies of democracy "from Aristotle to Bryce," [62] Almond and Verba, as Foucault predicts, present their work as discontinuous, wholly new, a break in these hermeneutic and critical traditions. It is an effort to formulate a "scientific theory of democracy" using survey research to objectify, classify, and subjectify individuals with "the most precise methods available." [63] They are not occupied by philosophical concerns about freedom, citizenship, or morality. On the contrary, Almond and Verba present their study of political culture as an expert-professional response to a cluster of policy problems—totalitarianism, fragile democracies, embattled liberalism, rapid decolonization—in a world experiencing a "participation explosion." In this world, new nations "are presented with two different models of modern participatory state, the democratic and the totalitarian." [64] If a democratic model is to take hold in new nations, Almond and Verba believe it needs more than the formal institutions and traditional theories of democratic life—it "requires as well a political culture consistent with it." [65] In the post-1945 era, the subject of these discourses shifts from one of colonialism, Westernization, and civilization to one of national liberation, modernization, and development.[66] At the same time, the form of individual subjectivity, as Almond and Verba note with the "participation explosion," moves from one of docile colonial subjects to that of mobilized citizens under either democratic capitalism or socialist collectivism.

Even though "Western social science has only begun to codify the operating characteristics of the democratic polity itself . . . and the understanding of their inner workings, operating norms, and social-psychological preconditions are only now being realized in the West," [67] Almond and Verba, as social scientists, recognize "we can put the questions in such a way as to get useful answers." [68] Political culture can serve as a conceptual technology for codifying "truthfully" the essential norms and preconditions of popular government, allowing one to build a "stable and effective democracy." Before the disciplinary technologies of empirical political analysis can grasp

> the problems of the diffusion of democratic culture, we have to be able to specify the content of what has to be diffused to develop appropriate measures for it, to discover its quantitative incidence and demographic distribution in countries with a wide range of experience with democracy.

With such knowledge we can speculate intelligently about "how much of what" must be present in a country before democratic institutions take root in congruent attitudes and expectations.[69]

The empirical manipulation made in these microapparatuses of truth generation by Almond and Verba "amounts to a series of experiments intended to test" their hypotheses about political culture and democracy. Yet, for Foucault, these operations also can become a new set of interpretations to impose another system of rules on mass behavior. And they compose the tools of registration, assessment, and classification that states employ in their attempts to create docile subjects.

The democratic and nondemocratic are defined through objectified classifications that establish the normal and abnormal. England and America set the norm of democratic governments, as Almond and Verba's hypotheses "draw 'lessons' from British and American history." [70] These lessons, however, serve as normalizing standards for all other nations, indicating "what attitudes and behavior must be present in other countries if they are to become democratic." [71] This imbricate relation of the totality and individual in biopower might seem overdone by Foucault. Yet, Almond and Verba focus on the exact same coupling of forces for "classifying objects of political orientation." [72] In examining "patterns of orientation toward political objects among members of the nation" to understand "the 'general' political system" and "at the other extreme . . . the 'self' as political actor" they define and classify two separate ranges of attitudes to discover the optimal distribution of preferable psychosocial traits in the undisciplined variance of mass political behavior.[73]

This coupling shows how empirical political analysis unconsciously might reveal the dynamics of biopower operating in contemporary societies as well as the discursive apparatus used in social sciences to objectify and manipulate its workings in disciplinary technologies. For Almond and Verba, the constructs of political culture "refer to the political system as internalized in the cognitions, feelings, and evaluations of its population." [74] These internalized disciplines include "attitudes toward the political system and its various parts, and attitudes toward the role of the self in the system." [75] This approach, then, constructs three new *things,* or objects of truth generation, in its classification of the types of political culture—the subject, the parochial, and the participant political cultures. It also sees only three categories of citizens—subjects, parochials, and participants—coexisting as configurations of psychic orientations in actual political systems. For Almond and Verba, a citizen-subject is not the moral subject of political theory classics. Instead, this type of citizen is passive and undemanding in the political system, while the citizen-parochial is ignorant of and expects nothing from the political system.[76] And, "in general, a parochial, subject or participant culture would be most congruent with, respectively, a traditional political structure, and a democratic political structure." [77] By compounding these classes with multiple subclasses of categories involving affective, cognitive, and evaluative orientations toward input, output, self, and system objects, the analysis builds its "grid of intelligibility" [78] from this range of political cultures to analyze real political systems.

Almond and Verba plainly admit they are motivated by a desire to describe a "civic culture " and the roles "it plays in the maintenance of a democratic political system." [79] However, they also hold that the classical ideals of political theory for democratic citizenship overemphasize a " 'rationality-activist' model of political culture." [80] The fully rational subject, guided by reason rather than emotion, in the well-informed calculation of public interest and principle simply does not constitute an adequate model for maintaining democracy. A civic culture assumes this inadequate classical image *"plus something else,"* namely, "an allegiant participant culture." For empirical political analysis, individuals should participate in politics, but "not give up their orientations as subjects nor parochials." [81] That is, they must behave *less* like classical moral subjects and *more* like clients of modern state bureaucracy to make democracy stable and effective.

The implication here is obvious. To maintain stability and legitimacy in a democratic system, their analytical artifact, "the civic culture," stresses the roles and orientations of a *parochial* and *subject* to " 'manage,' or keep in place the participant political orientations." [82] Traditional attitudes of following and obedience must be blended with modern attitudes of participation and self-assertion in sound democracies. Affirming Huntington's diagnosis of the "democratic distemper" [83] in the 1970s as a "creedal passion," which allegedly was marked by excessive mass participation, Almond and Verba suggest that "by itself this participant-rationalist model of citizenship could not logically sustain a *stable* democratic government." [84] A civic culture for democratic societies, therefore, must stress a new scientifically normalized balance "in which political activity, involvement, and rationality exist but are balanced by passivity, traditionality, and commitment to parochial values." [85] Discovering and, then, possibly controlling anomalies in individual citizens as well as in many nations' body politic is the disciplinary intent of this microapparatus of truth generation. The "civic culture," then, is clearly something less than Rousseau's "civic virtue."

This celebration of apathy by empirical political analysis is frequently criticized by normative political theory.[86] However, like Marcuse's critique of "one-dimensionality," Foucault's critique goes far beyond these observations. Given his view of the human sciences, Foucault would argue that empirical political analysis not only "finds" apathy to be a common behavior, it actually constitutes a system of rules for creating and legitimating apathy, docility, and passivity in mass politics. Thus he maintains that power should not be discussed in terms of its negative influences. "In fact," he suggests, "power produces; it produces reality; it produces domains of objects and rituals of truth. The individual and the knowledge that may be gained of him belong to this production." [87] Consequently, Foucault would hold that apathy is not an outcome of power that social scientists merely discover; instead, apathetic docility is a product of power that social scientists help to manufacture, albeit imperfectly, within the powerful dominant system of normalizing rules by defining "activism" as an anomalous mode of behavior.

The disciplinary intent of Almond and Verba's "political anatomy" of the citizenry, then, is disposed toward generating docility and passivity, or, at least, classifying these behaviors as *normal* when and where they already exist. The "civic culture" construct might constitute a "small cell of power within which the separation, coordination and supervision of tasks" are "imposed and made efficient." [88] Normalization through criteria of cross-national comparison is the strategy of political culture analysis. Passivity, traditionalism, and parochialism are separated as tasks of citizenship to be coordinated with the requisite balance of political activity, involvement, and rationality in the supervisory gaze of social science. "Discipline," again, "is the unitary technique by which the body is reduced as a 'political' force at the least cost and maximized as a useful force." [89] By analytically partitioning the psychocultural substance of citizens and the citizenry into subject, parochial, and participant components and recombining them in empirical scientific systems of truth, the state can guarantee passivity, traditionality, and parochialism with discursive operations aimed at constraining individual action. Thus the citizen can be made useful cheaply, by limiting his or her freedom, voice, and power in favor of and as part of expert-administered stability.

Political culture is studied scientifically to understand how it creates and maintains "stable and effective democracy." [90] Unlike political theorists, Almond and Verba do not believe that the "rational activist model" of democratic citizenship promotes stability or effectiveness. Instead, they affirm the power/knowledge of expert discourses, "the elites," over the common people, "the ordinary citizen," in holding that political culture must implant or enforce orientations in the masses that accommodate them to elite power. That is, if "elite power is to be achieved, quite contradictory attitudes and behavior are to be expected of the ordinary man." [91]

Docility, discipline, and amenability to control are the ideals of the democracy of biopower. Or, as Almond and Verba argue, if

> the alternate pole of elite power is to be achieved, quite contradictory attitudes and behavior are to be expected of the ordinary man. If elites are to be powerful and make authoritative decisions, then the involvement, activity, and influence of the ordinary man must be limited. The ordinary citizen must turn power over to elites and let them rule. The need for elite power requires that the ordinary citizen be relatively passive, uninvolved, and deferential to elites. [92]

As subjects in and of the apparatus of biopower, citizens must accept being subject to and subjects of elite power. The ideal democratic citizen is not a rational activist, but a parochial subject whose passivity en masse creates stability. Under the dictates of biopower, as Almond and Verba scientifically observe, "the democratic citizen is called on to pursue contradictory goals: he must be active, yet passive; involved, yet not too involved; influential, yet deferential." [93] Having been objectified, scientifically assessed, and psychosocially classified, citizens merge into the currents of biopower as data points in a code of power/knowledge manufactured from their behavior. Here, then, one finds that the anonymous instruments of power and the forces they exert over citizens from within

> are coextensive with the multiplicity that they regiment, such as hierarchical surveillance, continuous registration, perpetual assessment and classification. In short, to substitute for a power that is manifested through the brilliance of those who exercise it, a power that insidiously objectifies those on whom it is applied; to form a body of knowledge about these individuals, rather than to deploy the ostentatious signs of sovereignty. [94]

Democratic institutions and techniques are not in doubt for empirical political analysis, but the "cohesions" of political culture for democracy are. That is, "a pattern of political attitudes and an underlying set of social attitudes that is supportive of a stable democratic process," which constitute the channels of biopower, become the object of their research.[95] The disciplinary technologies of biopower, running through the rituals of power in schools, prisons, clinics, armies, architecture, or workplaces, generate these "subtler cultural components" behind democratic institutions.[96]

Political culture discourse is one mode of power/knowledge connecting the individualization of micropolitics and the totalization of macropolitics. An individual's political attitudes and social motivations as well as their relation to the larger structures and procedures of political systems, Almond and Verba argue, can best be delimited in political culture. "In other words, the connecting link between micro- and macropolitics is political culture."[97] Since certain psychological tendencies in individuals are needed to operate a political regime, and given that political systems cannot work without particular psychological qualities in individuals, the discourse of political culture/political socialization ties the two realms strategically together. It reveals the individual plane of political psychology to the social plane of system organization by mapping out attitudinal and behavior tendencies in the cultural structure of the system.

Here, then, control might be found. "Thus any polity," Almond and Verba proclaim, "may be described and compared with other polities in terms of (1) structural-functional characteristics, and (2) its cultural, subcultural, and role-cultural characteristics. Our analysis of types of political culture is a first effort at treating the phenomena of individual political orientation in such a way as to relate them systematically to the phenomena of political structure."[98] The "dividing practices" now can be exercised on citizens and states, dividing the cases into types of political culture—variant mixes of subject/parochial/participant culture—and classifying individual subjectification within them against the norms embedded in political institutions.

Moreover, an analysis of any particular nation's political culture can be subdivided further into its *system, process,* and *policy cultures.* "System culture" would encompass "attitudes toward the legitimacy of the regime and its various institutions, and attitudes toward the legitimacy and effectiveness of the incumbents of the various political roles."[99] "Process culture" denotes "attitudes toward the self in politics (e.g., parochial-subject-participant), and attitudes toward other political actors (e.g., trust, cooperative competence, hostility)," while "policy culture" is "the distribution of preferences regarding the outputs and outcomes of politics, the ordering among different groupings in the population of such political values as welfare, security and liberty." [100] In drawing these substantive implications out of political culture, empirical analysis attempts to mark the accessible pressure points on the body politic and political subjects for instrumental control. Ultimately, political culture discourse is working toward creating a more consistent, predictive framework of analysis. In "relating" these subspheres of subjectivity together, political culture/political socialization discourse can begin to plot the "constraints" in popular attitudes toward political institutions and policies. "Thus, in a given situation," Almond speculates, "attitudes toward foreign policy, domestic economic policy, and racial segregation may be parts of a consistent ideology; for most individuals in this group, if one knew how they stood on foreign policy one could predict their views on taxation, on busing, and the like." [101] Normalizing control, then, might be exerted not only over individual subjects' attitudes about their polity and their own political personae, but also over their "freedoms of choice" in determining policy preferences.

To maintain a democratic political system, as Almond and Verba indicate, American, British, Italian, German, and Mexican attitudes can be divided, objectified, classified, and manipulated to indicate that the norms of civic culture are most powerful in America and Britain—because "these two nations most closely approximate the model" considered as the ideal—and the most tenuous in Mexico, Italy, and Germany—since in these nations "there are important deviations from these ideal patterns." [102] In other words, the civic culture "appropriate for maintaining a stable and effective democratic political process can best be appreciated if we consider the impact of deviations from this model." [103] Normalization agendas in the model, posed in terms of substantive precedents in certain democratic nation-states, both identify the deviants and prescribe corrections for deviance.

Conclusions

As this partial interpretation of political culture and individual subjectivity illustrates, the present-day naturalistic use of such concepts fits into the logic of power, knowledge, and truth that Foucault outlines. While there are non-Marxological elements and conceptual weaknesses in Foucault's approach, his categories of interpretation do cast an interesting light on contemporary political science. [104] As unsophisticated as it might seem now, a work like Almond and Verba's *The Civic Culture* may represent an important discursive attempt to create detailed, sophisticated, "specific intellectual" knowledge about the organization of individual subjectivity by modern states. Such works suggest that *statecraft* is a form of *soulcraft*. Thus their self-presentation in this microapparatus of truth is one of creating order, making citizens, building nations in a world of flux lest totalitarian regimes displace democratic institutions. Consequently, social scientific *soulcraft* also can become a form of modern technocratic *statecraft*. Political culture ultimately involves the micrological socialization of power/politics, while political socialization also presumes a particular macrological culture of power/politics. "The modes of circulation, valorization, attribution and appropriation of discourses," Foucault states, "vary with each culture and are modified within each." [105] Thus one perhaps must study discourses, like political theory and empirical political analysis, according to their "modes of existence" or "social relationships." [106] In particular, one must recognize that traditional political theory usually has been a hermeneutic and critical product of definite authors, who were or are "specific intellectuals" often aspiring to serve as "universal intellectuals," while empirical political analysis is interconnected completely with the works of "specific intellectuals" with a direct, localized relation to scientific knowledge production in the modern state, which often casts their work in the role of the "universal intellectual" that Foucault definitely resists. [107]

Political culture, as Almond states, "is not a theory; it refers to a set of variables which may be used in the construction of theories." [108] Political culture discourse, in turn, can be seen as a construct of specific intellectuals, who may be generating power/knowledge in their empirical political analysis within the biopower networks of the state. Foucault clearly embraces the idea of specific intellectuals, seeing this path as the correct one to follow. Individual subjectivity, on the other hand, is often an idea tied to intellectuals as "bearers of universal values" speaking to those individual subjects capable of articulating and acting upon ultimate priorities to order their social relations. [109] The discourses of political culture and political socialization, then, are fragments of a larger naturalistic discourse that appears enmeshed within the present bureaucratic-corporate political economy of "truth" about modernization and development. As reductionist categories within predictive theories for producing "true" and "false" statements about political stability, legitimacy, and support, the political culture/political socialization discourse can be seen as a new system of rules. Hence its interpretation tends to complement the "general politics" of truth in the East-West struggle for power by affirming disciplinary practices underpinning liberal capitalist democracies.

The most troubling dimension in these "true" and "false" propositions adduced by empirical political analyses is the lack of critical perspective. In making the ambiguous more definite, they affirm that "what is, should be," because democracy might be the most stable and effective when its normalized subjects remain within the disciplines of biopower. Trusting elite authority and accepting disciplinary technologies, the subject is trained to behave as an "allegiant participant." The ideal citizen is not too active, not too assertive, not too rational. Maintaining the "cohesions" of stable government is a more salient goal for democracy than helping good citizens create a good society. Thus many "specific intellectuals" doing empirical political analysis can generate truths appropriate to the regime and subjects of biopower. Real "rationality-activist" democratic citizens are not "what is," because so few persons are always actively participatory. Hence they "should not be." Empirical political analysis, at the same time, affirms that elite power cannot accommodate popular input effectively, and such mass political activity usually leads to social instability. The disciplinary technologies, then, work toward producing "stable and effective" democracy from passivity, apathy, and parochial deference by normalizing behavior into these appropriate tracks of modern democratic citizenship. Deviations from this norm can be diagnosed, in turn, as political disorders, like a "creedal passion" or the "democratic distemper."

Such thematizations of mass attitudes and individual beliefs for new nations in the Third World also signify their growing integration into the lifeworld of "Western man." Developing the requisite political culture can be seen as part of Third World citizens and states

> gradually learning what it meant to be a living species in a living world, to have a body, conditions of existence, probabilities of life, an individual and collective welfare, forces that could be modified, and a space in which they could be distributed in an optimal manner. For the first time in history, no doubt, biological existence was reflected in political existence, the fact of living was no longer an inaccessible substrate that only emerged from time to time, amid the randomness of death and its fatality; part of it passed into knowledge's field of control and power's sphere of intervention.[110]

The biopower that Foucault describes is essential to the evolution of modern Western capitalism, which could not continue developing without this "controlled insertion of bodies into the machinery of production and the adjustment of the phenomena of population to economic processes" both at home and in the Third World.[111] Political culture, as the vector of individual and social orientations toward objects of power, constitutes one of the "methods of power capable of optimizing forces, aptitudes and life in general without at the same time making them more difficult to govern" in any society and for any individual integrated into the reproduction of modern transnational capitalism.[112]

In conclusion, as the ongoing CIA and USIA searches for "social science analysts" suggest, it is clear that such professional discourses about political culture and its scientific analysis might play a significant role in the political administration of civil society. From Foucault's perspective, "rules are empty in themselves, violent and unfinalized; they are impersonal and can be bent to any purpose. The successes of history belong to those who are capable of seizing these rules, to replace those who had used them, to disguise themselves so as to pervert them, invert their reading and redirect them against those who had initially imposed them." [113] The microapparatuses of truth, like Almond and Verba's conceptual construction of political culture, perhaps have assisted the development of an empirical/predictive discourse for loosely managing regime stability through such systems of rules.

Once the grids for psychosocial definition and behavioral classification are set out by empirical analysis, normalizing scientific analysis and public policies can try to assure stability through trained passivity and quietism. Such scientific analysis is not always accurate, and the political manipulation of attitudes is not always effective. Resistance, as I have argued in Chapters 5, 6, and 7, is possible. Still, the cumulative impulse in naturalistic social scientific research ensures that the analytical apparatus continually works to improve its results. To attain "stable and effective democracy," political elites and state personnel struggle to manipulate the individual attitudes and predispositions that empirical political analysis discloses in political culture studies. Foucault's frameworks, then, provide powerful interpretative insights into how the "truth" constructs of empirical political analysis can be seen as interoperating with normalizing disciplinary technologies for "making citizens" in modern political regimes in both the developing and the developed countries.[114]

Notes

1. Paul Rabinow, "Introduction," *The Foucault Reader* (New York: Pantheon, 1984), 15.

2. Michel Foucault, "Truth and Power," *Power/Knowledge: Selected Interviews and Other Writings, 1972-1977*, ed. by Colin Gordon (New York: Pantheon, 1980), 125-133.

3. See Stephen K. White, "Foucault's Challenge to Critical Theory," *American Political Science Review* 80, no. 2 (June 1986), 419-432.

4. Michel Foucault, *Discipline and Punish: The Birth of the Prison* (New York: Vintage, 1979), 221.

5. Michel Foucault, *The History of Sexuality*, vol. 1, *An Introduction* (New York: Vintage, 1980), 139.

6. Michel Foucault, "Afterword: The Subject and Power," *Beyond Structuralism and Hermeneutics* (2nd ed.), Hubert L. Dreyfus and Paul Rabinow (Chicago: University of Chicago Press, 1983), 208.

7. Ibid.

8. Foucault, *Discipline and Punish,* 190.

9. Foucault, "Afterword," 213.

10. Ibid., 212.

11. Foucault, *History of Sexuality,* 139.

12. Michel Foucault, "On Governmentality," *Ideology and Consciousness* 6 (Autumn 1979), 10.

13. Ibid.

14. Ibid.

15. Foucault, *History of Sexuality,* 143.

16. Foucault, *Discipline and Punish,* 198.

17. Ibid., 220.

18. Ibid.

19. Ibid., 221.

20. Ibid., 220-221.

21. Ibid., 200.

22. Foucault, "The Eye of Power," *Power/Knowledge,* 156.

23. Foucault, *History of Sexuality,* 144.

24. Ibid.

25. Ibid., 145.

26. Ibid., 144.

27. Foucault, "Truth and Power," *Power/Knowledge,* 133.

28. Ibid.

29. Ibid., 131-132.

30. Ibid., 132.

31. Ibid., 133.

32. Ibid.

33. See Foucault, *History of Sexuality*; *Discipline and Punish*; *The Birth of the Clinic: An Archaeology of Medical Perception* (New York: Vintage, 1975); and *Madness and Civilization* (New York: Vintage, 1973).

34. *American Political Science Association Personnel Service Newsletter* 28, no. 10 (July 1984), 4.

35. *American Political Science Association Personnel Service Newsletter* 30, no. 4 (December 1985), 13.

36. *American Political Science Association Personnel Service Newsletter* 30, no. 7 (March 1986), 7.

37. Richard E. Dawson and Kenneth Prewitt, *Political Socialization* (Boston: Little, Brown, 1969), vii.

38. Ibid.

39. Foucault, "Nietzsche, Genealogy, History," *Foucault Reader,* 85.

40. Foucault, *Discipline and Punish,* 194.

41. Michel Foucault, "Appendix: The Discourse on Language," *The Archaeology of Knowledge* (New York: Pantheon, 1982), 234.

42. Foucault, "Nietzsche, Genealogy, History," 86.

43. Dreyfus and Rabinow, *Beyond Structuralism,* 105.

44. Ibid., 120.

45. See Gabriel A. Almond and Sidney Verba, *The Civic Culture: Political Attitudes and Democracy in Five Nations* (Princeton, NJ: Princeton University Press, 1963).

46. See Charles E. Merriam, *The Making of Citizens* (New York: Teachers College Press, 1966).

47. Ibid., 36.

48. Ibid., 35.

49. Almond and Verba, *The Civic Culture,* 4.

50. Ibid.

51. Gabriel A. Almond and Sidney Verba, eds., *The Civic Culture Revisited* (Boston: Little, Brown, 1980).

52. Verba, "On Revisiting the Civic Culture," *Civic Culture Revisited,* 409.

53. Ibid., 397.

54. Almond, "The Intellectual History of the Civic Culture Concept," *Civic Culture Revisited,* 1-36.

55. Verba, "On Revisiting," 407.

56. Foucault, "On Governmentality," 11.

57. Gabriel Almond, James S. Coleman, and Lucian W. Pye, "Foreword," *Political Socialization,* Dawson and Prewitt, vi.

58. Foucault, *History of Sexuality,* 143.

59. Almond and Verba, *The Civic Culture,* 9.

60. Ibid., 9-10.

61. Ibid., 12. Marcuse's discussion of "the research of total administration" buttresses this point. In appraising democratic practices, "the criteria for judging a given state of affairs are those offered by (or, since they are those of a well-functioning and firmly established social system, imposed by) the given state of affairs. The analysis is 'locked'; the range of judgment is confined within a context of facts which excludes judging the context in which the facts are made, man-made, and in which their meaning, function, and development are determined. Committed to this framework, the investigation becomes circular and self-validating. If 'democratic' is defined in the limiting but realistic terms of the actual process of election, then this process is democratic prior to the results of the investigation." Herbert Marcuse, *One-Dimensional Man* (Boston: Beacon, 1964), 116.

62. Ibid., 10.

63. Ibid., 12, viii.

64. Ibid., 4.

65. Ibid., 5.

66. See Samuel P. Huntington, *American Politics: The Promise of Disharmony.* (Cambridge, MA: Harvard University Press, 1981).

67. Almond and Verba, *The Civic Culture,* 5.

68. Ibid., 9.

69. Ibid., 9-10.

70. Ibid.

71. Ibid., 10.

72. Ibid., 15.

73. Ibid.

74. Ibid., 14.

75. Ibid., 13.

76. Ibid., 18-19.

77. Ibid., 21.

78. Dreyfus and Rabinow, *Beyond Structuralism,* 121.

79. Almond and Verba, *The Civic Culture,* 31.

80. Ibid.

81. Ibid., 32.

82. Ibid.

83. Huntington, *American Politics,* 85-220.

84. Almond, "An Intellectual History," 161.

85. Almond and Verba, *The Civic Culture,* 32. As Marcuse concludes, "Proclaiming the existing social reality as its own norm, this sociology fortifies in the individuals the 'faithless faith' in the reality whose victims they are: nothing remains of ideology but the recognition of that which is—model of behavior which submits to the overwhelming power of the established state of affairs." Marcuse, *One-Dimensional Man,* 119-120.

86. Lawrence Joseph, "Democratic Revisionism Revisited," *American Journal of Political Science* 25, no. 4 (November 1981), 160-178.

87. Foucault, *Discipline and Punish,* 194.

88. Ibid., 221.

89. Ibid.

90. Almond and Verba, *The Civic Culture,* 473.

91. Ibid., 478.

92. Ibid.

93. Ibid., 478-479.

94. Foucault, *Discipline and Punish,* 220.

95. Almond and Verba, *The Civic Culture,* vii.

96. Ibid., 5.

97. Ibid., 33.

98. Ibid., 33-34.

99. Almond, "An Intellectual History," 29.

100. Ibid., 28.

101. Ibid.

102. Almond and Verba, *The Civic Culture,* 493, 495.

103. Ibid., 493.

104. White, "Foucault's Challenge," 419-432.

105. Michel Foucault, "What Is an Author?" *The Foucault Reader,* ed. by Paul Rabinow (New York: Pantheon, 1984), 117.

106. Ibid.

107. Foucault, "Truth and Power," 126.

108, Almond, "An Intellectual History," 26.

109. Foucault, "Truth and Power," 132.

110. Foucault, *History of Sexuality,* 142.

111. Ibid., 141.

112. Ibid.

113. Foucault, "Nietzsche, Genealogy, History," 86.

114. Whether or not Foucault's position allows one to resist these tendencies effectively is another question. See William Connolly, "Discipline, Politics, and Ambiguity," *Political Theory* 11, no. 3 (August 1983), 325-341; and Charles Taylor, "Foucault on Freedom and Truth," *Political Theory* 12, no. 2 (May 1986), 152-183.

Index

Acton, H. B., 25, 46, 47, 65
Adler, Franklin, 89
Adorno, Theodor W., 122, 126, 161
Advanced capitalism, 10-16, 39-46, 57, 63-65, 70-78, 128-152, 159-178, 211-237, 242-265
Africa, 12-13, 14, 166, 167, 172, 179, 185-207, 212, 215, 220, 250
Agger, Ben, 5, 154, 156
Agro-managerialism, 32, 59
AID (Agency for International Development), 168, 216
Almond, Gabriel, 239, 252-263, 265, 267-268
Amin, Samir, 238
Ananke, 146, 148, 155
Ancient society, 23, 24, 29, 30-33, 43-46, 54, 59, 60, 64
Anderson, Perry, 206, 208, 210
Anthropology, 9, 15, 31, 215-226, 242-254
Arato, Andrew, 16, 179
Aron, Raymond, 180, 238
Aronowitz, Stanley, 16
Artificial negativity, 12, 15, 152, 159-178
Asia, 13, 29, 33, 34, 39, 59-60, 166, 167, 172, 174, 179, 212, 215, 220, 250
Asiatic society, 23, 24, 29, 30-33, 43-46, 54, 59-60, 64
Avineri, Shlomo, 23, 46
Axelos, Kostas, 46, 65

Baran, Paul, 40, 49

Barber, Benjamin, 121, 127
Bell, Daniel, 152
Bendix, Reinhard, 239, 240
Benhabib, Seyla, 16
Biopower, 244-265
Bober, Martin, 46
Boggs, Carl, 5, 88, 207
Bookchin, Murray, 121, 127, 181
Bordiga, Amadeo, 80-84, 86, 90
Bourgeoisie, 24-26, 29, 34-46, 49, 54, 70, 72-73, 75-88, 112-117, 187-203, 187-197
Bourgeois society, 54-57, 60-65, 72-73, 74-88, 96-100, 112-117, 159-161
Braverman, Harry, 66, 68, 179
Breines, Paul, 153
Bronner, Stephen, 16
Brzezinski, Zbigniew, 50, 68
Bukharin, Nikholai, 47, 66, 71
Burawoy, Michael, 66, 68
Bureaucracy, 14-16, 30-33, 39-43, 45-46, 57-65, 70-88, 150-152, 159-178, 203-207, 219-238, 244-265
Burnham, James, 178

Cabral, Amilcar, 12-13, 14, 15, 185-210, 211, 212, 215, 241
Callinicos, Alex, 16, 46
Capitalism, 9-16, 23, 24, 29, 36-43, 44-46, 52, 54, 60-61, 64
Cassirer, Ernest, 95, 122

CGL (General Confederation of Labor),
    69, 70, 79
Chaliand, Gerard, 186, 207, 210
Chilcote, Ronald H., 207
China, 39, 48, 49, 220, 231, 243, 250
Chronocentricity, 220, 227, 229-233, 237
CIA (Central Intelligence Agency), 166,
    174, 250, 251, 285
Clark, Martin, 76-90
Class, 9-16, 29-44, 53-65, 69-88, 94-121,
    128-134, 159-178, 192-197, 203-207,
    241-254, 258-265
Cohen, G. A., 21, 43, 46, 47-48, 65
Cold War, 12, 14, 16, 45, 158, 166-178,
    213, 214, 249-265
Coleman, James S., 239, 267
Colonialism, 185-207, 211-238, 254-265
Colonization, 187-197, 211-226, 242-254,
    262-265
Communism, 23, 25, 29, 43, 44-46, 70-87,
    128-134, 150-152, 159-168, 201-205,
    211-219, 249-265
Comparative politics, 13, 14, 16, 211-238,
    249-265
Corporate capitalism, 57-65, 129-145, 150-
    152, 159-178, 212-226, 228-238, 249-
    265
Critical theory, 10-16, 93-94, 118-121,
    122, 128-134, 145-152, 159-182, 215-
    238
Croce, Benedetto, 66, 71
Cultural hegemony, 72-74, 80-88, 187-
    207, 211-238, 242-265
Cultural studies, 10, 16, 185-203, 211-238,
    242-265

Dahrendorf, Ralf, 57, 59, 67
Darwin, Charles, 28, 53
Davidson, Basil, 188, 207, 208, 209
Democracy, 9-16, 70-87, 100-121, 128-
    145, 150-152, 197-203, 211-212, 216-
    219, 249-265
Development, 12-16, 29-43, 57-65, 150-
    152, 161-178, 187-251, 211-238, 249-
    265
Discipline, 242-265

Domination, 9-16, 39-46, 57-65, 80-88, 93-
    121, 128-145, 161-176, 187-203, 205-
    207, 215-238, 242-247, 249-265
Drucker, Peter, 48, 179

Early capitalism, 10, 23-24, 33-39, 43-46
Ellul, Jacques, 48, 66
Elshtain, Jean Bethke, 127
Elster, Jon, 46
Emancipation, 9-16, 63-65, 70-88, 93-99,
    118-121, 128-134, 150-152, 176-179,
    201-204, 236-238
Engels, Frederick, 10, 22, 23, 24, 35, 42,
    43, 45, 46-47, 56, 59, 60, 65, 66, 67,
    70, 100, 112, 124, 126, 240
England, 37, 38-39, 42, 215, 222, 228,
    257, 262
Enlightenment schema, 11, 15, 93, 96-100,
    112-127, 118-121, 122, 135-145, 215-
    219, 222-226, 242-249
Entrepreneurial capitalism, 128-130, 135-
    136, 158-166
Eotechnics, 30, 33-37, 43-46, 49
Eros, 133, 134, 139, 141, 146, 147, 149
Ethnocentricity, 227, 228-229, 237
Europe, 10, 11, 12, 14, 21-25, 29, 30, 33-
    39, 42, 43-46, 53, 59, 64, 93, 147,
    161, 163, 167, 172, 179, 187, 189-
    190, 194-196, 203, 206-207, 213,
    214, 215, 216, 217, 218, 219, 220,
    223, 244
Ewen, Stuart, 68, 182

Fanon, Frantz, 205, 207, 211
Fascism, 87-88, 129, 215-216, 254
Fay, Brian, 16
Feudalism, 23, 24, 29, 33-37, 44, 45-46,
    52, 54, 59
Fordism, 43, 57, 63, 64, 76, 157, 162
Forester, John, 16
Foucault, Michel, 13, 64, 241-268
Fourth World, 15, 207, 211, 213, 214, 225
France, 37, 42, 215, 222, 247
Frank, Andre Gunder, 238
Frankfurt School, 11-17, 93, 129-134, 159-
    161, 176-178
Franklin, Benjamin, 27, 53

Freud, Sigmund, 11, 128, 129, 130-134, 145-150

Galbraith, John Kenneth, 40, 49, 240
Gaventa, John, 181
Gebhardt, Eike, 16, 179
Genealogy, 13, 252-254, 262, 265
Germany, 42, 128, 179, 180, 215, 216, 228, 262
Giddens, Anthony, 46, 65
Goldman, Lucien, 67
Goulder, Alvin, 16-17, 182
Gramsci, Antonio, 10-11, 14, 46, 64, 68, 69-90, 120, 153, 157, 187, 198-203, 206-207, 208, 209
Gross, David, 181
Guinea-Bissau, 185-207

Habermas, Jurgen, 67, 152, 155, 156, 182
Hegel, Georg Wilhelm Friedrich, 46, 71, 83, 100, 124, 131, 149
Heidegger, Martin, 129, 130, 131, 134, 154
Held, David, 16, 153
Hilferding, Rudolf, 40, 49, 67
Historical materialism, 10-11, 21-65, 94-117, 130-150, 159-166
Hook, Sidney, 46, 65
Horkheimer, Max, 46, 67, 122, 126, 153
Huntington, Samuel, P., 50, 226, 227, 228, 239, 258, 267, 268
Husserl, Edmund, 129, 130, 154

India, 42, 48, 49, 172, 220, 231, 232
Industrial capitalism, 10-16, 23-24, 44-46, 51-65, 93
Industrial revolution, 10-11, 14-15, 26, 30-46, 54, 57, 62-65, 130-140, 159-176, 230-238, 244-247, 262-265
Informationalism, 11, 14, 236-237
Instrumental rationality, 9-16, 21, 58, 128-130, 135-145, 160-178, 219-238, 242-249
Intellectuals, 70-74, 80-88, 128-134, 160-178, 192-197, 217-238, 241-265
Italy, 10, 14, 69-90, 215, 262

Jacoby, Russell, 16, 182

Japan, 39, 42, 45, 64, 167, 179, 181, 215, 216, 220, 223, 228, 230
Jay, Martin, 16, 153, 155
Joseph, Lawrence, 5, 268

Kautsky, John, 5, 238
Kautsky, Karl, 70
Kellner, Douglas, 16, 153, 154
Kirchheimer, Otto, 67
Kolakowski, Leszek, 16
Korsch, Karl, 153

Labriola, Arturo, 70
Landes, Joan B., 127
Latin America, 13, 166, 167, 182, 212, 215, 220, 249
Latouche, Robert, 34, 48-49
Lefebvre, Henri, 46, 65, 68, 182
Leiss, William, 68, 155, 156, 182
Lenin, V. I., 47, 66, 77, 83, 86, 88, 89, 144, 153, 193, 194, 203
Liberation, 11-16, 70-74, 80-88, 100-121, 128-152, 176-178, 197-204
Lichtheim, George, 16, 51
Logos, 133, 138, 141, 142, 148, 149, 155, 156
Lukacs, Georg, 22, 23, 46, 104, 122-123, 124, 147, 153, 208

Mallet, Serge, 67
Mandel, Ernest, 40, 49, 57, 67
Manufacture, 23, 25, 29, 33-37, 61, 62
Mao Tse-Tung, 150, 193, 194, 231
Marcuse, Herbert, 11-12, 14, 15, 23, 46, 64-65, 67, 94, 120, 128-158, 159, 161, 180, 248, 259, 267, 268
Marx, Karl, 9-16, 21-65, 66-68, 94, 100, 111, 112, 120, 126, 147-148, 150, 155, 236, 240
Marxism, 9-16, 21-65, 69-88, 94, 100-101, 128-135, 159-161, 185, 192-197, 203, 217, 219, 241, 262
Marxologies, 9-16
Mattick, Paul, 153
McLellan, David, 46, 65, 66
Means of production, 9-11, 21-46, 52-65
Merriam, Charles E., 253, 267

Methodology, 10-16, 22-26, 53-57, 70-74, 100-111, 130-134, 187-197, 215-226, 241-249

Metrocentricity, 13, 218, 219, 226-238

Mezzogiorno, 69, 87

Mill, John Stuart, 229, 230, 239

Miller, James, 121, 127, 181

Mills, C. Wright, 16, 65

Mode of production, 10-11, 21-46, 52-65

Modernity, 15, 220-226, 230-233, 242-265

Modernization, 13, 211-238

Modernizationism, 13, 217-238

Monopoly capitalism, 15-16, 40, 44-46, 63-65, 84-88, 130-145, 150-152, 158-178, 181

Mumford, Lewis, 10-11, 21, 29-46, 47-50, 51, 53, 54, 66, 157

National liberation, 14-16, 185-207, 226-238, 249-262

NATO (North Atlantic Treaty Organization), 213

Neotechnics, 14, 30, 39-43

Neumann, Franz, 67

New Left, 150, 151, 152, 169-171

Normalization, 237, 242-265

OECD (Organization for Economic Cooperation and Development), 213, 214

One-dimensionality, 12, 14-16, 64, 100-120, 130-150, 159-178, 215-238, 242-265

O'Neill, John, 16

Organization of production, 10-11, 22, 51-65

Outsiders, 12, 15, 128-132, 134, 144, 148, 149, 150, 151, 152, 164-166

Packenham, Robert, 181, 238

Paggi, Leonardo, 70-71, 88

PAIGC (African Party for the Independence of Guinea-Bissau and Cape Verde), 185-207

Paleotechnics, 30, 37-43, 44

Panopticon, 246-249

Party, 72-74, 75-87, 130-134, 150-152, 167-171, 197-203

PCI (Italian Communist Party), 69, 78, 90, 206

Perestroika, 45, 168

Performance principle, 145-150

Phillips, Kevin P., 68

Piccone, Paul, 5, 12, 17, 88, 89, 131, 154, 158, 178, 179, 207

Plekhanov, G. V., 70, 71

Political culture, 13-14, 211-238, 249-265

Political economy, 10-11, 14, 16, 22-26, 43-46, 53-57, 94, 159-178, 187-203, 219

Political science, 13-14, 16, 211-240, 241-268

Political theory, 10-16

Pollock, Friedrich, 67

Portugal, 185-207, 220

Post-Fordism, 64

Postimperialism, 13, 223

Power, 9-16, 29-33, 43-46, 57-65, 70-87, 100-120, 130-150, 159-178, 187-205, 215-226, 233-238, 241-265

Primitive accumulation, 25, 29, 33-37

Primitive cooperation, 23, 25, 29, 33-37, 51-63

Primitive society, 23, 25, 29, 31-33, 43-46, 54

Productive forces, 9-11, 21-46, 47-48, 51-65

Productive relations, 9-11, 21-46, 47-48, 51-65

Productivism, 76, 77, 78, 79, 80

Proletariat, 24-26, 29, 34-46, 48-49, 61-64, 69-88, 128-134, 160-178

Prototechnics, 30-33

PSI (Italian Socialist Party), 69, 70, 74, 79, 81, 83, 90

Pye, Lucian, 239, 240, 267

Ratio, 137, 138, 139, 142, 148, 149, 155, 156

Rationalization, 9-16, 22-46, 51-53, 57-65, 76-80, 84-87, 94-118, 130-150, 161-176, 211-238, 241-265

Reed, Adolph, Jr., 68, 158, 181

Reich, Wilhelm, 157

Reification, 9-16, 53-65, 70-80, 94-118, 135-150, 159-166, 177-178, 219-226, 242-254
Risorgimento, 69
Roemer, John, 46
Rostow, W. W., 50, 216, 229, 238
Rousseau, Jean-Jacques, 11, 12, 15, 65, 93-127, 128, 251, 259
Russia, 37, 39, 74, 75

Scandinavia, 37, 43, 228, 230
Schiller, Friedrich, 129, 142
Schmidt, Alfred, 47, 66
Schoolman, Morton, 153, 156
Schwartz, Joel, 122, 127
Scientific management, 39-43, 57, 63-65, 74-80, 84-86, 130-145, 159-178, 242-249, 262-265
Shapiro, Jeremy, 142, 156, 157
Shklar, Judith, 94, 95, 122, 123, 124
Socialism, 10, 11, 12, 13, 39-43, 44-46, 70-74, 128-150, 203-207
Sociology, 9, 15
Sombart, Werner, 38
Soviet Union, 45, 82, 89, 130, 147, 166, 167, 168, 169, 187, 214, 220
State, 24, 25, 31-33, 51-65, 73, 74, 75-80, 81-88, 112-121, 128-134, 150-152, 157-178, 187-207, 215-226, 242-265
Steel, Ronald, 180, 238
Subjectivity, 9-16, 72-87, 94-120, 128-152, 161-178, 187-203, 211-238, 242-265
Surveillance, 13-14, 211-226, 242-265
Sweezy, Paul, 40, 49

Tasca, Angelo, 80, 82, 83

Taylorism, 76-80, 84, 162
Technics, 10, 21-22, 27-29, 30-46, 52-65, 135-145
Technique, 10, 27, 51-65, 69
Technocentricity, 227, 233-238
Technology, 10-11, 21, 24-25, 26-29, 30-46, 51-65, 69, 130-145, 150-152
Third World, 12, 13, 134, 151-152, 166, 167, 168, 169, 174, 207, 211, 213, 214, 217, 222, 225, 250, 251, 264, 265
Tools, 10, 27, 30-33, 52-53
Tucker, Robert C., 23, 46, 47, 52, 65

United States, 11, 12, 13, 14, 15, 37, 41, 42, 45, 86, 128, 129, 130, 147, 159-178, 211-238, 241-265
USIA (United States Information Agency), 168, 249, 250, 251, 265

Veblen, Thorstein, 24, 25, 48, 51, 63
Verba, Sidney, 252-261, 263, 265, 267, 268

Wallerstein, Immanuel, 179
Warren, Scott, 16
Weber, Max, 57, 67
Wellmer, Albrecht, 17, 155
Westernization, 150-152, 161-176, 187-203, 211-238, 242-265
White, Stephen K., 5, 17, 266, 268
Wittfogel, Karl, 32, 37, 67
Wolfe, Alan, 68
Workers councils, 74-80
Work relations, 24, 53-65, 70-74

Yergin, Daniel, 180

Zeitlin, Irving M., 47

About the Author

Timothy W. Luke is Professor of Political Science at the Virginia Polytechnic Institute and State University. His articles have appeared in *Social Research, New Political Science, Studies in Comparative International Development, Critical Studies in Mass Communication, Current Perspectives in Social Theory, Philosophy of the Social Sciences, American Political Science Review, Journal of Politics,* and *International Studies Quarterly.* His most recent book is *Screens of Power: Ideology, Domination and Resistance in Informational Society* (University of Illinois Press, 1989).

state/caup — 57